ERRATA
(The Plant Kingdom, 3rd edition)

P. 35, Fig. 2.29: Art reversed in *a* and *c*.

P. 51, Fig. 3.12: In caption, lines 3 and 4 are transposed.

P. 56, Fig. 3.18: On art at *d*, for "Basidiocarp" read "Basidium."

P. 57, Fig. 3.19: Caption: for (*a*) "*Lycoperdon sp.*" read "*Scleroderma cepa.*"

P. 61, Fig. 4.1: Add *a* to art at left and *b* to art at right.

P. 65, Fig. 4.5: Art reversed in *a* and *b*.

P. 72, Fig. 4.14: On part *g*, add leader to operculum (at tip of capsule).

P. 75, Fig. 4.19: Caption omitted; add: "*Sphagnum squarrosum*, sporophytes enlarged."

P. 81, Fig. 5.6: On art, all leaders should end 1/8 in. to the right of their present terminations.

P. 84, Fig. 5.11: Caption (*c*) should read: "White pine (*Pinus strobus*), transection at junction of two annual rings."

P. 86, Fig. 5.14: On art, change "Prm" leader to "AM"; delete "AM" and leader below.

P. 87, Fig. 5.15: On art, all leaders should end ¼ in. to right of their present terminations.

P. 90, Fig. 5.21: On art, leaders "Vtrs" and "Sto" should end 3/16 in. to the right of their present terminations; leader "Vlos" should terminate on elongate cells to the right and below its present termination; the four leaders at the extreme right should terminate 1/8 in. below their present levels.

P. 94, Fig. 6.1: On art, add leader from "Spg" to enlarged tip above, right.

P. 94, Fig. 6.4: On art, leader "Sto" should terminate in nearest gap in stem perimeter.

P.102, Fig. 6.16: On art, leader "Mcspg" should end ¼ in. to the right of its present termination.

P.156, Fig. 9.13: On part *b*, leader from "Locule" should terminate in stippled brown area.

PRENTICE-HALL FOUNDATIONS
OF MODERN BIOLOGY SERIES

WILLIAM D. MCELROY
AND CARL P. SWANSON, *editors*

BATES   *Man in Nature, 2nd edition*

BOLD   *The Plant Kingdom, 3rd edition*

BONNER AND MILLS   *Heredity, 2nd edition*

DETHIER AND STELLAR   *Animal Behavior, 3rd edition*

GALSTON   *The Life of the Green Plant, 2nd edition*

HANSON   *Animal Diversity, 2nd edition*

MCELROY   *Cell Physiology and Biochemistry, 2nd edition*

SCHMIDT-NIELSEN   *Animal Physiology, 3rd edition*

SUSSMAN   *Growth and Development, 2nd edition*

SWANSON   *The Cell, 3rd edition*

WALLACE AND SRB   *Adaptation, 2nd edition*

WHITE   *Chemical Background for the Biological
Sciences, 2nd edition*

THE PLANT KINGDOM

3rd edition

HAROLD C. BOLD
Professor of Botany, The University of Texas, Austin

PRENTICE-HALL, INC.

ENGLEWOOD CLIFFS, NEW JERSEY

TO M. D. B.

FOUNDATIONS OF MODERN BIOLOGY SERIES   WILLIAM D. MCELROY
AND CARL P. SWANSON, *editors*

C—13-680371-7
P—13-680363-6
Library of Congress Catalog Card Number   74-110091

Current printing   10   9   8   7   6   5   4   3   2   1

PRENTICE-HALL INTERNATIONAL, INC., *London*
PRENTICE-HALL OF AUSTRALIA, PTY. LTD., *Sydney*
PRENTICE-HALL OF CANADA, LTD., *Toronto*
PRENTICE-HALL OF INDIA PRIVATE LTD., *New Delhi*
PRENTICE-HALL OF JAPAN, INC., *Tokyo*

FOREWORD

THIS SERIES, FOUNDATIONS OF MODERN BIOLOGY, WHEN LAUNCHED A number of years ago, represented a significant departure in the organization of instructional materials in biology. The success of the series provides ample support for the belief, shared by its authors, editors, and publisher, that student needs for up-to-date, properly illustrated texts and teacher prerogatives in structuring a course can best be served by a group of small volumes so planned as to encompass those areas of study central to an understanding of the content, state, and direction of modern biology. The twelve volumes of the series still represent, in our view, a meaningful division of subject matter.

This edition thus continues to reflect the rapidly changing face of biology; and many of the consequent alterations have been suggested by the student and teacher users of the texts. To all who have shown interest and aided us we express thankful appreciation.

WILLIAM D. MCELROY
CARL P. SWANSON

IN PREPARING THIS THIRD EDITION, THE WRITER HAS NOT DEVIATED markedly from the plan of the two earlier editions. The major changes in this enlarged edition are (1) a modest expansion of the information presented about illustrative genera; (2) greater attention to the relationships between plants and human affairs; (3) emphasis of certain important biological concepts; (4) inclusion of the results of recent research; and (5) augmentation and improvement of the illustrations. Although the text is designed to emphasize the plants themselves, important syntheses and concepts have received due attention. While the author does not share Mr. Thomas Gradgrind's philosophy of education,* he is of the opinion that current emphasis in some writing and teaching on "discovery, concepts, and principles" may have provided students with shadow instead of substance, with a superstructure lacking adequate foundation, or with stone instead of bread! The writer hopes, on the contrary, that the reader, in some cases on his own initiative, but in

---

* In Charles Dickens' *Hard Times:* "Now, what I want is, Facts. Teach these boys and girls nothing but facts. Facts alone are wanted in life. Plant nothing else, and root out everything else . . . stick to facts, Sir!"

most instances with his instructor's guidance, will be able to formulate concepts and make syntheses more successfully on the basis of this encounter with substantial data. The student's foundation will be the more secure if he has been able to study the living plants and their structures in the laboratory, or *at the very least,* if he has had access to appropriate colored transparencies illustrating them.

The author is grateful for the reception accorded the earlier editions of *The Plant Kingdom;* he has especially appreciated the many readers' and teachers' comments, both adverse and favorable, that he has received in the past, and he will continue to welcome such comments. Finally, he acknowledges with appreciation the critical and helpful comments of his colleagues, Professors C. J. Alexopoulos and H. J. Arnott of The University of Texas at Austin, and of Professor H. P. Banks of Cornell University. Mr. Geza Knipfer's continuing assistance with some of the art work has been of great value.

HAROLD C. BOLD

CONTENTS

FOREWORD   *v*   PREFACE TO THE 3RD EDITION   *vii*

1 UNITY AND DIVERSITY OF PLANTS   *1*

*Classification of plants   2   Unity versus
diversity of plants   3*

2 ALGAE   *11*

*Form and organization of algae   14   Cellular
organization of algae   16   Reproduction of algae   18
Notes on some divisions of algae   22   Evolution
of algae   36*

3 BACTERIA, SLIME MOLDS, AND FUNGI   *38*

*Bacteria   40   Myxomycota: the slime molds   43
Acrasiomycota: the cellular slime molds   45
Fungi   46*

60   **4   NONVASCULAR LAND PLANTS: LIVERWORTS, HORNWORTS, AND MOSSES**

Liverworts   61   *Hornworts*   67   *Mosses*   69
Evolution of nonvascular land plants   76

77   **5   ORGANIZATION OF VASCULAR PLANTS**

Axes: stems and roots   79   *Leaves*   87
Adaptations of vascular plants   91

92   **6   SEEDLESS VASCULAR PLANTS: I**

Psilophytes   93   *Club and spike mosses*   96
Arthrophytes   106   *Summary*   109

111   **7   SEEDLESS VACULAR PLANTS: II**

Ferns   111   *Summary of seedless vascular plants*   122

124   **8   GYMNOSPERMS**

Reproduction of gymnosperms   126   *Representative
gymnosperms*   128   *Fossil gymnosperms*   140

141   **9   ANGIOSPERMS**

External morphology of flowers   142   *The reproductive
process in angiosperms*   147   *Fossil angiosperms*   159

160   **10   CONCLUSION**

Organization of the plant body   160   *Reproduction*   162
Classification and the evolutionary development of plants   165

170   **GLOSSARY**

181   **SELECTED READINGS**

INDEX   *183*

THE PLANT KINGDOM

1 UNITY
AND DIVERSITY
OF PLANTS

OUR ENVIRONMENT IS CHARACTERIZED BY RICHLY DIVERSIFIED PLANT LIFE
on which we depend for our very existence. The air we breathe contains
a continuously adequate level of oxygen only because it is continually
replenished by green, chlorophyllous plants. Furthermore, plants, both
aquatic and terrestrial, are the foundation of the food chain for the
animal kingdom. Plant protoplasm and its products are the basic sources
of the energy and the building blocks with which animal protoplasm is
synthesized. The widely diverse activities of such achlorophyllous organisms as bacteria and fungi are also of great significance to the biological
world.

At first glance, we are likely to be impressed with the diversity
of plants that populate the earth. The green scum on certain ponds, the
duckweed on others, the lichens, fungi, liverworts, mosses, ferns,
conifers, and flowering plants—some of which populate even the most
inhospitable areas of the earth, both land and sea—are all elements
of this diversity and form the subject matter of the present volume.
We shall survey this diversity and emphasize the various important
biological principles that are particularly well illustrated by each of

the several plant groups. Such questions as the origin of life, the great variety of living organisms, and the nature of their interrelationships will also be considered. We shall devote some attention as well to extinct plants known to us only as fossil remains. These topics may best be discussed in connection with plants themselves. One topic, however, the classification of plants, requires immediate consideration.

CLASSIFICATION OF PLANTS

Classifications of organisms are man-made; they do not exist in nature. There are two types of classification systems of living organisms. In the first and oldest type, *artificial systems,* organisms are grouped together for convenience of identification. Such groupings do not imply actual kinship and hence are not *phylogenetic.* Examples of this type of classification are the division of plants into beneficial and harmful, into herbaceous and woody, or into evergreen and deciduous. As students of plant structure (called *morphologists*) became impressed with the basic similarity in the body plans of certain plants, they began to group them into *natural systems;* after the impact of Charles Darwin's exposition of organic evolution, the categories of these systems were interpreted to be phylogenetic. Phylogenetic classifications, which are designed to emphasize genetic relationships among living organisms, are based on carefully evaluated evidence of several types. The more important types are fossil records, geographical distributions, and comparative studies of living plant structure, function, biochemistry, development, and chromosomal and genetic constitution.

Darwin's publication of *The Origin of Species* in 1859 gave great impetus to natural classification systems, and a number of new schemes purporting to show phylogenetic relationships were proposed. However, classifications differ with the classifiers' appraisals of available evidence of relationship, sought in the comparative study of both living and fossil plants. Our knowledge of the latter, of course, will at best always be incomplete. Classifications of plants (and animals), therefore, are in a constant state of flux and are subject to continuing criticism and disagreement, for they represent only approximations. Classifications are continually being modified as new evidences for or against a postulated relationship between groups are discovered. Several systems of plant classification are summarized comparatively in Table 1.1. In addition, the table lists common, anglicized names for the several groups and estimates the number of species in each. The three systems of classification shown in Table 1.1 are in themselves good evidence that agreement has not yet been reached regarding the lines of relationship among plants. Like science itself, classification of plants is not static but subject to modification as new data emerge. Of course, this table is *not* meant for memorization but for reference to alternative schemes of classification of the plants that are discussed in Chapters 2 to 9 and in other books.

As Table 1.1 indicates, certain groups of plants have vernacular names, such as algae, fungi, bacteria, liverworts, mosses, ferns, seed plants, and flowering plants. Examples of these are illustrated in the chapters that follow. In considering such an assemblage of plants, one is at once impressed by their differences in habitat and structure, and by their seeming diversity of function. Although the diversity of these organisms is indeed the subject matter of this volume, there are also common attributes that are shared nearly universally by living organisms. Some of these unifying attributes of plants (and animals) are (1) cellular organization; (2) metabolic phenomena; (3) sexual reproduction; (4) genetic phenomena; and (5) adaptation.

1   Cellular organization   In 1838 and 1839, the botanist M. J. Schleiden and the zoologist Theodor Schwann published their theory that the cell (Figure 1.1) is the universal unit of organization in plants and animals. They arrived at this conclusion as a result of numerous studies by themselves and by other investigators who had been working with the light microscope from the time of its invention in 1590. This basic cell theory has become the generally accepted explanation of the organization of living organisms.* Furthermore, with the exception of

* See in this series C. P. Swanson, *The Cell* (3rd ed.) (Englewood Cliffs, N.J.: Prentice-Hall, Inc., 1969).

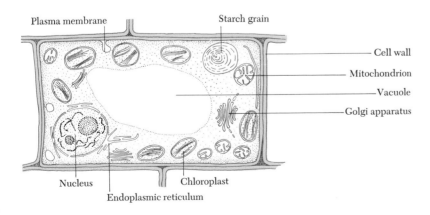

Plasma membrane   Starch grain

Cell wall

Mitochondrion

Vacuole

Golgi apparatus

Nucleus   Chloroplast

Endoplasmic reticulum

Figure 1.1   Generalized diagram of a plant cell. [Modified from W. T. Keeton.]

EICHLER, 1883 (WITH MODIFICATIONS)		TIPPO, 1942		
Plant kingdom		*Plant kingdom*		
A	*Cryptogamae*			
Division 1	*Thallophyta*	*Subkingdom 1*	*Thallophyta*	
Class 1	*Algae*			
	Cyanophyceae	*Phylum 1*	*Cyanophyta*	
	Chlorophyceae	*Phylum 2*	*Chlorophyta*	
		Phylum 3	**Euglenophyta**	
	Phaeophyceae	*Phylum 4*	*Phaeophyta*	
	Rhodophyceae	*Phylum 5*	*Rhodophyta*	
	Diatomeae	*Phylum 6*	*Chrysophyta*	
		Phylum 7	**Pyrrhophyta**	
Class 2	*Fungi*			
	Schizomycetes	*Phylum 8*	*Schizomycophyta*	
		Phylum 9	**Myxomycophyta**	
		Phylum 10	*Eumycophyta*	
	Eumycetes		**Class 1**	**Phycomycetes**
	Lichens		**Class 2**	**Ascomycetes**
			Class 3	**Basidiomycetes**
		Subkingdom 2	**Embryophyta**	
Division 2	*Bryophyta*	*Phylum 11*	*Bryophyta*	
Class 1	*Hepaticae*	*Class 1*	*Hepaticae*	
Class 2	*Musci*	*Class 2*	*Musci*	

[a] Only groups with currently living plants are included. The black typeface indicates categories newly introduced or made more explicit in successively more modern systems of classification. The colored typeface indicates categories used again in essentially the same form, under the same or a different name. When the name of a group is used later at a higher rank, as is Chlorophyceae, the name of

BOLD, 1970 [b]		COMMON NAMES [c]	APPROXIMATE NUMBER OF LIVING SPECIES
Plant kingdom			
		Algae	*19,000*
Division 1	*Cyanophycophyta*	*Blue-green algae*	
Division 2	*Chlorophycophyta*	*Green algae*	
Division 3	*Euglenophycophyta*	*Euglenoids*	
Division 4	**Charophyta**	**Charophytes**	
Division 5	*Phaeophycophyta*	*Brown algae*	
Division 6	*Rhodophycophyta*	*Red algae*	
Division 7	*Chrysophycophyta*	*Chrysophytes (diatoms, etc.)*	
Division 8	*Pyrrhophycophyta*	*Dinoflagellates*	
		Fungi (sensu lato)	*50,000*
Division 9	*Schizomycota*	*Bacteria*	
Division 10	*Myxomycota*	*Slime molds*	
Division 11	**Acrasiomycota**	*Cellular slime molds*	
		Fungi (sensu stricto)	
Division 12	**Chytridiomycota**	*Posteriorly uniflagellate fungi*	
Division 13	**Oomycota**	*Water molds and others*	
Division 14	**Zygomycota**	*Bread molds and others*	
Division 15	*Ascomycota*	*Sac fungi*	
Division 16	*Basidiomycota*	*Club fungi*	
Division 17	**Deuteromycota**	*Imperfect fungi*	
Division 18	*Hepatophyta*	*Liverworts and hornworts*	*6,000*
Division 19	*Bryophyta*	*Mosses*	*14,000*

the lower group is usually retained as a subsidiary under the higher. Although approximately equal to "Division," "Phylum" is not recognized as a category by the International Code of Botanical Nomenclature.

[b] This book.

[c] — indicates no common inclusive name.

Table 1.1 *A comparative summary of some classifications of the plant kingdom* (continued)

EICHLER, 1883 (WITH MODIFICATIONS)	TIPPO, 1942
Division 3 *Pteridophyta*	
	Phylum 12 Tracheophyta
	Subphylum 1 Psilopsida
Class 1 *Lycopodinae*	*Subphylum 2 Lycopsida*
Class 2 *Equisetinae*	*Subphylum 3 Sphenopsida*
	Subphylum 4 Pteropsida
Class 3 *Filicinae*	Class 1 *Filicinae*
B *Phanerogamae*	
Division 4 *Spermatophyta*	
Class 1 *Gymnospermae*	*Class 2 Gymnospermae*
	Subclass 1 Cycadophytae
	Subclass 2 Coniferophytae
Class 2 *Angiospermae*	Class 3 *Angiospermae*

blue-green algae and bacteria (see Figures 2.6 and 3.2), such cellular components as nuclei, nuclear membranes, cytoplasm, mitochondria, Golgi bodies, and the endoplasmic reticulum (Figures 1.1 and 1.2) are present in almost all plant and animal cells.

2 *Metabolism* In living organisms, the many chemical activities carried on, collectively called *metabolism,* offer additional evidence of unity. Such processes as energy release in respiration seem to be universally the same in living organisms, as do many of the pathways of chemical synthesis and degradation.* Further, many enzymes (the catalysts of metabolic processes in living organisms) are similar in various types of protoplasm.

3 *Sexual reproduction* No matter how diverse organisms may be—algae, elephants, daffodils, or human beings—four phenomena are almost always involved in sexual reproduction: (1) union of cells; (2)

* See in this series W. D. McElroy, *Cellular Physiology and Biochemistry* (2nd ed.) (Englewood Cliffs, N.J.: Prentice-Hall, Inc., 1964).

BOLD, 1970		COMMON NAMES	APPROXIMATE NUMBER OF LIVING SPECIES
Division 20	Psilophyta	Psilophytes	8
Division 21	Microphyllophyta	Club mosses	1,000
Division 22	Arthrophyta	Horsetails and sphenopsids	10–25
Division 23	Pterophyta	Ferns	9,500
Division 24	Cycadophyta	Cycads	100
Division 25	Ginkgophyta	Maidenhair tree (Ginkgo)	1
Division 26	Coniferophyta	Conifers	550
Division 27	Gnetophyta	—	71
Division 28	Anthophyta	Flowering plants	250,000
		APPROXIMATE TOTAL:	350,000

union of their nuclei;* (3) intermingling of two sets of nuclear components (chromosomes with their genetic materials); and (4) reassortment of genes at *meiosis* (reduction division). These phenomena are connected with another unifying principle, the phenomenon of inheritance, the laws of which are the province of genetics.† In the plant kingdom only the blue-green algae and the euglenoids seem to lack sexual reproduction.

4 Genetic and developmental phenomena The life of each individual cell, the differentiation of cells in the development of complex multicellular organisms, and, finally, the transmission of hereditary traits are governed—in *all* organisms—by deoxyribonucleic acid (DNA) in interaction with the cytoplasm through the agency of ribonucleic acid

---

* In some organisms, the nuclei merely remain side by side, and the chromosomes do not become associated until the zygote divides.

† See in this series D. M. Bonner, *Heredity* (2nd ed.) (Englewood Cliffs, N.J.: Prentice-Hall, Inc., 1964).

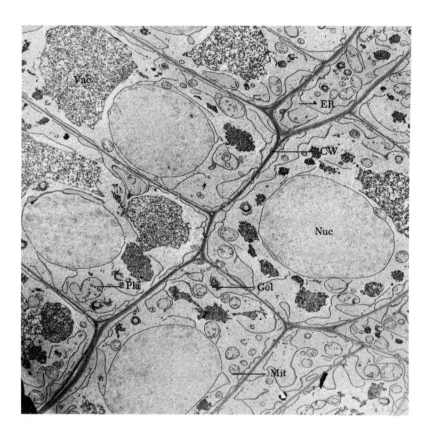

Figure 1.2 **View of cells of root tip of water hyacinth, Eichhornia crassipes (electron micrograph, × 1,770).** *ER, endoplasmic reticulum; Gol, Golgi apparatus; Mit, mitochondrion; Nuc, nucleus; Pla, plastid; Vac, vacuole; CW, cell wall.* [Courtesy of Professor H. J. Arnott.]

(RNA). The specific pattern of genetic organization is responsible for the structural and functional attributes of the cell as it develops in a given environment.

5   *Adaptation*   Another manifestation of the unity of living organisms is *adaptation,* the capacity of organisms, both as individuals and as continuing, sexually reproducing populations, to survive in their changing environment. Adaptations are both morphological (structural) and physiological (functional), two aspects of organisms that usually are intimately connected. Living things must be attuned to their environment; those that are not become extinct.*

How, then, are the diversities among living organisms to be reconciled with the equally apparent and striking similarities just enumerated? Modern biology answers this seeming paradox with the concept of

* See in this series B. Wallace and A. M. Srb, *Adaptation* (2nd ed.) (Englewood Cliffs, N.J.: Prentice-Hall, Inc., 1964).

organic evolution.* According to this explanation, diversity has arisen secondarily. It is deviation from original unity and has occurred throughout the more than 3 billion years during which life has existed on this planet. The living organisms we see about us are the present actors on an ancient stage. With passage of time, the settings have changed and so have the actors. They have become transformed in some respects as they acted. Many have dropped out; many others have become so changed over the ages through selection and new combinations of mutations as to be scarcely recognizable. We are thus driven to speculation regarding their origin. That such spontaneously occurring changes, or mutations, have occurred and are occurring in living organisms is no longer subject to question. We can observe them taking place on a small scale in nature at present, and we can induce their occurrence with suitable stimuli, such as irradiation and chemical agents. During many generations of sexually breeding populations, certain combinations of mutations were selected and became dominant, and in time the species changed. This is postulated, through extrapolation, to be the fundamental explanation of all the diversity of present-day organisms and the cause of their modification from their ancestors. Since the sequence of occurrence and inheritance of many of the changes cannot be followed completely and unequivocally, the story of the *course* of organic evolution in the past will probably remain incomplete. The point to note here is that a survey of diverse types of plants may tend to obscure the fact that present diversity sprang from earlier unity.

In such considerations, we are finally brought face to face with the ultimate question of the origin of life itself. Did it arise but once, or more than once? How was the first life organized? What was the nature of its nutritive and metabolic processes? For a long time, it was taken for granted that answers to these questions must be relegated to the realm of speculation, but recent and significant experiments indicate that the origin of life may be subject to experimental analyses. In a series of investigations wherein various mixtures of gases—methane, ammonia, hydrogen, and water vapor—were enclosed in chambers in which electricity was discharged, the production of amino acids, which are building units in the proteins of living organisms, was achieved in entirely nonliving systems. Thus the distinction between the inorganic and organic has become irrelevant.

Early speculators usually postulated that the most primitive living organisms must have been those that could thrive in an environment that contained only inorganic, low-energy compounds; according to this,

* See in this series E. D. Hanson, *Animal Diversity* (2nd ed.) (Englewood Cliffs, N.J.: Prentice-Hall, Inc., 1964).

such organisms must have possessed a tremendous range of enzymes, enabling them to convert such substances into protoplasm. Quite the opposite view is now more widely accepted. This postulates that the first organisms lived in a medium supplied with complex, high-energy molecules that they could utilize directly or with a minimum of change. As the supply of these complex substances became critically low, alternate pathways of protoplasmic synthesis evolved. These enabled primitive organisms to build up their substance from increasingly less complex building units.

According to one point of view, chlorophyllous, photosynthetic organisms are less primitive than achlorophyllous organisms like most bacteria, fungi, and animals. On the other hand, it is quite possible that some achlorophyllous organisms evolved from green organisms by losing their ability to produce chlorophyll. Such a change can be experimentally produced in certain unicellular algae like *Euglena* (see page 33) by high temperature. Comparative studies of the nutrition of microorganisms are shedding a good deal of light on these questions. The origin and relationships of diverse living organisms and of their variations in structure, nutrition, and metabolism constitute the subject matter of organic evolution, which postulates that living things are related to one another through common ancestry. It is the purpose of the present volume to survey these diversities in orderly fashion and thus, hopefully, to provide some insight into the range and activities of members of the plant kingdom.

ALTHOUGH NO ONE CAN DESCRIBE THE ORGANIZATION OF PRIMITIVE LIFE with absolute certainty, the fossil record strongly indicates that organisms much like certain modern algae lived more than 3 billion years ago. This is not to state categorically that algae were the earliest living organisms. The fossil record is incomplete and always will be, but there is every indication that algae, along with bacteria and certain fungi, are extremely ancient organisms; at least some of them have persisted with little modification from their progenitors (Figure 2.1). For this reason and because of the relative simplicity of most algae, we shall begin our survey of the diversity of the plant kingdom with these plants. Furthermore, algae provide elegant material for laboratory demonstrations of many fundamental biological phenomena.

What are algae? Where do they grow? What do they do and what are they good for? In the following pages we shall attempt to answer these questions about algae (and later, about every group of plants we consider). To the layman, algae are "pond scums," "seaweeds" (even when they grow in fresh water!), and, too often, "mosses." To the biologist, they are chlorophyllous organisms characterized by having

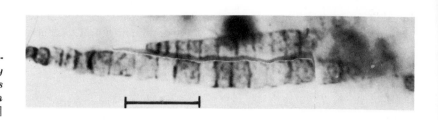

Figure 2.1   Palaeolyngbya bargho-
orniana, a Precambrian, presumably
blue-green, alga from Australian rocks
about 1 billion years old. Scale shown
represents 1 µm. [After J. W. Schopf.]

one of the following (Figure 2.2): (1) gametes (see page 18) but no specialized sex organs (this is characteristic of certain unicellular algae); (2) unicellular sex organs; or (3) multicellular sex organs in which every cell forms a gamete. In these respects, they differ from all other green plants. This definition may seem technical, but it is so of necessity, for science, in its dedication to accuracy, requires strict definition.

Algae live in both salt and fresh water; they also occur on and within soil and on moist stones and wood, as well as in association with fungi and certain animals. With respect to "what they do" and "what they are good for," algae are of paramount importance as primary producers of energy-rich compounds that form the basis of the food cycle of all aquatic animal life. In this connection, the *planktonic* (water-suspended) algae are especially important, since they serve as food for many animals. It has been estimated, for example, that about 90 percent of the photosynthesis on earth is carried on by aquatic plants; the planktonic algae are primarily responsible for this. Furthermore, algae oxygenate their habitat while they are photosynthesizing, thus increasing the level of dissolved oxygen in their immediate environment.

Figure 2.2   Sexual reproduction in
algae and nonalgae, diagrammatic.
(a) Chlamydomonas sp.; the organisms
themselves function as gametes. (b)
Oedogonium sp.; the gametes are
borne in special unicellular gametangia
(male, below, and female, above). (c)
Multicellular (plurilocular) gametan-
gium of Ectocarpus, a brown alga;
every cell is fertile. (d, e) Sex organs
of a bryophyte (diagram): (d) the male
organ or antheridium; (e) the female
organ or archegonium. Note the sterile
cells surrounding the fertile ones.

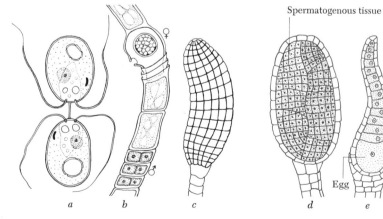

In addition, certain blue-green algae—like some bacteria, but unlike most other plants—can employ gaseous nitrogen from the atmosphere in building their protoplasm, and in this way contribute significantly to the nitrogenous compounds in the water and soils where they live. This activity is called *nitrogen fixation.*

In addition to these basic biological activities, algae have proved useful to man in a number of ways. More than 70 species of marine algae (seaweeds) are used as food, mostly by oriental peoples (although several of the red algae are sold as food supplements in the United States). Certain brown and red marine algae produce large amounts of hydrocolloids (water-holding substances) as intercellular secretions. Of these, *algin* (from brown algae) and *agar* and *carrageenin* (both from red algae) are used commercially. These hydrocolloidal substances are extracted from the algae and then dried and powdered. Upon rehydration, they are used as stabilizers in chocolate milk, ice cream, prepared icings and fillings, toothpaste, and so forth. Agar is used in biological studies to solidify culture media.

Another type of algae, the diatoms (see Figures 2.28 and 2.29), which populated ancient seas (and occur in lakes and oceans today), are also of economic value. The cells of ancient diatoms, covered with siliceous walls, settled to the sea bottom upon death; the walls were deposited in extensive layers of "diatomaceous earth," which is now of use in filtration, in insulation, in paint (as an ingredient), in silver polish (as a fine abrasive), etc.

In some instances, however, algae may become noxious, particularly when they are offensive to the eye or nose. The appearance of a great concentration of algae under favorable growth conditions produces *water blooms,* which render reservoirs and recreational bodies of water temporarily unusable. The occurrence of large mats of floating algae may result in the death of many fish from lack of oxygen, since at night the algae not only compete with the fish for this gas but form a blanket that reduces oxygenation of the water from the atmosphere. Furthermore, toxic products from algae as well as from some bacteria associated with them in water blooms may poison livestock and fish. The familiar phenomenon of the so-called *red tides* that kill fish are associated with the abundance of an alga, *Gonyaulax.*

Finally, we must note one further aspect of the use of algae, namely, their increasing importance in basic biological research, in such areas as reproduction, metabolism, genetics, and so forth. The unicellular algae are especially useful here, because of their small size and the ease and rapidity with which large populations may be grown.

Let us now turn from general considerations to more specific data concerning algae. Hundreds of genera* of algae are known, and our knowledge of them is constantly being augmented. In older systems of classification (see Table 1.1), the algae were considered to be a uniform group; of late, the term "Algae" has been abandoned as designating a formal taxon in classification, and the taxon has been replaced by a number of divisions based on the diversity of certain structural and biochemical attributes. These are summarized in Table 2.1. It should be apparent from this table that the several groups of algae differ in pigmentation, food reserves, wall composition, number and nature of organs of locomotion, and habitat. The end of this chapter cities genera from these algal groups to illustrate important phenomena.

FORM AND ORGANIZATION OF ALGAE

The algae range from minute, simple types, as exemplified by unicellular species, to very large and complex ones, for example the kelps.

Some biologists group unicellular, motile algae together with unicellular, motile animals in a separate kingdom (neither plant nor animal, but including attributes of both), namely, Protista. Usually these unicellular algal cells move by beating the water with one or more protoplasmic extensions called *cilia* or *flagella* (see Figure 2.3).

The green algae (Chlorophycophyta) have the most complete range of body type, for they include not only unicellular but also colonial, filamentous, membranous, and tubular genera. The association of organisms in colonies (see Figures 2.8 and 2.11a) and filaments (see Figures 2.9a and 2.12), probably originates, during ontogeny (development of the individual), by failure of the cells to separate after their division. These associations often are so loose that a colony may be shaken apart into fragments, even into individual cells. In some instances, however—for example, in certain species of *Volvox* (see Figure 2.11a)—the individual cells of the colony are bound together by connections that

* Genera (singular, *genus*): one of the categories of classification (each of which is a *taxon*) prescribed by the International Code of Botanical Nomenclature. This code recognized the following taxa in ascending order: *species, genus, family, order, class,* and *division.* In illustration of these, the alga *Chlamydomonas eugametos,* is classified as follows:

Division: Chlorophycophyta
Class: Chlorophyceae
Order: Volvocales
Family: Chlamydomonadaceae
Genus: *Chlamydomonas*
Species: *Chlamydomonas eugametos*

It is conventional to italicize the generic and specific names in print.

Table 2.1   Major algal groups and their noteworthy characteristics

DIVISION	COMMON NAME	PIGMENTS[a]	STORED PHOTO-SYNTHATE	MAJOR COMPONENTS OF CELL WALL	FLAGELLAR NUMBER, LENGTH, AND POSITION[b]	HABITAT[c]
Chlorophycophyta	*Green algae*	*Chlorophylls a and b*	*Starch*	*Cellulose plus pectin*	*2–8, or many; equal; apical*	*fw, bw, sw, t*
Charophyta	*Stoneworts*	*Chlorophylls a and b*	*Starch*	*Cellulose plus pectin*	*2; equal; apical*	*fw, bw*
Euglenophycophyta	*Euglenoids*	*Chlorophylls a and b*	*Paramylon*	*No cell wall*	*1–8; equal; apical or subapical*	*fw, bw, sw, t*
Chrysophycophyta	*Golden algae (including diatoms)*	*Chlorophyll a (some have c and/or e)*	*Oil, chrysolaminarin*	*Pectin plus silicon dioxide; cellulose in some*	*1–2; unequal or equal; apical*	*fw, bw, sw, t*
Phaeophycophyta	*Brown algae*	*Chlorophylls a and c*	*Mannitol, laminarin*	*Cellulose plus algin*	*2; unequal; lateral*	*fw (rare), bw, sw*
Pyrrhophycophyta	*Dinoflagellates, in part*	*Chlorophylls a and c*	*Starch*	*Cellulose or no cell wall*	*2; 1 trailing and 1 girdling*	*fw, bw, sw*
Rhodophycophyta	*Red algae*	*Chlorophylls a and d, phycocyanin, phycoerythrin*	*Floridean[d] starch*	*Cellulose, other polysaccharides*	*None*	*fw (some), bw, sw (most)*
Cyanophycophyta	*Blue-green algae*	*Chlorophyll a, phycocyanin, phycoerythrin*	*Cyanophycean[e] starch*	*Peptidoglycans (mucopolysaccharides)*	*None*	*fw, bw, sw, t*

[a] In addition to the chlorophylls, phycocyanin, and phycoerythrin listed in the table, all the algae contain carotenes and xanthophylls. The abundance of the latter may mask the chlorophylls in some, such as the Phaeophycophyta and Chrysophycophyta.
[b] In motile cells, when such are produced.
[c] fw, fresh water; bw, brackish water; sw, salt water; t, terrestrial.
[d] Stains wine-red with iodine.
[e] Glycogenlike.

suggest the apparent protoplasmic continuity through the cell walls of so-called higher plants (see Figure 1.2).* The repeated division of a single cell and its descendants in the same direction without separation of the cells produces a filament (see Figures 2.9 and 2.12), which may be branched or unbranched. Algae may also be composed of sheets of cells, one or more layers thick; these are membranous or leaflike (see Figure 2.15). Certain green and yellow-green algae are composed of solitary or interwoven tubes (see Figures 2.16 and 2.17), which are not partitioned into individual cells. In complexity of form and in size, the kelps (see Figure 2.19) of the brown algae (Phaeophycophyta) are probably unsurpassed by any other algae. Some of these enormous marine plants, which thrive in the cold waters off the American Pacific coast and elsewhere, exceed 150 ft (feet) in length. The presence of phloemlike, presumably conducting cells in kelps suggests the more complex land plants.

Algae differ in growth patterns, too. Growth in such algae as *Oscillatoria* (see Figure 2.9*a*), *Spirogyra* (see Figure 2.14), and *Ulva*, the sea lettuce (see Figure 2.15) is generalized because increase in cell number and size is not confined to a specific region of the plant. In contrast, growth in other algae, such as *Fucus* (see Figure 2.20*a*), and all land plants is localized, usually at the apexes.

CELLULAR ORGANIZATION OF ALGAE

With the exception of blue-green algae (Cyanophycophyta; see Figure 2.6), cellular organization in algae (see Figure 2.5) does not differ fundamentally from that in other plants, although there are variations in detail among the several groups. Pigmented bodies, the *chloroplasts* (see Figures 2.3*a* and 2.5), are conspicuous organelles of algal cells. The plastids vary in form and pigmentation in the diverse genera and classes of algae (see Table 2.1). The algal nucleus, however, is often not conspicuous in the living condition because it is concealed by the more prominent plastids.

* The significance of these connections is often cited in discussions dealing with organizational questions. Do multicellular organisms and their complex activities represent merely the total sum of the individual cells of which they are composed, and their cellular activities? The presence of intercellular connections in multicellular organisms is interpreted by some biologists as evidence that there is supracellular unity and that the organism is the significant biological unit. Multinucleate, nonseptate organisms, such as *Rhizopus*, the black mold (see Figure 3.12), and the tubular green algae, support this view. Furthermore, electron microscopy has demonstrated that cellular continuity through nonliving walls is even more extensive than previously observed with the light microscope.

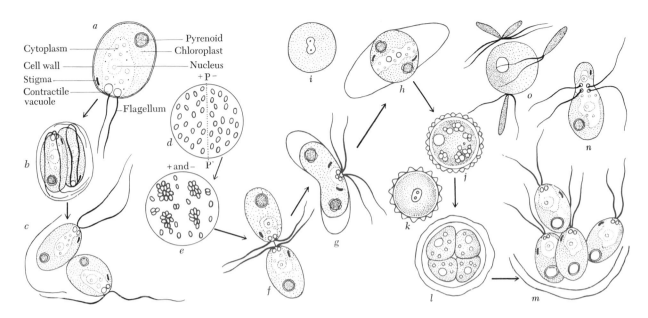

Figure 2.3 **The structure and reproduction of Chlamydomonas.** *(a–c) Asexual reproduction in Chlamydomonas moewusii. (a) Single individual. (d–m) Sexual reproduction in C. moewusii (see also Figures 2.4 and 2.5). (d) + and − mating types separated along P–P'. (e) Clump formation after mating types have been mixed. (f–h) Gamete pairing and union. (i) Union of gamete nuclei. (j, k) Zygotes (diploid nucleus visible in k). (l, m) Zygote germination after meiosis. (n) Chlamydomonas sp., heterogamy. (o) Chlamydomonas sp., oogamy: nonmotile egg surrounded by sperm.*

Motile algal cells, which may or may not be walled, have one or more flagella and may possess a *stigma*, or "red eyespot" (Figure 2.3a). This stigma may be the site of light perception, and recent work has demonstrated that the wavelengths absorbed by the eyespot pigment coincide with those that stimulate changes in the organism's orientation to light. *Contractile vacuoles*, like those in protozoa, occur in the motile cells of many algae (Figure 2.3a).

As mentioned above, Cyanophycophyta differ in their cellular organization from all other algae (see Figure 2.6), being in some respects more like bacteria (see Figures 3.1 and 3.2) than algae. (1) The nuclear material, DNA, is not partially separated from the cytoplasm, as it is in other plants, by a readily demonstrable membrane; (2) nucleoli, mitochondria, Golgi apparatus and endoplasmic reticulum are absent; (3) the pigmented areas of the cytoplasm are organized differently from those of other algae, lacking membrane-enclosed plastids; and (4) large, watery vacuoles are absent from the cells. Because of their cellular organization, the blue-green algae and the bacteria are said to be prokaryotic and sometimes are classified together.

Cell division in unicellular algae (see Figures 2.3*b,c* and 2.7) results in multiplication of individuals, as it does in other unicellular organisms. Colonies and filaments may fragment, the several fragments subsequently developing into new organisms. Algae may also produce several types of specialized reproductive cells, among them motile *zoospores* (see Figure 2.12) and several types of nonmotile spores. All these methods of increasing the number of individuals in the population are *asexual* (nonsexual), for they do not involve cellular or nuclear union.

Sexual reproduction occurs commonly in algae with the exception of only two groups, Cyanophycophyta and Euglenophycophyta, in which it has not yet been observed. Since the unicellular alga *Chlamydomonas* is especially favorable for the study of sexuality, we shall consider the reproductive process in that organism in some detail in the following paragraphs.

Chlamydomonas (Figures 2.3 to 2.5) is a motile member of the division Chlorophycophyta. In populations of *Chlamydomonas* where sexually mature and compatible individuals are present,* the sexual process begins with clumping or aggregation (Figures 2.3*e* and 2.4*b*) of cells attracted to each other by chemical substances diffused from their flagella. From these clumps, paired individuals emerge (Figures 2.3*f* and 2.4*b*). In some species, each pair is connected by a cytoplasmic strand and is actively propelled by the two flagella of one member of the pair; in others, the uniting cells are not actively motile. Cells that unite in sexual reproduction are called *gametes*. As the sexual process continues, the delicate cell walls are dissolved at the point where the two gametes are closest together, and in a process called *plasmogamy,* the contents of the two cells flow together, producing a *zygote* (Figures 2.3*g–k* and 2.4*c,d*). Sooner or later, the two nuclei brought together in the zygote unite (Figure 2.3*k*); this nuclear union is termed *karyogamy*. This, of course, results in an association of two sets of parental chro-

---

* When sexually compatible individuals are present in a culture (population) that has developed from one individual (a *clonal culture*), the culture is said to be *bisexual;* when the compatible mating types develop only from different clonal cultures or individuals, the cultures or individuals are said to be *unisexual*.

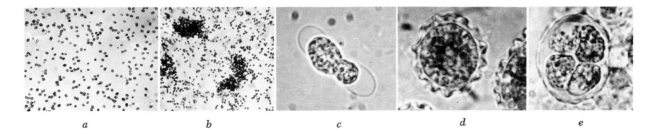

a   b   c   d   e

Figure 2.4   **The sexual reproduction of Chlamydomonas moewusii, photomicrographs.** *(a) Sexually mature cells of one mating type (−). (b) The same shortly after adding + gametes (note clumps of gametes and free pairs). (c) Uniting gametes, enlarged (flagella not shown). (d) Dormant zygote. (e) Germinating zygote, showing the four cells produced after meiosis. (Compare with Figure 2.3).*

mosomes and their genes within a single nucleus (*diploid*, 2*n*). In the process just described for *Chlamydomonas*, several phenomena are present that characterize almost all sexual reproduction. These are: (1) the union of cells; (2) the union of nuclei; (3) the association of chromosomes and genes; and (4) meiosis, to be discussed below. The parental chromosomes, however, retain their identity and do not unite in the fusion nucleus.

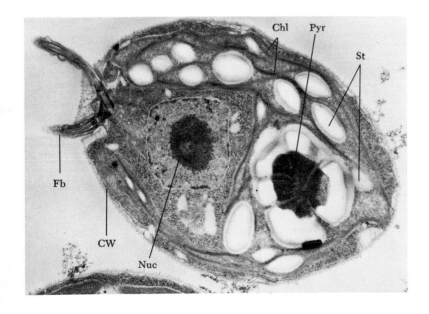

Figure 2.5   **Chlamydomonas reinhardtii Dang.** *Electron micrograph of median longitudinal section of a cell (× 7,190) Chl, chloroplast; CW, cell wall; Fb, flagellum; Nuc, nucleus; Pyr, pyrenoid; St, starch. [After D. L. Ringo.]*

ALGAE

In *Chlamydomonas,* the uniting gametes are the young organisms themselves (Figures 2.2*a* and 2.3*f*). In multicellular organisms, by contrast, the gametes are special cells of the mature organism, formed for the specific function of reproduction (Figure 2.2 *b,c*).

Several other features of the sexual process in *Chlamydomonas* illustrate important biological principles. A number of species produce gametes that are apparently not distinguishable as "male" and "female" and hence are termed *isogamous* (Figure 2.3*f–h*); other species of *Chlamydomonas* and most other organisms produce gametes that are clearly distinct from each other in size (Figure 2.3*n,o*) and these are designated male and female. Such gametes are called *heterogamous,* or *oogamous* if the larger one lacks flagella.

Among algae and other organisms, development of the zygote may follow one of two paths (see the accompanying diagram): (1) the

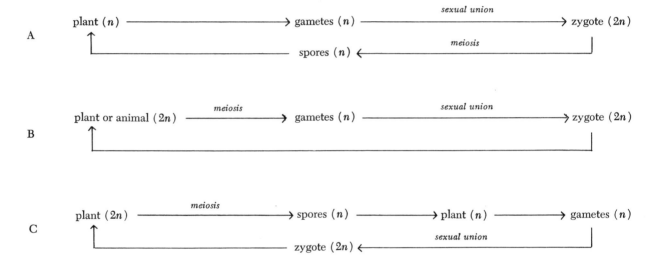

parental chromosomes and genes, brought together in the zygote nucleus, may segregate by *meiosis,* a special type of nuclear division. In this process, the chromosome number (2*n*) is divided in half (*haploid, n*) and genetic segregation occurs (life cycle A); or (2) the chromosomes may remain associated, each set then duplicating itself in nuclear divisions called *mitoses.* In mitosis, the original chromosome number is preserved by reduplication and segregation of genes does not usually occur (life cycles B and C).*

* For further discussion of meiosis and mitosis, see in this series C. P. Swanson, *The Cell* (3rd ed.) (Englewood Cliffs, N.J.: Prentice-Hall, Inc., 1969).

In the first alternative above (life cycle A), four haploid (n) cells arise as a result of meiosis.* This occurs in *Chlamydomonas* and certain other algae and fungi. But in the second alternative above (life cycles B and C), when the zygote nucleus undergoes mitotic, rather than meiotic, division, nuclei result with twice the chromosomal and genic complement of the gametes; such nuclei are diploid ($2n$). This second alternative, involving mitotic divisions of the zygote nucleus, occurs almost universally in the animal kingdom, in certain algae and fungi, and in the more complex plants having sexual reproduction.

In life cycle C, in which the zygote and its descendants also divide mitotically to form a diploid organism, meiosis may give rise to haploid spores rather than to gametes as in life cycle B. Each haploid spore develops into a haploid phase (a free-living plant or merely haploid tissue), which at maturity forms gametes. Life cycle C includes two alternating phases or individuals that differ in both chromosome number and type of reproductive cell produced. In this type of cycle the diploid, spore-producing phase has been designated as the *sporophyte* and the haploid, gamete-producing phase, the *gametophyte*. Accordingly, three fundamental patterns of reproductive or life cycle, summarized in the diagram, occur among algae and, in fact, among all living organisms.

The origin of the sexual process is unknown, but the study of simple algae such as *Chlamydomonas* has provided certain clues. That sexual reproduction is not necessary to maintain a race is clear from the fact that in certain organisms, gametes that fail to unite may develop into new haploid individuals; this is an example of *parthenogenesis*. Recent researches indicate that although the sexual process in plants is a manifestation of profound physiological changes within the organism, it may be evoked or modified by manipulation of certain external factors such as temperature, duration of illumination, and amounts of carbon dioxide and nitrogen available. It is clear also that the sexual process is the basic mechanism of evolution, for it affords the opportunity in all populations where it occurs to initiate new combinations of genes and to transmit them to subsequent generations. The importance of this process in bringing together two or more favorable mutant genes in one organism, and its effect on survival and evolution, can scarcely be overestimated. Conversely, the unfavorable combinations of genes that arise in sexual reproduction play a decisive role in the elimination of individuals and species through evolutionary competition with more favorable genetic combinations.

---

* In some cases, one or more of the nuclear products of meiosis may disintegrate.

In concluding this introduction to the algae, let us direct our attention again to their classification (Tables 1.1 and 2.1). The major groups of algae are blue-green algae (Cyanophycophyta), green algae (Chlorophycophyta), brown algae (Phaeophycophyta), and red algae (Rhodophycophyta). Except for the diatoms of the Chrysophycophyta, the remaining groups are smaller, yet they contain numerous economically important and biologically interesting organisms. We shall consider these divisions one by one.

CYANOPHYCOPHYTA   The blue-green algae were named for the color of the cells of many of the species, although this color is by no means universal. They occur in marine, fresh, and brackish waters, as well as in terrestrial and subterranean environments. A number of blue-

Figure 2.6 **Blue-green algae.** *(a) Electron micrograph of a section through several cells of the filamentous alga Plectonema boryanum. Note concentric photosynthetic lamellae, PL, and central, diffuse nucleoplasm, Nucp. [After K. M. Smith, R. M. Brown, D. A. Goldstein, and P. L. Walne.] (b) Diagram of the organization of a blue-green algal cell as revealed by the electron microscope. Note ingrowing septum of dividing cell, right. [After J. C. McMenamin.]*

a

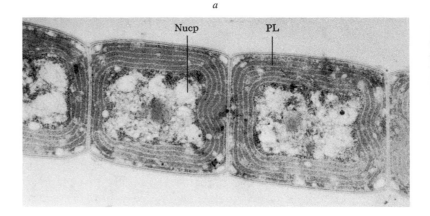

b

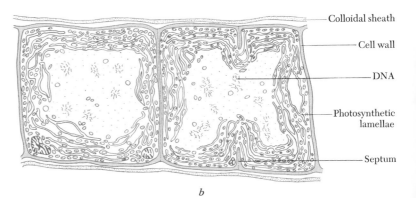

green algae live in and around hot springs, where they color surrounding rocks with their deposits. In addition to the attributes cited in Table 2.1, blue-green algae differ from other algae in lacking membrane-bounded nuclei, in the organization of the pigmented cytoplasm, and in lacking mitochondria, Golgi apparatus, endoplasmic reticulum, and large, aqueous vacuoles (Figure 2.6). The cell structure is thus much like that of bacteria (see Figures 3.1 and 3.2). The photosynthetic lamellae are not enclosed by membranes to form plastids, as in the green algae and other plants. The walls of some blue-green algae have been shown to contain various substances such as α,ε-diaminopimelic and muramic acids, which are present also in the walls of Gram-negative bacteria. Furthermore, several D-amino acids occur only in the walls of blue-green algae and certain bacteria. The DNA in blue-green algae is dispersed within the cell, which is hence said to be *prokaryotic*. Unicellular, colonial, and filamentous forms of blue-green algae occur.

The unicellular blue-green algae such as *Chroococcus* (Figure 2.7) multiply by repeated cell division or binary fission, followed by separation of the division products as individual cells. Failure of such cells to separate explains the colonial type of organization, as in *Merismopedia* (Figure 2.8), in which cell division in two planes results in growth of the colonies, which may reproduce by fragmentation. Reproduction by fragmentation occurs also in filamentous forms such as *Oscillatoria*, *Nostoc*, and *Anabaena* (Figure 2.9). The filaments of many species of *Oscillatoria* are motile, as are the fragments, called *hormogonia*, of many filamentous blue-green algae. The mechanism of their motility has never been adequately explained. Specialized thick-walled cells called *spores* or *akinetes* are produced by some filamentous genera, many of which also produce *heterocysts*, transparent thick-walled cells of uncertain function. (Figure 2.9*b*). It has been recently suggested that heterocysts are the site of nitrogen fixation in blue-green algae; a number of heterocystous blue-green algae fix nitrogen in a manner similar to that of certain bacteria (see page 42).

Sexual reproduction has so far not been observed in blue-green algae. Several reported indications of genetic interchange have not been supported by unequivocal evidence, nor has reported transduction by a blue-green algal virus.

CHLOROPHYCOPHYTA   The green algae have many attributes in common with the more complex land plants, as is indicated by the data in Table 2.1. They are as widespread in occurrence as blue-green algae, but are predominant in bodies of fresh water; many of the tubular and membranous forms, however, are marine. There are unicellular, colonial, filamentous, membranous, and tubular genera among the green algae, and sexual reproduction ranges from isogamous to oogamous. In addi-

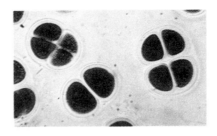

Figure 2.7   Chroococcus turgidus, a unicellular blue-green alga, in division.

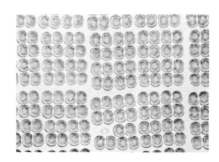

Figure 2.8   Merismopedia sp., a colonial blue-green alga. The colony is a flat sheet of cells one layer thick.

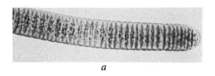

a

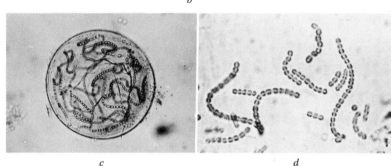

Akinete

Vegetative or somatic cell

Heterocyst

b

Figure 2.9   *Filamentous blue-green algae. (a) Oscillatoria sp. Note lack of differentiation. (b) Anabaena sp. Note the thick-walled, dormant spore, or akinete. (c) Nostoc sp.; filaments within colloidal matrix. (d) Nostoc; individual filaments. Note cells in division.*

c

d

Figure 2.10   *Unicellular green algae. (a–c) Chlorococcum sp., a zoospore-producing organism. (a) Vegetative cell. (b) Zoosporangium. (c) Zoospore. (d) Chlorella sp. and (e) Eremosphaera viridis, both nonzoospore producers.*

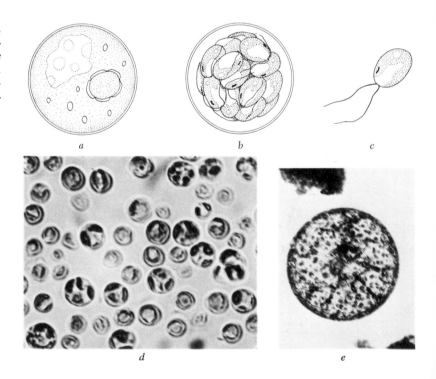

a

b

c

d

e

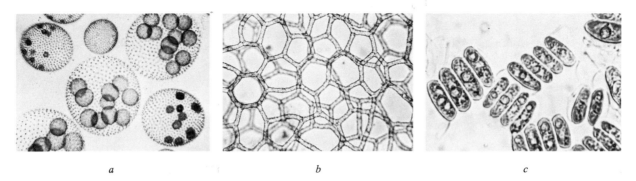

a   b   c

Figure 2.11   **Colonial green algae.** *(a) Volvox aureus, colonies motile (note daughter colonies within parent colonies). (b) Hydrodictyon reticulatum, the "water net," a zoospore producer. (c) Scenedesmus sp.*

tion, asexual reproduction by flagellate spores, called *zoospores* (see Figure 2.12*b,c*), occurs in many genera.

The reproduction of *Chlamydomonas* (see Figures 2.3 and 2.4), a motile green alga, has already been described in some detail. Its eukaryotic cellular organization is illustrated by electron microscopy in Figure 2.5 and explained in the figure caption. The presence of a pigmented stigma or red eyespot is characteristic of many motile algal cells and is somehow related to their phototactic responses (movements stimulated by light).

Nonmotile, unicellular green algae may (*Chlorococcum;* Figure 2.10*a–c*) or may not (*Chlorella, Eremosphaera;* Figure 2.10*d–e*) reproduce by forming zoospores. Colonial organization among green algae is exemplified by *Volvox* (Figure 2.11*a*), *Hydrodictyon* (Figure 2.11*b*), and *Scenedesmus* (Figure 2.11*c*), in which daughter colonies arising within each cell of a parental colony reproduce the species. Zoospores are produced either singly or in multiples of two by the cells of such filamentous green algae as *Ulothrix* (Figure 2.12) and *Oedogonium* (Figure 2.13*a*), which are anchored to the substrate by holdfast cells. The sexual reproduction of *Ulothrix* is isogamous, while that of *Oedogonium* is oogamous. In *Oedogonium,* the large, nonmotile eggs are

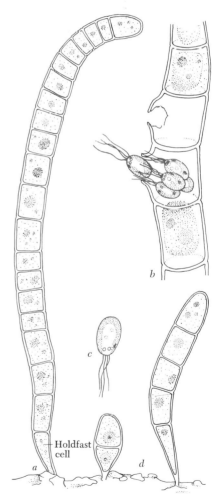

Figure 2.12   **Ulothrix sp., a filamentous green alga.** *(a) Mature vegetative plant. (b) Zoospore formation. (c) Zoospore. (d) Development of quiescent zoospore into young filament.*

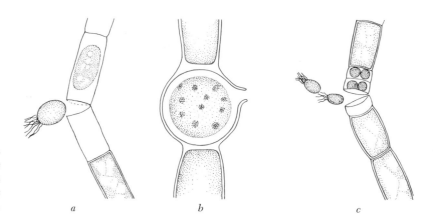

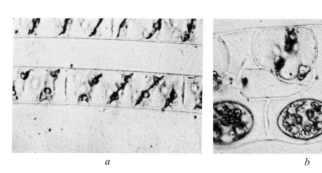

Figure 2.13 *Oedogonium sp., a fila-mentous green alga. (a) Zoospore formation. (b) Female plant with oogonium containing egg. (c) Male plant with antheridia liberating sperm.*

a   *b*   *c*

Figure 2.14 *Spirogyra sp., a fila-mentous green alga. (a) Vegetative filaments (note the single twisted chloroplast in each cell). (b) Sexual re-production by conjugation (note ovoidal zygotes).*

a   *b*

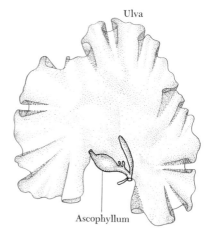

Ulva

Ascophyllum

produced within specialized cells, the *oogonia* (Figure 2.13*b*), which open at maturity by pores or fissures; the multiflagellate sperms develop within small boxlike cells (Figure 2.13*c*), the *antheridia*.

A number of unbranched filamentous green algae such as the familiar *Spirogyra* (Figure 2.14) have elaborate chloroplasts and reproduce sexually by a conjugation process that consists of the union of ameboid gametes (Figure 2.14*b*). All the genera of green algae so far discussed have a life cycle of type A (see diagram on page 20); the sea lettuce, *Ulva* (Figure 2.15), a membranous green alga widespread in marine waters, has a life cycle of type C.

Finally, mention must be made of a group of largely tropical, marine

Figure 2.15 *Ulva lactuca (the "sea lettuce"), a membranous green alga attached to Ascophyllum, a brown alga.*

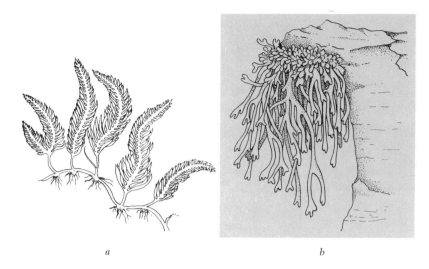

a   b   c

Figure 2.16   *Tubular green algae. (a) Caulerpa sp. (b) Codium sp. (c) Enlarged view of surface of Codium.*

green algae in which the sometimes large and elaborate plant bodies are composed of continuous multinucleate tubes (Figure 2.16), which are often interwoven. The life cycle in these forms is of type B. Of special interest and importance in biological research is the genus *Acetabularia* (Figure 2.17), the mermaid's parasol or wine goblet;[*] this genus grows in tropical and subtropical waters, attached to calcareous substrates such as shells.

PHAEOPHYCOPHYTA   The brown algae (Table 2.1) are almost exclusively marine. The simplest among them are branching filaments; unicellular and colonial types are unknown. In this group are also coarse plants like the kelps (see Figure 2.19) and rockweeds, such as *Fucus* (see Figure 2.20). Both the complexity of organization and the size of the kelps exceed those of other algae and, indeed, those of many land plants.

Ectocarpus (Figure 2.18) grows attached to coarser marine algae, shells, rocks, and submerged woodwork. The cells of the branching filaments contain brown, bandlike plastids. Two kinds of reproductive organs are formed during the type C life cycle. On the Massachusetts

[*] See in this series C. P. Swanson, *The Cell* (3rd ed.) (Englewood Cliffs, N.J.: Prentice-Hall, Inc., 1969).

Figure 2.17   *Acetabularia crenulata.*

coast, the diploid plants (Figure 2.18*a–c*) produce enlarged, unicellular zoosporangia in which meiosis occurs. As a result, within these *unilocular* zoosporangia are formed 32 to 64 laterally biflagellate, haploid zoospores (Figure 2.18*c*). These develop into the haploid sexual plants (Figure 2.18*d*), which are, except for their gametangia, similar to the diploid plants. The haploid plants develop multicellular (hence, *plurilocular*) gametangia, which produce gametes (Figure 2.18*e,f*); the zygotes then formed develop into the diploid plants. Certain other types of life cycle have been reported for species of *Ectocarpus* from Naples and from the Isle of Man.

Among the kelps, *Laminaria* (Figure 2.19*a*), one of the smaller genera, often 3 to 10 ft long, is widely distributed. The plant consists of a flattened blade that may be branched, connected to a rather massive, branching holdfast that anchors the organism to the rocky bottom. Growth occurs at the junction of blade and stipe, both of which are quite complex internally. The life cycle of *Laminaria* corresponds to type C but in this case the haploid and diploid phases are markedly dissimilar. The plant itself is the diploid sporophyte, on the surface of which unilocular zoosporangia develop. After meiosis, these liberate 32 to 64 zoospores that develop into microscopic filamentous gameto-phytes, which produce the eggs and sperm (Figure 2.19*b,c*). After

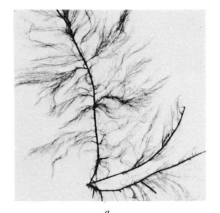

a

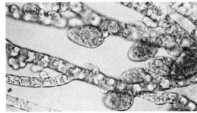

b

Figure 2.18 **Ectocarpus sp., a filamentous brown alga.** *(a) Habit of growth, natural size. (b) Diploid plant (sporophyte) with unilocular zoosporangia. (c) Enlarged view of zoosporangia. (d) Haploid plant (gametophyte) with plurilocular gametangia. (e) Single plurilocular gametangium. (f) Gamete (note unequal, lateral flagella).*

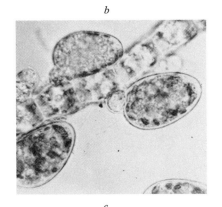

c

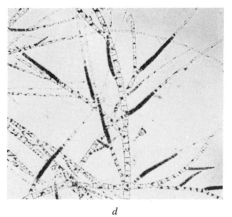

d

e

f

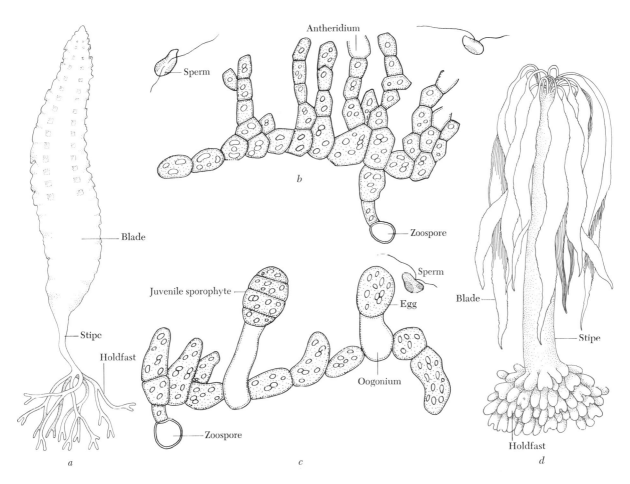

Figure 2.19   *Two kelps. (a–c) Laminaria agardhii. (a) The sporophyte. (b) Male gametophyte. (c) Female gametophyte. (d) Postelsia palmaeformis. The holdfast is also known as a haptera.*

union of these gametes, the zygotes develop into new *Laminaria* plants (Figure 2.19*c*). This type of life cycle occurs in all the kelps.

The rockweed, *Fucus* (Figure 2.20*a*), and the gulfweed, *Sargassum* (Figure 2.21) have life cycles of type B. The diploid plants produce oogonia and antheridia in special chambers or conceptacles (Figure 2.20*b,c*). Meiosis occurs in the young sex organs so that the sperm and eggs are haploid. The zygotes develop into a new generation of diploid plants.

RHODOPHYCOPHYTA   The red algae (see Table 2.1) are also largely

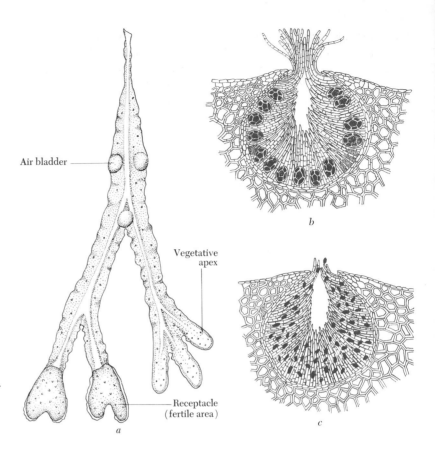

Air bladder

Vegetative
apex

Receptacle
(fertile area)

a

b

c

*Figure 2.20   Fucus vesiculosus, rock-
weed. (a) Habit of growth. (b) Section
of oogonial conceptacle, each oogonium with eight eggs. (c) Section of
antheridial conceptacle.*

marine, although a number of freshwater forms occur. Some of the red
algae are especially beautiful, both in nature and when mounted as
herbarium specimens on white paper. In a number of red algae, the
process of sexual reproduction is quite complicated. In the more complex cases, three sequential phases occur in the reproductive cycle,
namely: (1) a haploid, sexual phase; (2) a diploid, spore-producing
phase; and (3) a haploid, spore-producing phase. This is exemplified by
Polysiphonia (Figure 2.22), and *Callithamnion* (Figure 2.23), common
marine red algae in which the life cycle is a modified form of type C.
There are haploid male and female gametophytes, which at maturity
bear sperm and eggs, respectively (Figure 2.23*a,b*): in the Rhodophycophyta the sperm are called *spermatia* and are produced in spermatangia; the eggs are produced in *carpogonia*, each of which has an
elongate receptive protuberance called the *trichogyne* (Figure 2.23*a*).
After fusing with neighboring cells and without undergoing meiosis,

the zygote gives rise to a mass of diploid *carpospores* within an urnlike container; the carpospores and their container are called a *cystocarp* (Figure 2.23c), and are borne upon the female plant. The carpospores develop into diploid plants (Figures 2.23d) similar, except in chromosomal constitution, to the sexual haploid plants. At maturity these diploid plants (*tetrasporophytes*) produce *tetrasporangia* (Figure 2.23d,e), each of which gives rise through meiosis to four spores called *tetraspores*. This rather complicated life cycle may be summarized as in the accompanying diagram.

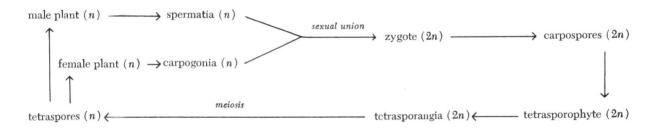

Figure 2.21   (Left) Sargassum filipendula, a brown alga related to Fucus.

Figure 2.22   (Right) Polysiphonia sp., a filamentous red alga, with branches of colorless male gametes. [Courtesy of Dr. Peter Edwards.]

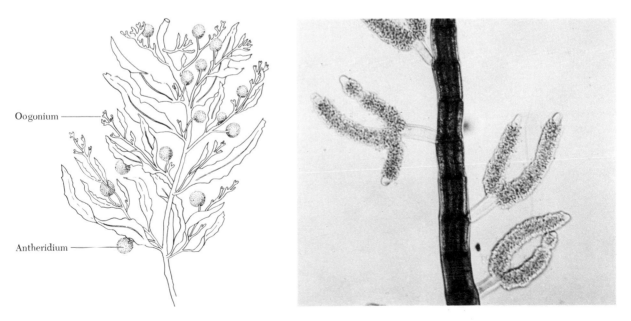

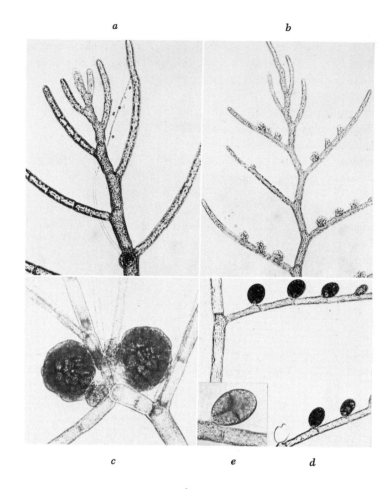

Figure 2.23 **Callithamnion byssoides (in culture), life history.** *(a) Female gametophyte (note extremely long trichogyne with spermatia attached). (b) Male gametophyte with clusters of spermatangia containing spermatia. (c) Two cystocarps (carposporophytes) resulting from fertilization, on female plant. (d) Tetrasporophyte with tetrasporangia, one empty, and (e) one enlarged.* [Courtesy of Dr. Peter Edwards.]

Figure 2.24 **Euglena mesnilii, a unicellular organism.** *(a) Living individual with short flagellum, Fla, and stigma, Sti, visible. (b, c) Stages in reproduction by cell division, here binary fission.*

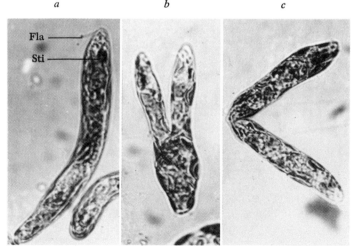

It should be emphasized that this type of life cycle differs essentially from type C only in the intercalation of the diploid carpospore (sometimes called carposporophyte) stage between the zygote and tetrasporophyte stages.

EUGLENOPHYCOPHYTA   Euglenoids (Table 2.1, Figures 2.24 and 2.25), which are unicellular and flagellate, are well known through such examples as *Euglena, Phacus,* and *Trachelomonas.* They may exhibit such animal-like attributes as contractile fibers at the cell surface, invaginations of the cell surface, contractile vacuoles, and changes of cellular form. Although their pigments are identical with those of Chlorophycophyta (see Table 2.1), Euglenophycophyta differ (from the green algae) in the nature of their storage products, their lack of cellulose walls, and in other details of cellular organization. Sexual reproduction in euglenoids is unknown.

Euglena (Figures 2.24 and 2.25) illustrates most of the attributes of the Euglenophycophyta. The cell undergoes continuous changes in form,

Figure 2.25   *Euglena granulata, electron micrograph.* Chl, *chloroplast;* Ca, *canal;* Fla, *flagellum;* Nuc, *nucleus;* Pe, *periplast;* Pyr, *pyrenoid;* Sti, *stigma.* [Courtesy of Professor H. J. Arnott.]

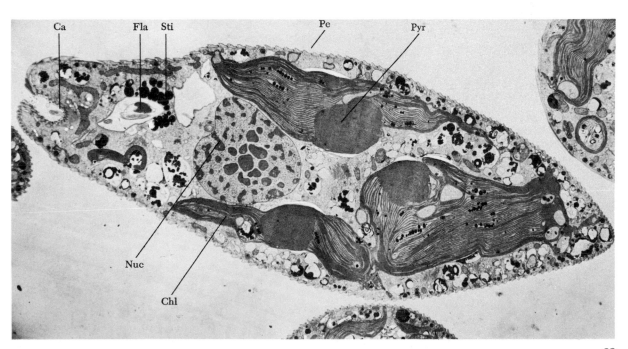

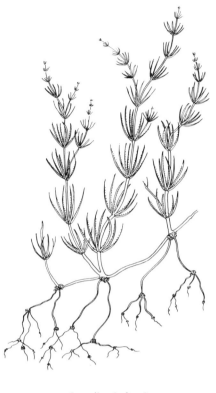

made possible by the pliable consistency of the surface layer of proto-plasm, the *periplast*, which often has characteristic spiral markings. The anterior pole of the *Euglena* cell (Figure 2.25) is colorless and contains a flasklike invagination, the *canal* and *reservoir*, at the base of which the two flagella are attached; only one flagellum is emergent. The granular stigma or red eyespot is prominent at the anterior end of the cell, as is a large contractile vacuole which empties into the reservoir. The form of the chloroplasts varies in the different species, but in all of them the large nucleus is central. *Euglena* does not ingest food, as some of its colorless, and thus more animal-like, relatives do. *Euglena* reproduces by binary fission (Figure 2.24*b,c*), and may undergo encystment.

CHAROPHYTA   Similar in pigmentation and in starch storage to both the Chlorophycophyta and green land plants, the Charophyta, here exemplified by *Chara* (Figure 2.26), differ considerably in organization from other algae. Stonewort plants are divided into nodes and inter-nodes, with whorled branches at the nodes. The long internodal cells, in which cytoplasmic streaming may be readily observed, may or may not be surrounded by corticating cells.

The oogonia and antheridia of the Charophyta (Figure 2.27) are complex and are covered with sterile cells; they are thus suggestive of the sex organs of green land plants. The site of meiosis (and hence the life cycle) of Charophyta has not yet been discovered.

DIATOMS   Class Bacillariophyceae of the Chrysophycophyta, the diatoms (Table 2.1, Figures 2.28 and 2.29), are organisms of great biological interest and economic importance. The cell walls of diatoms are impregnated with varying amounts of silicon dioxide. These walls (*frustules*) persist after the death of the protoplasts within, and vast deposits of them from ancient seas today furnish us with *diatomaceous earth*, which has many important uses (among others, in filtration).

Two series of diatoms have been distinguished on the basis of their symmetry: (1) the bilaterally symmetrical, or pennate, types; and (2) the radially symmetrical, or centric, types. Pennate diatoms are abundant in both fresh and salt water, whereas the centric type is most abundant in marine waters.

All diatom cells are composed of two slightly overlapping cell walls (shells or frustules composed of two *valves;* Figure 2.29). They multiply

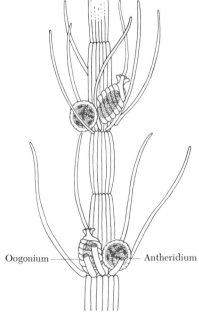

Oogonium ———— ———— Antheridium

Figure 2.26   *(Top) Chara sp. Note whorled branching and rhizoidal system.*

Figure 2.27   *(Bottom) Chara sp.: sex organs.*

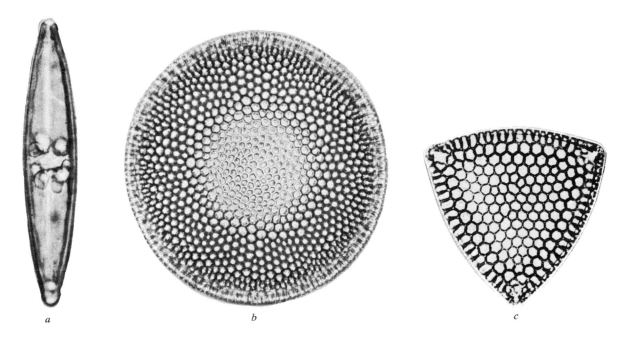

Figure 2.28   *Chrysophycophyta, diatoms. (a) Navicula sp. (b) Coscinodiscus sp. (c) Triceratium sp.*

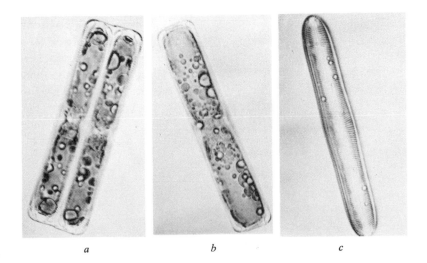

Figure 2.29   *Pinnularia sp. (a) Valve view. (b) Girdle view. (c) Cell division.*

by a longitudinal cell division in which one daughter cell uses the slightly smaller valve as a cover, while the other uses the larger one in the same way. Thus, in many diatoms, cell division results in diminution of size in part of the population.

Diatoms are apparently diploid, and meiosis precedes their sexual reproduction. In most pennate diatoms, the valves are thrown off as one or two amoeboid gametes from paired individuals conjugate. The resulting zygote enlarges considerably before it secretes entirely new walls. In some centric diatoms, reproduction is oogamous; a small uniflagellate sperm unites with another cell's protoplast, which functions as an egg.

Chemical analysis of Precambrian shales (see Table 6.1) has provided abundant evidence that the crude oil and other matter present in the shales represent carbon compounds originating from photosynthesis; this photosynthesis may be inferred to have been performed by algae. The fossil record has provided little evidence regarding the origin, interrelationships, and course of evolution of the algae. There is direct evidence that blue-green and probably green algae were among the earliest living organisms, already present on the earth more than 3 billion years ago (see Figure 2.1); because of their prokaryotic cellular organization, the blue-green algae are different from all the other groups and most probably are more closely related to bacteria. The resemblance of these ancient fossil algae to currently living (extant) species is remarkable in some cases.

With respect to the eukaryotic algae, the occurrence of unicellular, flagellate, motile stages in many otherwise nonmotile organisms suggests that they evolved from a flagellate ancestry. These flagellates probably diversified during the course of evolution into the variety of organisms discussed in earlier pages. Increase in size sometimes involved cellular differentiation and consequent specialization in the plant body, as in the kelps (for example, *Laminaria*); at other times tissue differentiation did not occur (for example, in *Ulva*, the sea lettuce). Type of sexual reproduction—isogamy, heterogamy, and oogamy—apparently evolved independently of body form. For example, all three patterns of sexual reproduction occur among the species of the single unicellular genus *Chlamydomonas*, while algae with more complex organization may exhibit isogamy (*Ulothrix*, *Ectocarpus*) or oogamy (*Oedogonium*, kelps, red algae). The algae also provide examples of increasing specialization and segregation of reproductive tissues from somatic or vegetative tissues. Thus, in unicellular organisms like *Chlamydomonas*, there is seemingly no morphological difference between young vegetative cells and gametes (see Figure 2.2*a*). By contrast, the reproductive function is localized in special organs (*Oedogonium;* see Figure 2.13*b,c*) or branches (*Ectocarpus;* see Figure 2.2*c*) in many algae.

Because of fundamental similarities, especially with respect to pigmentation and stored photosynthate, between the Chlorophycophyta and the land plants (so-called higher plants), it is generally considered that the former represent the ancestral line from which the latter evolved. Current evidence indicates that the other divisions of algae did not evolve beyond the algal level.

It is hoped that these pages have given you some insight into what algae are and how useful they are, both economically and biologically. The reference works listed under Selected Readings at the end of the book contain more complete accounts of these exceedingly important and interesting members of the plant kingdom.

3 BACTERIA, SLIME MOLDS, AND FUNGI

CHLOROPHYLLOUS PLANTS, USING LIGHT ENERGY, ARE ABLE TO CONVERT low-energy compounds—namely, carbon dioxide and water—into energy-rich carbohydrates in the process of photosynthesis. From simple sugars or fragments of them as basic units, with the addition of inorganic materials absorbed from the soil or the water in which they are bathed, green plants are able to synthesize their protoplasm. They are said to be *photoautotrophic*, therefore, because they use light energy to build living matter from inorganic substances. Of organisms lacking chlorophyll, the great majority are dependent on the complex substances manufactured by green plants for the materials with which to build their bodies; these organisms are *heterotrophic*. The distinction between these groups is not absolute. Certain green plants can live heterotrophically in light and darkness when supplied with appropriate organic compounds.

Some heterotrophic organisms, called *parasites*, require the living protoplasm of their hosts or grow upon them, sharing their metabolites. Others are *saprophytic*, requiring either nonliving protoplasm or the nonliving products of protoplasm. They thus occur in soil, in water-containing organic matter, and upon inadequately protected wood, textiles, and foods. The saprophytic heterotrophs are the main agents in degrading the complex products of other organisms and in causing decay of their bodies after death. Thus, decaying organic materials are broken down in many stages to carbon dioxide, water, and many other inorganic compounds, a common pool of substances that can be incorporated anew into the bodies of other organisms. The processes of degradation are especially striking as one digs down carefully through layers of undisturbed forest litter. Were it not for the activity of heterotrophs making available elements bound up in other organisms, life would be limited by a grave shortage of certain materials, especially available nitrogen.

A third group of heterotrophic organisms, which includes most animals, ingests protoplasm or its products; these are called *phagotrophic* or, sometimes, *holozoic*.

A few bacteria, although lacking chlorophyll, can synthesize their protoplasm from low-energy inorganic compounds by using the chemical energy released in oxidation of these compounds (see page 42). Organisms of this type are said to be *chemoautotrophic*. It should be emphasized that the same essential major chemical elements—carbon (C), hydrogen (H), oxygen (O), phosphorus (P), potassium (K), nitrogen (N), sulfur (S), calcium (Ca), iron (Fe), and magnesium (Mg)—are present in the protoplasm of most living organisms. Differences, however, prevail in the degree of complexity of carbon and nitrogen compounds required for the synthesis of protoplasm. Autotrophic organisms start with simple compounds of these substances—carbon dioxide (CO_2), water (H_2O), ammonia (NH_3), and nitrates (NO_3^-). In summary, autotrophs may be photoautotrophic or chemoautotrophic, depending on the primary source of their energy.

In the preceding paragraphs, we have, in effect, classified living organisms on the basis of their nutrition. With few exceptions, heterotrophic members of the plant kingdom comprise those organisms known as bacteria, slime molds, and fungi (see Table 1.1). Most of these organisms are structurally as simple as or even simpler than the algae. It has been suggested by certain biologists that some of the fungi may have derived from algae by loss of chlorophyll. Others consider protozoa as ancestral to fungi, for some fungi, like protozoa, are phagotrophic.

Although united by their common lack of chlorophyll and consequent lack of photoautotrophic nutrition (except in the case of certain bacteria), considerable diversity exists among the bacteria, slime molds, and fungi, which accordingly are classified as separate groups (see Table 1.1). The increasingly long list of common attributes shared by bacteria and blue-green algae has impelled some to classify these organisms together in a group, Prokaryota, an allusion to their lack of membrane-bounded nuclei and (in the blue-green algae) plastids.

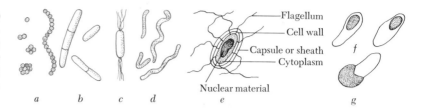

Figure 3.1   Bacteria. (a) Cocci. (b) Bacilli, two in division. (c) Polar-flagellated bacillus type. (d) Spirillum. (e) Cellular organization of a peritrichous bacterium. [After E. E. Clifton.] (f) Spore formation. (g) Spore germination.

Flagellum
Cell wall
Capsule or sheath
Cytoplasm
Nuclear material

a   b   c   d   e   f   g

Bacteria are probably the most simple and minute living organisms with cellular organization. Bacterial cells are usually less than 8 μm (micrometers)* in length and may be as little as 0.5 μm in width. The cells of bacteria may be of three types: (1) spherical, the *cocci* (singular, *coccus*); (2) rod-shaped, the *bacilli;* or (3) spiral-shaped, the *spirilla* (Figure 3.1*a–d*). The first two may be joined to form colonies or filaments. The individual cells, like those of blue-green algae, differ from other plants in nuclear organization and in lacking large aqueous vacuoles (Figures 3.1*e* and 3.2). Bacterial cells contain DNA, the almost universal basis of

* A micrometer is 0.001 mm or about 0.00004 in.

Figure 3.2   Bacillus aneurinolyticus, electron micrograph. DNA, region of deoxyribonucleic acid. [Courtesy of Dr. James Whitliff.]

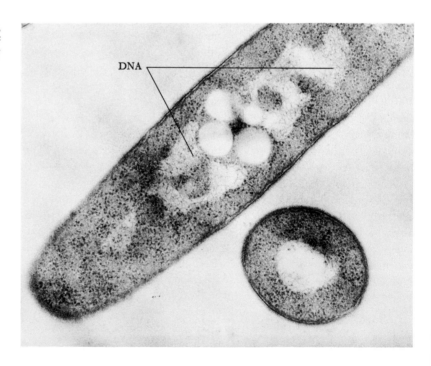

DNA

heredity, but it is not localized within a nuclear membrane; furthermore they lack other membrane-bounded organelles such as mitochondria, Golgi apparatus, and endoplasmic reticulum. Some genera have flagella (Figure 3.1c,e), and consequently can move. Certain types form thick-walled spores (Figure 3.1f,g) that are remarkably resistant to desiccation and unfavorable environmental conditions and are not unlike some blue-green algal spores.

Bacteria multiply by a cell division that may be repeated rapidly, as often as once every 15 to 20 min (minutes). It has been estimated that if one bacterial cell and its progeny were to continue multiplying at this rate for 24 hr (hours), the number of individuals produced would be 1×10^{21}, with a total group weight of 8,000 lb (pounds)! Why, then, is the world not overrun by bacteria? The answer, of course, lies in their requirement for a specialized environment, their competition with other microorganisms—namely algae, fungi, protozoa, and other bacteria—and finally, their accumulation of toxic products. Biologists sometimes lose sight of these facts in applying to natural situations conclusions that are based on pure cultures of microorganisms.

That certain bacteria also have a mechanism for genetic interchange was first demonstrated in 1946 by Joshua Lederberg and Edward L. Tatum when they cultivated together populations of two mutants of the colon bacillus *Escherichia coli;* each of the mutants was unable to synthesize two (of four) substances required in nutrition and metabolism. One required biotin and methionine, while the other required threonine and leucine; each could synthesize the two substances required by the other. Out of each billion cells from the culture of mixed mutants planted in a medium lacking all four required substances, approximately 100 colonies appeared. This is a clear manifestation that genetic interchange had occurred between individuals in the cultures of mixed mutants. This evidence of interchange of genes is incontrovertible, although the satisfactory demonstration of this change cytologically has been belated.[*] One example of the evidence is presented in Figure 3.3.

That relatively simple morphology does not preclude physiological and biochemical complexity is strikingly evident in the bacteria. A few are chemoautotrophic and photoautotrophic in nutrition. The former obtain energy from oxidations to build their protoplasm from entirely inorganic units. Two nitrifying bacteria, *Nitrosomonas* and *Nitrobacter,* exemplify chemoautotrophic types; they obtain their energy as indicated in the following reactions.

Figure 3.3 **Cytological evidence of genetic interchange in the bacterium Escherischia coli.** *Note connection between individuals of morphologically distinct strains.* [Courtesy of Dr. Thomas F. Anderson, after F. Jacob and E. L. Wollman.]

---

[*] For another mechanism of bacterial interchange of genetic materials, see in this series D. M. Bonner and S. E. Mills, *Heredity* (2nd ed.) (Englewood Cliffs, N.J.: Prentice-Hall, Inc., 1964).

Nitrosomonas:

$$NH_4^+ + 2O_2 \longrightarrow 2H_2O + NO_2^- + \text{energy}$$

Nitrobacter:

$$NO_2^- + \tfrac{1}{2}O_2 \longrightarrow NO_3^- + \text{energy}$$

Photosynthetic bacteria, such as *Rhodospirillum,* although photoautotrophic, carry on a type of photosynthesis quite different from that of plants that have chlorophyll *a,* for in these bacteria, which contain bacteriochlorophyll,* no free oxygen is released, and hydrogen is provided by donor substances other than H_2O, such as hydrogen sulfide (H_2S) or alcohol, with low expenditure of energy.

The vast majority of bacteria are heterotrophic, and their widespread chemical activities, catalyzed by myriads of enzymes, constitute the major areas of research in current microbiology and bacteriology. As they affect mankind, bacterial activities are both harmful and beneficial, but the beneficial ones probably exceed the harmful.

Bacteria cause diseases in both plants and animals. These *pathogenic* types affect their hosts adversely by robbing them of vital metabolites, by enzymatically destroying host tissues, and sometimes by secreting poisons. It is significant that some bacteria themselves are subject to the ravages of pathogens in the form of bacterial *viruses,* called *bacteriophages,* which destroy the bacterial cells. Nonpathogenic bacteria can be bothersome too, for they are instrumental in spoiling foods and in causing decay in materials man desires to preserve.

The activities of bacteria in spoiling foods are only a special example of their universal activities in decay and degradation, processes accomplished by many types of bacteria and fungi through their enzymes. These processes culminate ultimately in the production of CO_2, H_2O, and many other inorganic compounds. The value of such destructive activities in freeing bound metabolites has already been cited (see page 39).

The importance of bacteria in maintaining soil fertility, especially in replenishing the element nitrogen, which is an essential part of proteins, is paramount. Certain bacteria, either living freely in the soil or in the roots of legumes (beans, clover, alfalfa, and so forth) or certain nonlegumes (alder, *Casuarina, Myrica*) use molecular nitrogen in synthesizing their protoplasm, thus tapping a source of nitrogen not available to most other organisms. (A number of blue-green algae func-

---

* Chlorophyll *a* occurs in all green plants. Certain accessory chlorophylls, such as chlorophyll *b,* differ in their side chains and absorption spectra. Bacteriochlorophyll differs from chlorophyll *a* in that its pyrrole rings II and IV are reduced and an acetyl group is present in side-chain position 2.

tion similarly.) Other bacteria oxidize NH_3 to nitrites (NO_2^-) and NO_3^-, thereby enriching the nitrogen supply in the soil and reducing the escape of gaseous NH_3 from it.

The cheese industry depends on the bacteriological fermentation of lactose, a milk sugar, and the production from it of lactic acid, which coagulates the milk proteins and forms curds (and whey). The formation of acetic acid (in vinegar) is effectively accomplished by other bacteria; this occurs in the souring of cider and wines. Numerous other potentially useful chemical activities of bacteria have been controlled for man's benefit.

Not the least important of these is the production by bacteria of mild *antibiotics** such as tyrothricin, bacitracin, subtilin, polymyxin B, and the production by certain filamentous, bacterialike organisms called Actinomycetes of powerful antibiotics such as streptomycin, aureomycin, and terramycin. The Actinomycetes are like fungi in having filaments and producing spores, but their biochemical attributes and nuclear and cellular organization link them more closely with bacteria.

Bacteria, like algae, are ancient organisms. They have been preserved as fossils, in spite of the delicacy of their cells, in precambrian strata at least 2 billion years old (Figure 3.4). Their manifold activities through the ages and at present emphasize their important role in the biological scheme. They are classified as plants largely because botanists made the early studies of bacteria. During the last 75 years, however, the study of bacteria has become a special area of biological science, *bacteriology,* and bacteria are often classified together with blue-green algae in a separate kingdom, Prokaryota.

Figure 3.4   *Precambrian fossil bacteria (bacilli), approximately 2 billion years old* $(\times 17,250)$. [After J. W. Schopf, E. S. Barghoorn, M. D. Maser, and R. O. Gordon; micrograph by M. D. Maser.]

MYXOMYCOTA: THE SLIME MOLDS

The slime molds (Figures 3.5 to 3.7) have been considered to be either "animal-like plants" or "plant-like animals," depending on whether a botanist or a zoologist is discussing them. The modern biologist finds such questions of less critical interest, in view of the remarkable uniformity of organization and function of living systems at the molecular level, although the question has meaning from an evolutionary perspective. Since slime molds have been classified both as fungi and as protozoa, we shall consider them in this book as a division separate from other fungi (see Table 1.1.)

However classified, slime molds are inhabitants of decaying plant

---

* Antibiotics are products of organisms (usually microorganisms) that arrest the development of one or more other organisms.

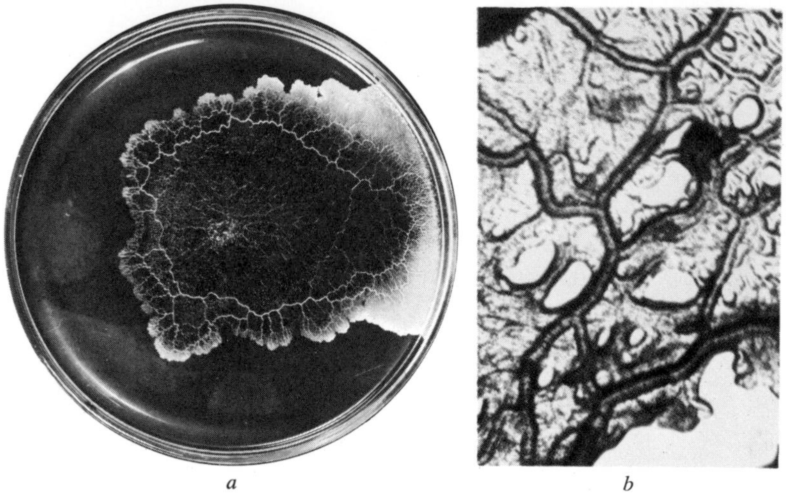

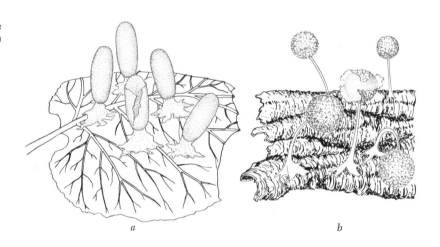

a   b

Figure 3.5   *Slime mold. (a) Plasmodium of Physarum polycephalum on agar in a Petri dish.* [Courtesy of C. J. Alexopoulos.] *(b) Portion of plasmodium magnified showing streams of unwalled protoplasm.* [Micrograph by M. D. Maser.]

Figure 3.6   ***Spore-bearing structures of slime molds.*** *(a) Diachea sp. (b) Lamproderma sp.*

a   b

materials such as moist logs, twigs, leaves, and so forth. In many of the Myxomycota, two flagellate isogametes unite to produce a motile, diploid zygote (Figure 3.7*c,d*). The zygote sooner or later loses its flagella and becomes ameboid as it moves over the substrate, engulfing bacteria and organic particles that are then digested in vacuoles. As this occurs, more protoplasm is synthesized, and the zygote nucleus divides mitotically. Repeated nuclear divisions of the resulting diploid nuclei, without accompanying cytoplasmic division, result in the development of a more or less extensive ameboid mass of protoplasm, the *plasmodium* (Figures

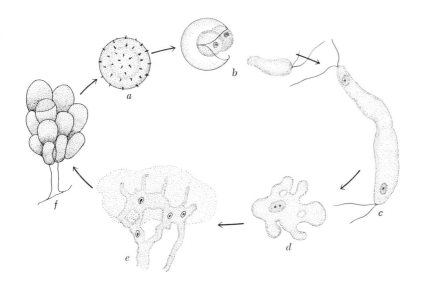

Figure 3.7 Life cycle of a slime mold. (a) Dormant spore. (b) Spore germination to form motile gametes. (c) Gamete union. (d) Zygote. (e) Portion of plasmodium (compare with Figure 3.5). (f) Sporangium. [Modified from C. J. Alexopoulos.]

3.5 and 3.7e). This is considered to be the *somatic* or *vegetative* phase of the life cycle.

Under suitable conditions of moisture and nutrition, plasmodia several square feet in area may arise. Sooner or later, localized upwellings of the plasmodium, with simultaneous dehydration, give rise to a spore-producing reproductive phase (Figures 3.6 and 3.7f); this varies in form in the different genera of slime molds. As the spore-bearing structures mature, meiosis occurs in the young spores; therefore the mature spores (Figure 3.7a) contain haploid nuclei. Upon dissemination, these spores germinate (on a suitably moist substrate) to form motile, flagellate gametes (Figure 3.7b). The stationary sporogenous phase, in contrast with the plasmodial one, is more typically plantlike. The naked, multinucleate plasmodia of some slime molds, which can readily be maintained and increased in the laboratory, have long been a favorite experimental material of biochemists and biophysicists, because they provide protoplasm for immediate chemical analysis without the complication of nonliving cellulose walls, and they are excellent for the study of stimulus, response, and protoplasmic synthesis.

Superficially similar to Myxomycota are the cellular slime molds, exemplified by *Dictyostelium* (Figure 3.8), which has been a frequent and fruitful subject of biological investigation. Although they apparently have the same type of life cycle, cellular slime molds differ from slime

ACRASIOMYCOTA: THE CELLULAR SLIME MOLDS

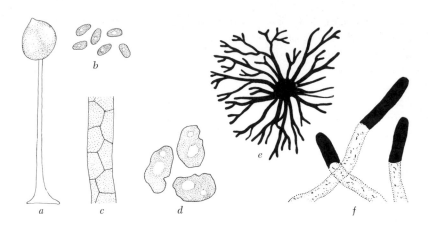

*Figure 3.8 **Dictyostelium sp.** (a) Stalked spore-bearing structure. (b) Spores. (c) Portion of stalk of (a) showing component cells. (d) Ameboid stage. (e) Streams of aggregating amebae. (f) Migrating pseudoplasmodia, or slugs, with slime trails behind.* [Courtesy of John T. Bonner, Kenneth B. Raper, and the Princeton University Press.]

molds in forming a *pseudoplasmodium,* a mass of individual, uninucleate amebae that have aggregated after leading an individual existence. This group of aggregated amebae, called the *slug,* builds a spore-producing structure composed of amebae, some of which then function as spores (Figure 3.8*a,b*). These continue the cycle at germination by forming amebae. The pseudoplasmodium is preceded by a nutritive phase in which individual amebae feed and multiply independently. Later, when they gather together to form the slug and finally, spores, the amebae abandon their completely independent existence. Thus, in the ontogeny of these organisms there occurs the formation of a "republic" or a "federation" by free-living individuals. This developmental pattern exemplifies a possible transition from unicellular to multicellular organisms, as suggested by some biologists.

FUNGI

Most fungi differ from the slime molds in lacking plasmodial stages and phagotrophic nutrition; they differ from the bacteria in their nuclear organization, in which respect they more closely resemble the algae (except blue-green algae) and higher plants. The plant bodies of fungi are among the simplest in the plant kingdom, being either unicellular or filamentous. In the latter case, the plant body is called the *mycelium;* the individual filaments are called *hyphae.* These hyphae may be composed of cells with one, two, or many nuclei, or they may be tubular, with no transverse walls (*coenocytic*), like certain algae (see page 27). The cell walls of most fungi are composed of chitin, whereas others contain cellulose and other polysaccharides. The mycelium spreads over and through the substrate or host, absorbing nutrients for growth by secreting enzymes that digest some of the components of the substrate (the soluble products then diffuse into the hyphae). Some fungi develop special absorptive branches, called *rhizoids* in saprophytic species, and *haustoria* in parasitic ones. In many fungi, the spore-producing filaments are raised above the remainder of the mycelium (see Figures 3.12 and 3.14).

Aquatic fungi with zoospores are considered primitive, and non-aquatic types with airborne spores are presumed to have arisen from them. Both saprophytic and parasitic organisms occur. The type of parasitism varies from superficial and facultative to systemic and obligate.*

In striking contrast with the relatively simple and unspectacular vegetative mycelium is the "fruiting body," which arises in some of the sac and club fungi (see Figures 3.16 and 3.18*a*)—including the familiar morels, mushrooms (toadstools), puffballs, and shelf fungi. It is important to remember, however, that the fruiting body of a fungus has been preceded by an extensive vegetative mycelium that has sometimes grown for months or years.

NOTES ON SOME DIVISIONS OF FUNGI   Like that of algae, the classification of fungi has undergone modification (see Table 1.1) with an increased tendency toward a polyphyletic system. The most recent change has been in the dismemberment of a single taxon which formerly included so-called algalike fungi (Phycomycetes, Phycomycota) and the elevation of its components to higher categories of classification. This abbreviated account of the fungi will discuss representatives of only the Chytridiomycota, Oomycota, Zygomycota, Ascomycota, and Basidiomycota, briefly mentioning the Deuteromycota and lichens.

Chytridiomycota   The Chytridiomycota are mostly aquatic organisms that occur in muds and on decaying plants and animals. They may parasitize aquatic plants and animals and even other fungi.

Among the simplest members of this group are the chytrids, here represented by *Rhizophydium globosum* (Figure 3.9), which lives saprophytically on the leaves and stems of submerged plants. This unicellular organism begins life as a posteriorly uniflagellate zoospore that settles

Figure 3.9   *Rhizophydium globosum, a chytrid, growing on the leaf cell of an aquatic plant.* Note release of zoospores.

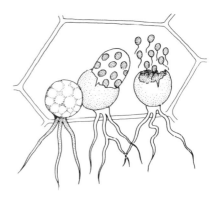

---

* These types of parasitism may be defined as follows: In superficial parasitism the parasite is on the surface of the host, and does not pervade the host as it does in systemic parasitism. In obligate parasitism no nutritive substitute can replace the living host; facultative parasites can grow on nonliving subtrates and also on living hosts.

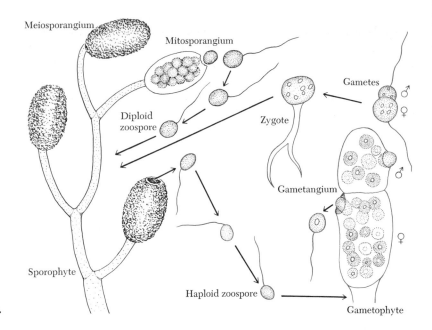

Figure 3.10   Allomyces macrogynus.

on the surface of the host cell and, at germination, produces a globose vegetative cell with rhizoidal appendages. At maturity, the vegetative cell becomes transformed into a zoosporangium from which released zoospores start new infections.

Allomyces (Figure 3.10), a widely distributed genus of Chytridiomycota, is of interest for a number of reasons. It is a mycelial organism that grows saprophytically on plant debris in aquatic habitats; it may be readily isolated from this debris by using small, boiled, split seeds (often hemp seed), as bait. The mycelium is coenocytic and only incompletely septate, except at the sites of gametangial and sporangial origin, where complete septa occur. Absorptive rhizoidal hyphae penetrate the substrate, functioning in anchorage. After a period of growth, the plants mature and produce reproductive organs (see diagram on next page).

The life cycle of *Allomyces macrogynus,* summarized in the accompanying diagram, is of type C (see page 20). Thick-walled, rust-colored *meiosporangia* as well as thin-walled *mitosporangia* are produced by the diploid plants (Figure 3.10). Both types of sporangia produce posteriorly uniflagellate zoospores. Those which are from the mitosporangia are diploid and grow into new diploid thalli if a suitable substrate is available, whereas haploid zoospores from the meiosporangia develop into mycelia, which produce gametangia (Figure 3.10). The male gametangia are orange at maturity. Heterogametes pair and undergo plasmogamy and karyogamy to form zygotes that develop directly into diploid mycelia. It has been demonstrated that a sexual hormone, *sirenin,* attracts the free-swiming male gametes to the female gametangia and gametes.

Oomycota The Oomycota are so called because their sexual reproduction is oogamous, involving the fertilization of large eggs by nuclei from a male hypha that functions like an antheridium. A few Oomycota are parasitic, causing economically important diseases such as grape and potato blights.

Achlya (Figure 3.11), one of the "water molds," is here chosen as a representative of the Oomycota. The numerous species of *Achlya* may be isolated readily from pond water and from soil submerged in water. The substrate in nature is often a dead insect, but boiled, split hemp seeds and other small seeds are favorite laboratory substrates. Most species of *Achlya* are saprophytic, but parasitism—on fish, for example—occurs in the related genus *Saprolegnia*. The mycelium of *Achlya* forms a radiating mass of branching, tubular, multinucleate, nonseptate filaments surrounding the substrate (Figure 3.11a), evidence of the efficiency of the absorptive rhizoids and the enzymes they produce. After a short period of development, the tips of certain hyphae are delimited by septa and function as zoosporangia (Figure 3.11b), each of which produces a large number of zoospores (Figure 3.11c). These encyst at the apex of the sporangium and biflagellate zoospores later emerge from the cysts, migrate to other available substrates, and there form new mycelia and zoosporangia.

Sexual reproduction is apparently initiated when growth depletes

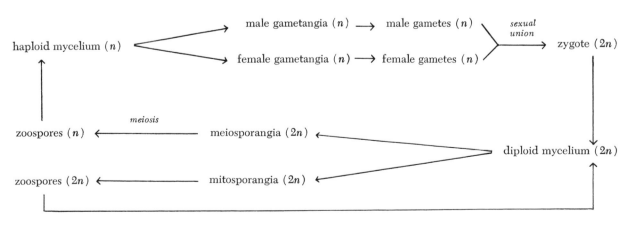

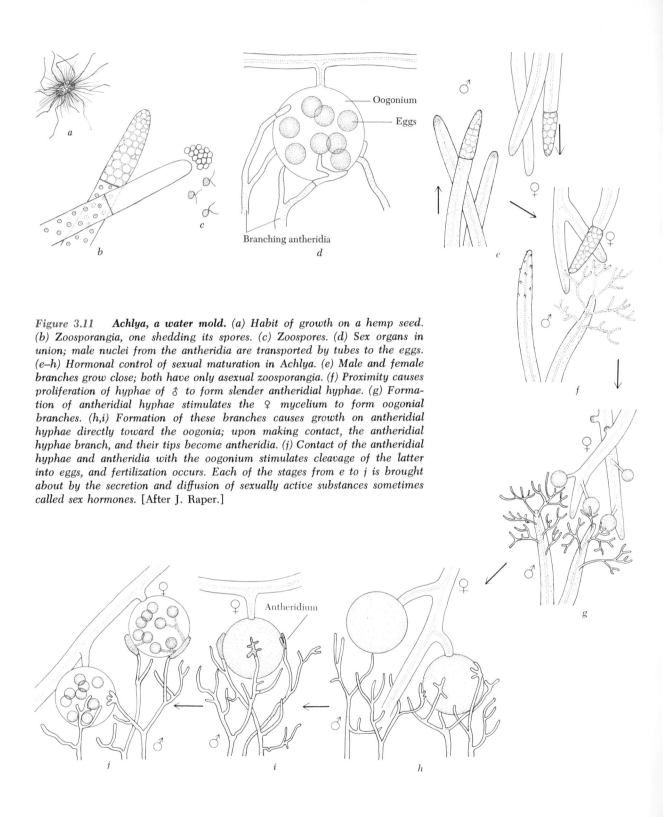

Figure 3.11   Achlya, a water mold. (a) Habit of growth on a hemp seed. (b) Zoosporangia, one shedding its spores. (c) Zoospores. (d) Sex organs in union; male nuclei from the antheridia are transported by tubes to the eggs. (e–h) Hormonal control of sexual maturation in Achlya. (e) Male and female branches grow close; both have only asexual zoosporangia. (f) Proximity causes proliferation of hyphae of ♂ to form slender antheridial hyphae. (g) Formation of antheridial hyphae stimulates the ♀ mycelium to form oogonial branches. (h,i) Formation of these branches causes growth on antheridial hyphae directly toward the oogonia; upon making contact, the antheridial hyphae branch, and their tips become antheridia. (j) Contact of the antheridial hyphae and antheridia with the oogonium stimulates cleavage of the latter into eggs, and fertilization occurs. Each of the stages from e to j is brought about by the secretion and diffusion of sexually active substances sometimes called sex hormones. [After J. Raper.]

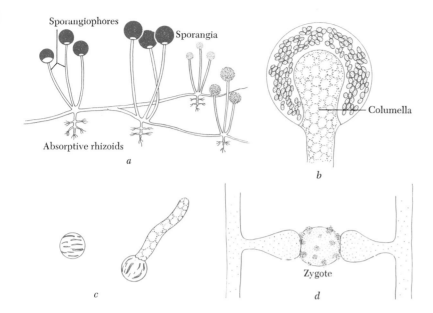

Sporangiophores

Sporangia

Columella

Absorptive rhizoids

a

b

Zygote

c

d

*Figure 3.12 **Rhizopus stolonifer,** "black mold of bread." (a) Habit of growth. (b) Median longitudinal section of sporangium with sterile, central columella covered by spores. (c) Spore germination. (d) Sexual stage with zygote.*

certain substances. Particularly interesting investigations have been made of this process as it occurs in the species *Achlya ambisexualis*. In this organism, in which the male and female sex organs (Figure 3.11*d*) are produced on separate individuals, the formation and functioning of the sex organs are controlled by chemical substances from the sterile male and female plants and later from their differentiated sexual branches themselves. The rather complex process is summarized in Figure 3.11*e–j*, which illustrates the orderly, progressive, and correlated steps in the production and union of sex organs. The chemicals that evoke these steps are termed *hormones*.

Zygomycota   The sexual reproduction of the coenocytic Zygomycota is by a conjugation process (Figure 3.12) that is in some respects similar to, but also different from, that of the alga *Spirogyra*. *Rhizopus stolonifer* (Figure 3.12), often called "Black Mold of Bread" (here chosen to represent the Zygomycota), consists of tubular, multinucleate hyphae differentiated into prostrate branches, absorptive *rhizoids*, and erect *sporangiophores*. The blackness of the walls of the myriad spores is responsible for the color of the mature fungus. If the spores fall upon a suitable substrate, they germinate and produce mature, sporebearing mycelia within 72 hr, under favorable conditions. It was in *Rhizopus* that *self-incompatability*, or *heterothallism*, of fungi was first demonstrated, early in the twentieth century. When compatible mating types grow close together, the sexual process results (Figure 3.12*d*); it is clearly affected by hormonelike secretions. Closely

BACTERIA, SLIME MOLDS, AND FUNGI

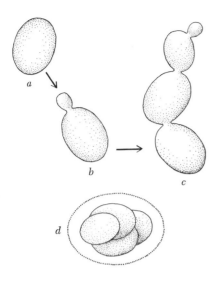

Figure 3.13 Saccharomyces cere-visiae, brewer's yeast, highly magnified. (a–c) Reproduction by budding. (d) Ascus containing ascospores.

growing, compatible + and − hyphae develop lateral branches which become contiguous. The ends of these, after contact, are delimited by septa and unite to form a black, dormant zygote, the compatible pairs (+ and −) of nuclei within it uniting. Unless both mating types are present, only asexual reproduction occurs. Meiosis is probably zygotic in *Rhizopus;* if so, its life cycle is of type A (see page 20).

Ascomycota The Ascomycota include several mostly saprophytic groups—the yeasts (Figure 3.13), the brown, green, and pink molds (Figure 3.14), and the morels and cup fungi (Figure 3.15)—as well as the parasitic powdery mildews (Figure 3.16). The ascus usually contains either four or eight *ascospores* (Figures 3.13*d* and 3.16). An *ascus* is a saclike cell within which ascospores are formed; some residual cytoplasm is not incorporated within the spores. The asci may be formed directly, or in a special fruiting body, the *ascocarp* (Figures 3.14*e*, 3.15, and 3.16).

Among the simplest Ascomycota are the yeasts, here exemplified by the brewer's yeast, *Saccharomyces cerevisiae* (Figure 3.13). Yeasts, which occur commonly in nature on ripening fruits, are simple unicellular organisms. Cellular multiplication by an unequal bipartition known as *budding* (Figure 3.13*a–c*) rapidly increases the population in suitable environments containing sugar. That *Saccharomyces* is an

Figure 3.14 Brown and blue-green molds. (a) Penicillium sp.; culture in a Petri dish of potato dextrose agar. (b) Aspergillus sp. (c–f) Penicillium sp. (c) Spore chains. (d) Germinating spore. (e) Section of ascocarp containing asci and ascospores. (f) Single ascus.

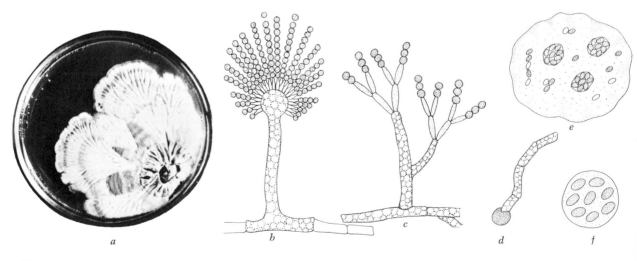

ascomycete is apparent by its production under certain conditions of ascospores in groups of four (Figure 3.13d). The yeast plant, of course, has been the servant of mankind from antiquity, both as a leavening agent and as a producer of ethyl alcohol from sugars. The degradation of the sugar involved, known as *fermentation*, is catalyzed by an enzyme complex called *zymase;* the process is intracellular, and is enhanced under anaerobic conditions. The low energy yield is evidence of the incomplete breakdown of sugar; much more energy still remains in the alcohol produced. Some yeastlike fungi are pathogenic and parasitize human beings. The life cycle of yeast is essentially of type C (see page 20).

Several genera of ascomycetous molds like *Aspergillus* and *Penicillium** (Figure 3.14) are significant for a variety of reasons. Most species are saprophytic and widespread on organic substrates; their airborne spores are everywhere. Flagellate motile cells do not occur in the life cycles of these fungi. Colonies of these genera often will grow on a piece of moistened bread exposed to the atmosphere and then covered by a glass tumbler, or on overripe fruit.

Aspergillus and *Penicillium* (Figure 3.14) belong to a group of brown and blue-green molds. Here again, the color resides in the spore walls, although certain species like *Penicillium chrysogenum* secrete a golden yellow pigment into the culture medium. The asexual spores are borne in chains on erect branches of the mycelium (Figure 3.14b,c). Some species produce closed ascocarps containing the asci and asco-spores (Figure 3.14e,f), presumably after sexual fusions. *Penicillium* is an especially important genus, since it affects human welfare in several ways. On the adverse side, certain species may cause respiratory infections, clothing mildew, and food spoilage (especially of citrus fruits and apples). Other species, though, have important roles in the manufacture of such cheeses as Roquefort and Camembert. Far overshadowing all other useful activities, however, is the production of the life-saving antibiotic *penicillin* by *Penicillium chrysogenum*.

Neurospora, a pink ascomycetous mold, has contributed heavily to our knowledge of the mechanism of heredity and gene action.†

The morels (Figure 3.15a) and cup fungi (Figure 3.15b,c) are Ascomycota that produce fleshy ascocarps in which asci are borne. The shallow cups of *Peziza* and other cup fungi are common on moist wood, in which the vegetative portion of the fungus ramifies as it digests the

* Strictly speaking, *Aspergillus* and *Penicillium* are Deuteromycota (see p. 57); however, some ascomycetous genera such as *Eurotium* and *Eupenicillium* have *Aspergillus* and *Penicillium* stages in their life cycle.

† For more on this matter, see in this series D. M. Bonner and S. E. Mills, *Heredity* (2nd ed.) (Englewood Cliffs, N.J.: Prentice-Hall, Inc., 1964).

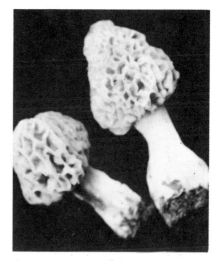

a

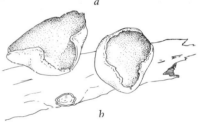

b

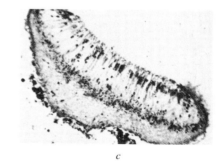

c

Figure 3.15 **Fungi.** *(a) Morchella sp., the morel. (b) Peziza sp., a cup fungus; ascocarp. (c) Pyronema sp., a cup fungus; section of ascocarp.*

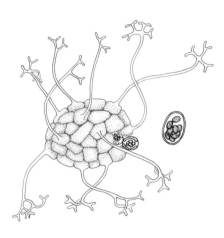

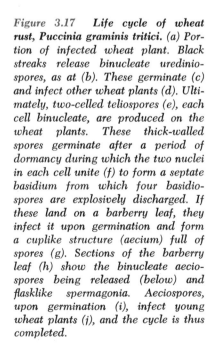

Figure 3.16 Microsphaera sp., a powdery mildew. Ascocarp (fruiting body) with appendages, slightly crushed, with detail of single ascus.

cellulose and lignin. The inner surface of the cup is lined with sterile hyphae (*paraphyses*) and columnar asci containing ascospores (Figure 3.15*c*).

Finally, the powdery mildews of the Ascomycota are widespread as obligate parasites upon many flowering plants. Their hyphae, which absorb food from the leaf cells, produce both asexual spores and ascocarps (Figure 3.16) containing asci and ascospores. Powdery mildews are common on plantain, roses, cereal grains, and lilacs, among others.

Basidiomycota To the Basidiomycota belong those fungi which produce *basidia* and *basidiospores* freely on the mycelium or in various types of fruiting structures, or *basidiocarps* (Figure 3.18*a* and 3.19). Basidia are either clublike hyphae, each (usually) with the four basidiospores borne at its apex (Figure 3.18*c*), or septate hyphae arising upon germination of thick-walled spores (Figure 3.17*f*). The Basidiomycota include the economically important parasitic rusts and smuts of cereal grains and other plants, the mushrooms and puffballs, and the pored shelf fungi, some of which destroy timber and lumber.

Among the Basidiomycota, the *rusts* are worth consideration for two

Figure 3.17 Life cycle of wheat rust, Puccinia graminis tritici. (a) Portion of infected wheat plant. Black streaks release binucleate urediniospores, as at (b). These germinate (c) and infect other wheat plants (d). Ultimately, two-celled teliospores (e), each cell binucleate, are produced on the wheat plants. These thick-walled spores germinate after a period of dormancy during which the two nuclei in each cell unite (f) to form a septate basidium from which four basidiospores are explosively discharged. If these land on a barberry leaf, they infect it upon germination and form a cuplike structure (aecium) full of spores (g). Sections of the barberry leaf (h) show the binucleate aeciospores being released (below) and flasklike spermagonia. Aeciospores, upon germination (i), infect young wheat plants (j), and the cycle is thus completed.

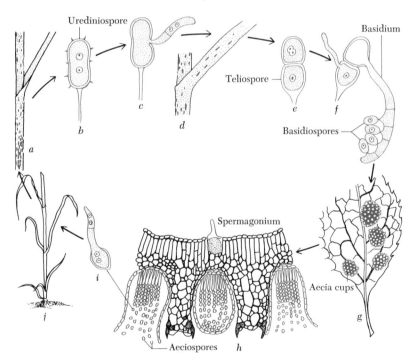

reasons: economically, they cause decreased yields in grains and other plants, and biologically they represent the classic examples of several striking phenomena. The wheat rust (Figure 3.17), a strain of *Puccinia graminis,* grows parasitically in the leaves and stems of wheat (other strains occur on other grains), absorbing materials from the wheat protoplasm. At maturity, the hyphae of *P. graminis* erupt in localized lesions on the host leaves and stems, producing large numbers of rust-colored spores that repeat the cycle, thus infecting many new plants. At least four additional types of reproductive cells are produced in the life cycle of this fungus, as summarized in the caption of Figure 3.17. A number of features of the wheat rust are significant. *Puccinia graminis,* like the powdery mildews of the Ascomycota, is a specialized parasite that has only recently been cultivated apart from its wheat host* or its alternate host. Apparently in nature the hosts supply it, during most of its life cycle, with the substances it requires to build its protoplasm. How this and similar host-parasite relationships have been initiated in the course of evolution is by no means clear. The specific requirement of wheat rust for wheat protoplasm is the more remarkable because in another phase of its life cycle (Figure 3.17g,h) the parasite is dependent on another host plant, the native American barberry, *Berberis vulgaris,* which is not closely related to wheat.

Mushrooms (Figure 3.18), the inedible and poisonous species of which are called "toadstools" by the layman, are saprophytes; they depend on wood and on soils rich in organic matter. The mushroom itself is the basidiocarp, or fruiting body, of the organism. It is preceded by and develops upon an extensive vegetative mycelium. Unlike most plants and animals, in which cells divide and redivide to form the tissues of the body, the mushroom is built up by complicated interwoven hyphae of the filamentous mycelium. The mushroom cap bears *gills* on its lower surface. The gills (Figure 3.18a–c), also composed of interwoven hyphae, produce the basidia and basidiospores (Figure 3.18c,d). Meiosis occurs in the basidium so that the basidiospores are haploid (*n*); these, upon germination, produce a *primary mycelium,* the cells of which are uninucleate. When compatible pairs of such mycelia are grown together, plasmogamous fusions occur between certain compatible cells, but nuclear union is delayed until basidia are formed. This plasmogamy initiates the *secondary mycelium,* with binucleate (*n* + *n*) cells from which the basidiocarp is formed. The common edible mushroom, *Agaricus campestris,* is grown commercially from "spawn," a mass of soil, manure, and rotting leaves that contains the

---

* A related rust fungus parasitizing cedar trees was previously cultivated apart from its host.

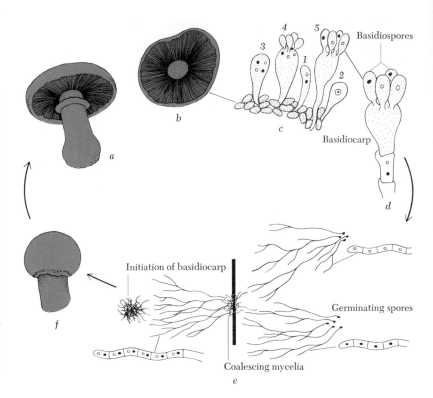

Figure 3.18 **Life cycle of a mushroom.** *(a,b) Fruiting structure, or basidiocarp, showing gills. (c) Portion of a gill: (1) binucleate basidium; (2) basidium after nuclear fusion; (3) basidium after meiosis; (4) early stage in formation of basidiospores; (5) mature basidiospores. (d) Basidium and basidiospores enlarged. (e) Spore germination and formation of young mushroom; the spores of two mating types germinating and the resulting primary mycelia coalescing to form the secondary mycelium from which a new basidiocarp will arise. Note enlargements showing both primary mycelia containing nuclei of the opposite mating types (shown as white and black) and segment of secondary mycelium with compatible nuclei brought together in the same mycelium. (f) Immature basidiocarp.*

mycelium of the fungus. When planted into properly prepared beds, the basidiocarps—that is, the mushrooms—develop after a period of vegetative growth of the mycelium.

Two additional features of mushrooms are of special interest—namely, the bioluminescence of some species and the hallucinogenic properties of others. The mycelium of certain mushrooms, both in laboratory cultures and in nature, is luminescent. This luminescence is mediated by the enzyme *luciferase* in the presence of luciferin as substrate. Substances bearing a similar name are also functional in the firefly, but evidence to date indicates these are of a different chemical nature.

The mushroom, *Psilocybe* * *mexicana,* and related species were and are valued for the ecstatic effects they generate when eaten. The chemical nature of the active substances is being investigated, and one of the hallucinogenic substances synthesized (psilocybin) is being used in the study of certain mental aberrations.

* Pronounced "sigh-lós-i-bee."

Puffballs (Figure 3.19a) are the fleshy (later dry) basidiocarps of fungi whose mycelium ramifies through rich soil and decaying stumps and lumber. The inside of the developing puffball contains many minute chambers lined with basidia, which form myriad spores. These spores are liberated by decay or compression of the dried basidiocarps.

Shelf and bracket fungi (Figure 3.19b) are the basidiocarps of wood-destroying fungi whose mycelia are within the host tree or the lumber that serves as substrate. Basidia line the numerous pores of these basidiocarps and are discharged from their cavities over long periods.

Finally, it is significant that in the majority of Basidiomycota, although a sexual process occurs, differentiated gametangia and gametes do not develop. This is, perhaps, but one step from isogamy (or as primitive), in which the gametes, although specially differentiated, are not morphologically distinguishable. These sexual processes of the algae and fungi are instructive with respect to the sexual process in general, because they are not obscured by secondary and supplementary phenomena.

Deuteromycota In Deuteromycota are classified a vast number of fungal species for which no sexual stages are known and which reproduce only by asexual spores. Their mycelia are septate, like those of Ascomycota and Basidiomycota. Both saprophytic and parasitic species are known; the latter are of economic importance as the etiological agents of diseases of cultivated plants such as celery, beans, onions, and apples, among others. Figure 3.20 illustrates one member of this vast assemblage.

Lichens Lichens (Figure 3.21) are dual organisms composed of an alga (green or blue-green) and a fungus. They are classified with Ascomycota or Basidiomycota, depending on their fungal component; in most lichens the fungus is a member of the Ascomycota. The nutritive relationships between the components have inspired much uncritical speculation, and the real relationships are only now being investigated by the techniques of pure culture. Recent work has shown that both the algal and fungal components of a lichen may lead independent existences in the same culture medium, even when placed in contact. Only when nutrition is minimal or subminimal and moisture is at a low level can the intimate association of fungus and alga be reestablished, forming a lichen.

Lichens may be encrusted on rocks or wood (*crustose*), or branched and emergent from the substrate (*fruticose*), or membranous and leaflike (*foliose*). The dual organism often is able to flourish in habitats where neither component could exist alone.

Lichens are propagated by windborne fragments that contain both alga and fungus. Each organism may also reproduce independently,

a

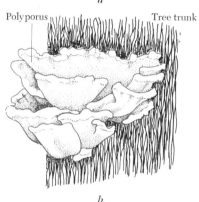
Polyporus   Tree trunk

b

Figure 3.19   *Fungi. (a) Lycoperdon sp., a puffball; basidiocarp on soil. (b) Polyporus sp., a shelflike pore fungus; basidiocarp on tree trunk.*

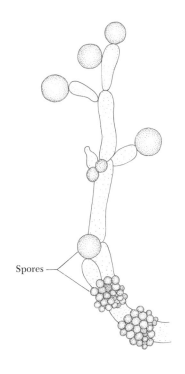

Spores —

*Figure 3.20 **Candida albicans, a member of the Deuteromycota.** Note spores of two different types.* [After C. J. Alexopoulos.]

liberating its reproductive cells from the lichen thallus; however, it is doubtful that new lichens are often synthesized from these in nature.

FOSSIL RECORD OF FUNGI   The fossil record of the fungi is not as clear as that of algae, but mycelial fungi were probably coexistent with algae and bacteria in the Precambrian (see Table 6.1 on page 98). Figure 3.22 illustrates a fossilized fungus from Carboniferous strata; well-preserved fossil fungi that parasitized Devonian plants have also been found.

IMPORTANCE OF FUNGI   The fungi, like the bacteria and slime molds, are of fundamental importance in medicine, industry, and other aspects of human welfare. The role of saprophytic fungi (and bacteria) in causing decay in moist habitats is of inestimable importance. On the one hand, were it not for their degradative activities in such habitats, vast quantities of nutrient materials would remain "locked up" in dead organisms and organic products, unavailable for recycling to other living organisms. On the other hand, these same degradative processes are of serious import in the preservation of cloth, insulation, lumber, and similar materials in moist environments.

*Figure 3.21   **Lichens.** (a) Several species on an oak branch; the fibrous, pendulous form at the right is a species of Usnea called "the old man's beard." (b) Algal cells (phycobiont) among fungal hyphae (mycobiont) of a lichen.*

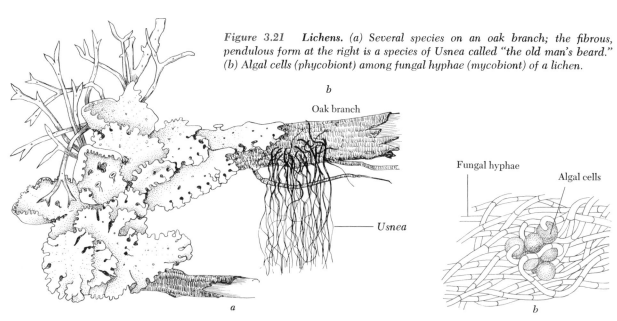

b

Oak branch

Fungal hyphae

Algal cells

Usnea

a

b

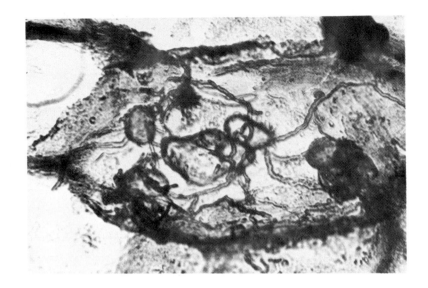

Figure 3.22 **Fossilized fungus in a rhizome of a Carboniferous plant.** [After H. N. Andrews and L. W. Lenz.]

Certain fungi have been of paramount importance in the development of the science of biochemical genetics. When subjected to mutagenic agents, these organisms have undergone a variety of genetic changes. These changes have been manifested in the chemical activities of the organisms, providing fundamental knowledge regarding the pathways of metabolism. Especially fruitful, in this connection, have been researches on the mold *Neurospora,* among others. Furthermore, parasitic fungi have directly inspired the genetic research that has provided mankind with many fungus-immune races of economically important plants. The fungi have been important, too, in the elucidation of the nature of specificity in host-parasite relationships.

4 NONVASCULAR LAND PLANTS: LIVERWORTS, HORNWORTS, AND MOSSES

IT IS GENERALLY BELIEVED THAT LIFE FIRST AROSE IN AN AQUATIC environment and that terrestrial plants and animals are the descendants of aquatic ancestors. Accordingly, land plants are considered to be the modified progeny of algae. In the plants that now populate and have in the past populated the earth, two diverse series are apparent, one possibly derived from the haploid and the other from the diploid algal ancestors. The plants of the first group, liverworts and mosses, are characterized by a lack of *vascular tissue*, that is, *xylem* and *phloem*, which, respectively, conduct water and food. The absence of vascular tissue probably accounts for the relatively small size of liverworts and mosses, as they do not have efficient systems for transporting water and food rapidly over any considerable distance. Plants in the second group have vascular tissue; this characteristic probably is correlated with the large size and complexity of many vascular plants, and their ability to live in harsh terrestrial habitats. To this group belong the ferns and other seedless vascular plants, as well as the seed-bearing plants.

Although liverworts, hornworts, and mosses are usually placed before the vascular plants in classifications of the plant kingdom (see

Table 1.1), they are not more ancient, according to present evidence from the fossil record (see Table 6.1 on page 98). Their place in systems of classification is probably inspired by their relative simplicity of form, their small size, and the lack of evidence that they are related to the vascular plants. A fossil liverwort and a fossil moss are illustrated in Figure 4.1.

Liverworts long ago received their rather curious name because the lobing of the plant bodies of some genera is suggestive of an animal liver. A number of botanists consider liverworts to be closely related to the mosses and classify them both in the division Bryophyta; others have challenged this view (see Table 1.1) because of differences between liverworts, hornworts, and mosses in the organization of both the gametophytic and sporophytic phases. Liverworts and hornworts, with a few conspicuous exceptions, seem to require moister conditions than do mosses, and grow on moist soil, rocks, and tree bark. The rhizoids of liverworts and hornworts, in contrast to those of mosses, are unicellular. The liverwort sporophyte is less complex than that of mosses and lacks a peristome (see page 72), which is present in the sporophyte of most mosses.

The essentials of organization of several commonly occurring liverworts, (*Ricciocarpus* and *Riccia*, *Marchantia*, and *Porella*) and of the hornworts will be presented in this section. The liverworts may be thallose,

LIVERWORTS

a

Figure 4.2 **Ricciocarpus natans, a thallose liverwort.**
(a) Plants floating on water (note dichotomous lobing and
the dorsal furrows). [Courtesy of Dr. W. C. Steere.] (b)
Transection of a plant in region of the antheridia. (c)
Median longitudinal section (m.l.s.) of single antheridium.
(d)Transsection of plant in the region of the archegonia.
(e) M.l.s. of an immature archegonium (f) M.l.s. of young
sporophyte within the enlarging archegonium (calyptra).
(g) M.l.s. of sporophyte at tetrad stage (note calyptra and
archegonial neck). Anth, antheridium; Arch, archegonium.

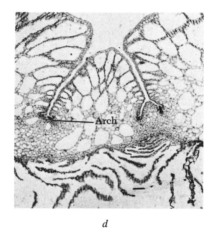

d

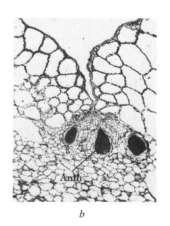

b

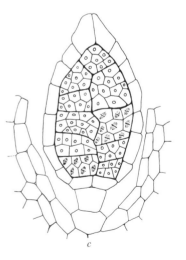

c

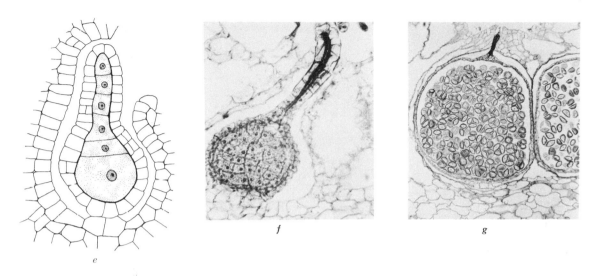

e

f

g

that is, without distinct axes and leaves (Figure 4.2*a*), or foliose (Figure 4.7*a*). The plant body of a nonvascular plant is often called the *thallus*.

RICCIOCARPUS AND RICCIA   The simplest of the thallose liverworts externally, *Ricciocarpus* (Figure 4.2) and *Riccia* (Figure 4.3), are more complex internally than one would expect. *Ricciocarpus natans* grows either floating upon quiet bodies of fresh water or resting on their muddy shores. *Riccia fluitans* is a submerged aquatic species that can be developed in aquaria, while most other species of *Riccia* form small rosettes, about 0.5 to 1 in. (inch), on moist soils.

Growth of these plants is strictly apical, and the pattern of development is *dichotomous*—that is, by equal lobing or branching into two parts. The aquatic plants lack rhizoids; the internal tissues are more or less spongy because of fissures and air chambers, but the plants are clearly differentiated into spongy (apparently photosynthetic) tissues and more compact storage tissues (Figure 4.2*b*).

At certain times of the year the *Ricciocarpus* plants become sexually mature, producing clearly distinguishable male and female gametangia on the dorsal surface, which may be infolded (Figure 4.2*b,d*). The male gametangia, which produce minute, biflagellate *sperm*, are called *antheridia* (Figure 4.2*c*); the female ones, called *archegonia* (Figure 4.2*d,e*), are approximately flask-shaped and at maturity contain single *eggs* within their bases. Accordingly, sexual reproduction here, as in all land plants, is oogamous. Unlike the gametangia of algae and fungi, archegonia and antheridia of land plants are composed of fertile cells surrounded by sterile ones (compare Figures 2.2 and 4.2*c,e*).

Figure 4.3   Riccia fluitans growing on inorganic agar medium.

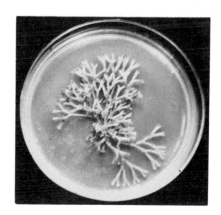

63

Ricciocarpus plants are *bisexual* in that *archegonia* and *antheridia* are both borne on one individual; depending on the particular species, *Riccia* plants may be bisexual or unisexual. In either case, the sperm, upon release from the mature antheridia, swim to those archegonia which are also mature. The maturity of the archegonia is evidenced by the disintegration and extrusion of the cells within the archegonial neck, making the egg available for union with the sperm. It is probable that here, too, as demonstrated in *Chlamydomonas, Oedogonium, Achlya* and ferns, a chemical secretion attracts the sperm to the archegonia.

In *Ricciocarpus* and *Riccia*, the zygotes undergo a number of mitoses and cytokineses, resulting in the development of a spherical mass of diploid tissues within the archegonium (Figure 4.2*f*). The archegonium is called a *calyptra* as it enlarges by cell division. Except for the superficial covering layer, the diploid cells, called *sporocytes* or *spore mother cells,* undergo two rapidly sequential nuclear divisions in which meiosis occurs, each giving rise to a tetrad of haploid cells (Figure 4.2*g*). These develop thick, impervious walls and separate from each other as *spores,* which are shed by decay of the gametophytic plants. After a period of dormancy they develop into new plants.

The reproductive cycle just summarized is basically the same in liverworts, hornworts, and mosses (and certain algae), in that it consists of two alternating phases, the haploid gametophyte and the diploid sporophyte. In *Ricciocarpus* and *Riccia*, the sporophyte consists of a sphere of diploid cells, located within the enlarged archegonium (calyptra) and the somatic tissues of the gametophyte. Chlorophyll is present within the cells of the sporophyte only in negligible amounts, if at all, and the sporophyte is clearly parasitic on the chlorophyllous gametophyte. Although the alternation of generations here is essentially similar to that of certain algae (those of life cycle C; see page 20), it differs in liverworts, hornworts and mosses in that the sporophytes of these groups are borne *within* or *upon* the gametophytes, and thus are

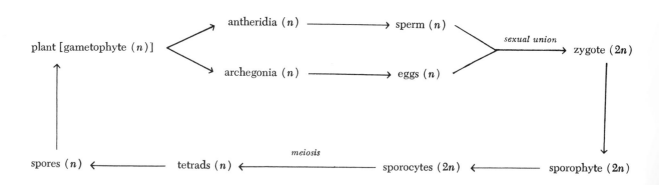

not free living.* The life cycle of liverworts and hornworts may be summarized as in the diagram on the previous page.

MARCHANTIA   *Marchantia* (Figures 4.4 to 4.6), the species of which occur on soil or on calcareous rocks, has a large, dichotomously branching, lobed plant body that is more complex internally than *Riccia* and *Ricciocarpus,* as it has highly specialized air chambers and pores differentiated from the compact storage tissue. Specialized branches, the *gemmae,* produced within cuplike structures on the plant's surface (Figure 4.4), are the mechanisms of dissemination and subsequent development of new gametophytic plants.

The archegonia and antheridia of *Marchantia* are borne on special branches, the stalked *archegoniophores* and *antheridiophores* (Figure 4.5). The sporophyte of *Marchantia* differs from those of *Riccia* and *Ricciocarpus* in its greater complexity and in its nutrition, abundant chloroplasts being present in its diploid cells through most of the developmental period. The complexity of the sporophyte (Figure 4.6) is apparent in its differentiation into *foot, stalk* (or *seta*), and *capsule* regions, and in the presence among the spores of specialized hygroscopic cells, the *elaters,* which are involved in spore dispersal.

* In certain red algae the diploid carposporophyte is also borne on the female gametophyte.

Figure 4.4 Marchantia polymorpha: vegetative plants with gemma cups.

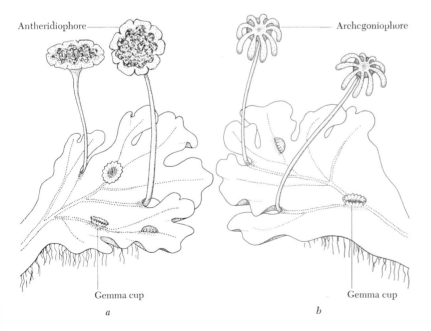

Antheridiophore

Archegoniophore

Gemma cup

Gemma cup

a

b

Figure 4.5   Marchantia polymorpha, sexually mature plants. (a) Female plants with archegoniophores. (b) Male plants with antheridiophores.

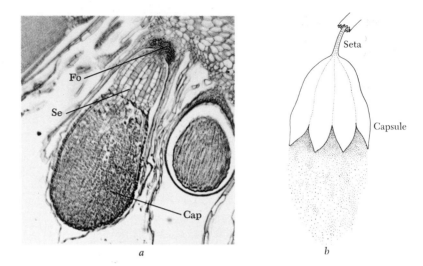

Figure 4.6   *Marchantia.* (a) Median longitudinal section of an immature sporophyte. (b) Older sporophyte with dehiscent capsule. Cap, capsule or sporangium; Fo, foot; Se, seta.

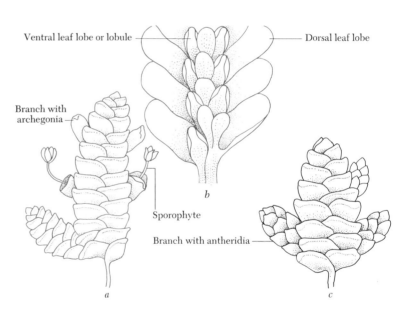

Figure 4.7   *Porella platyphylloidea, a leafy liverwort.* (a) Female plant with dehiscent sporophytes, dorsal aspect. (b) Portion of the same, ventral view. (c) Male plant, dorsal view.

PORELLA   *Porella* (Figure 4.7), some species of which grow on tree bark while others grow on wet stones, is representative of the leafy liverworts. The *Porella* plant consists of apically growing axes with three rows of leaves, the ventral row being smaller than the two dorsal series. The leaves of the dorsal series have infolded ventral lobes (Figure 4.7b), which explain the appearance of five rows of leaves suggested by superficial examination. The growth of the plants in dense mats and the overlapping of the leaves and lobes are both effective in holding water by capillary action.

The individual plants are unisexual, the archegonia and antheridia being borne on lateral branches of limited growth (Figure 4.7a,c). The chlorophyllous sporophytes are like those of *Marchantia* in having foot, seta, and capsule regions, as well as elaters. They differ in certain details of development and in the regular opening of the *Porella* capsules into four segments or valves (Figure 4.7a). The germinating spores ultimately give rise to new plants. Although superficially similar to mosses because of their axes and leaves, the leafy liverworts are readily distinguishable by their sex organs and sporophytes.

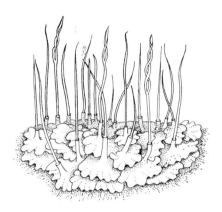

Figure 4.8 **Anthoceros sp., a hornwort. Gametophytes with maturing sporophytes.**

Figure 4.9 **Anthoceros sp. Median longitudinal section of sporophyte, diagrammatic.** [From H. C. Bold, *Morphology of Plants*, 2nd ed. (New York: Harper and Row, Publishers, 1967).]

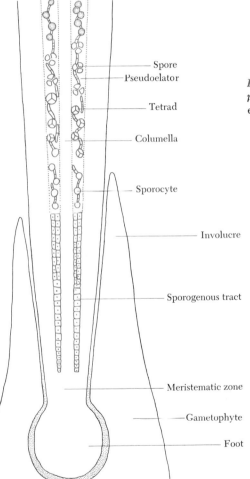

Spore
Pseudoelator
Tetrad
Columella
Sporocyte
Involucre
Sporogenous tract
Meristematic zone
Gametophyte
Foot

NONVASCULAR LAND PLANTS: LIVERWORTS, HORNWORTS, AND MOSSES

67

The hornwort *Anthoceros* (Figure 4.8) and its related genera, because of their striking differences from liverworts, are by some classified as a group coordinate in rank with the liverworts and mosses. The gametophytes of *Anthoceros* are multilobed thalli that grow closely appressed to moist soil and rock. They lack internal differentiation, except for ventral mucilage chambers (in some species), which usually contain a nitrogen-fixing species of the blue-green alga *Nostoc*. The cells of *Anthoceros* contain single, massive plastids, unlike the liverworts, in which many lenticular plastids are present in each cell.

Depending on the species of *Anthoceros,* the plants are unisexual or bisexual. The archegonia and antheridia are embedded within the dorsal tissues of the thallus; the antheridia, yellow-orange at maturity, are exposed in cavities. Fertilization, by sperm, of numerous archegonia results in the production of many chlorophyllous, needlelike sporophytes (Figure 4.8). These are unlike those of both liverworts and mosses in their continuing development from actively dividing cells between the foot and base of the sporophyte (Figure 4.9). The spores, accordingly, are produced over a period of several months; the mature spores are shed at the apex while newly produced sporocytes are continually undergoing meiotic divisions below. Much of the sporophyte is composed of actively photosynthetic cells and a central strand of elongate cells, the *columella.* Functional *stomata* with *guard cells* (see page 90) are present on the epidermal cells of the sporophyte. The spores give rise to new gametophytes, the life cycle being similar to that of liverworts.

Figure 4.10   Mosses. (a) Polytrichum sp.; female plants, ♀, with maturing sporophytes, Spph. (b) Funaria sp.; female branches, ♀, with developing sporophytes. Note peaked calyptras, Cal.

a   b

Mosses are widespread in rainy and humid places, but rare in more arid zones. Only a few species are adapted to survive a long drought, although many can successfully withstand temporary desiccation. The individual moss plant (Figures 4.10 and 4.11) consists of a slender leafy axis, either erect or prostrate, that may or may not have multicellular absorptive branches called rhizoids.* It is characteristic of mosses that they rarely occur as individuals but form extensive groups or colonies on moist soil, rocks, and wood. The largest mosses are natives of the Southern Hemisphere and may exceed a foot in length, as in the case of *Dawsonia,* but in the Northern Hemisphere the large species of the "haircap moss," *Polytrichum,* do not usually surpass 6 to 8 in. (Figures 4.10 and 4.11). Mosses growing on soil are important in preventing erosion.

It is convenient to begin consideration of the moss life cycle with the spore. Like other land plants, mosses produce airborne spores that are usually able to withstand desiccation for long periods.† Most spores

*We should distinguish among the terms *rhizoid, rhizome,* and *root.* Rhizomes are elongate, fleshy, nonvertical stems often growing upon the surface of the soil. Rhizoids are rootlike in performing the functions of anchorage and absorption. They lack root caps and xylem and phloem, which characterize roots; they may be unicellular, as in liverworts and ferns, or multicellular, as in mosses.

†Certain algal spores and zygotes, as well as the spores of nonaquatic fungi, also may be airborne.

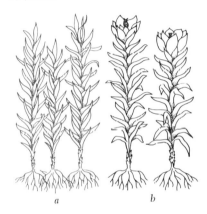

Figure 4.11 *Polytrichum sp. (a)* *Three female,* ♀, *and (b) two male,* ♂, *plants.*

Figure 4.12 *Funaria sp. (a) One ungerminated and several germinating spores. (b) Portion of protonema, Prne, with bud that will develop into leafy plant. (c) Young leafy shoots attached to protonema.*

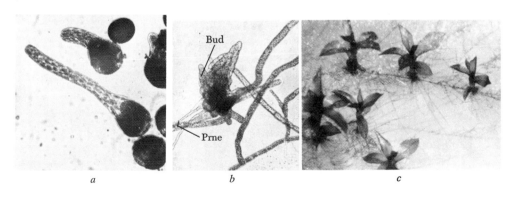

a

b

c

are widely distributed in the atmosphere, and those that come to rest upon favorable, moist surfaces then absorb water and renew their growth in the process called germination (Figure 4.12a). The spores of many mosses develop into prostrate filamentous systems that branch profusely. The cells of these filaments are filled with lenslike chloroplasts. Cells of the filaments are separated from each other by oblique walls. The system of branching filaments that develops from the germinating spore is known as the *protonema* (Figure 4.12b,c). After a period of development, during which extensive surfaces may be covered, the protonema forms *buds* (Figure 4.12b), which grow into *leafy shoots* (Figure 4.12c). It has recently been shown that growth hormones of the cytokinin group (benzyladenine and related compounds) are active in inducing a bud formation that does not occur in their absence.

At the bases of the leafy shoots, the protonema serves as a rhizoidal system; however, additional rhizoids develop on the leafy axes. Although moss leaves and stems may achieve considerable internal complexity, vascular tissues are absent; water is absorbed directly through the surfaces of the leaves and stems in many genera. In most populations, the densely aggregated plants tenaciously hold considerable amounts of water by capillary action. A few mosses grow in annual cycles, but the majority produce leafy shoots that persist for a number of growing seasons; such species are said to be *perennial*.

At certain times of the year, the tips of moss plants become fertile (Figure 4.11), producing sex organs. As in all land plants, reproduction is oogamous, the female gamete being a nonmotile egg cell and the male gamete, a small, motile (biflagellate) sperm. The antheridia (Figure 4.13a) and archegonia (Figure 4.13b) are multicellular as in liverworts, and the gametes are covered by a sterile cellular layer.

Figure 4.13 **Sexual reproduction in mosses. (a, b)** Mnium sp.: (a) median longitudinal section of apex of ♂ plant with numerous antheridia, Anth, and sterile filaments among them; (b) m.l.s. of apex of ♀ plant with archegonia, Arch, and interspersed sterile filaments and archegonial neck. (c, d) Funaria sp.: (c) antheridium, Anth, shedding sperm, Spe; (d) enlarging archegonium or calyptra, Cal, containing young sporophyte, Spph.

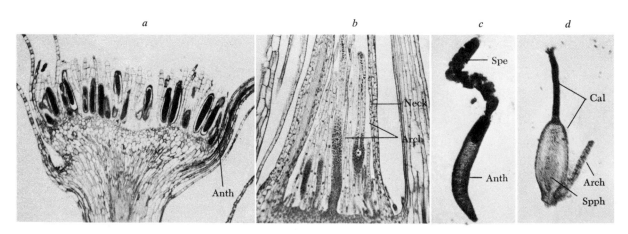

In some species of mosses, both antheridia and archegonia are present on the same individual, whereas in others, such as *Polytrichum* (Figure 4.11), the individual leafy shoots are unisexual. Fertile bisexual apexes as well as male apexes of unisexual moss plants are often recognizable because the leaves form a sort of cup about the sex organs (Figure 4.11*b*).

During heavy dews or rainfall, mature antheridia discharge their sperm (Figure 4.13*c*), some of which may reach the vicinity of an archegonium; in species with unisexual leafy plants, the contact may be accomplished by means of splashing rain drops. The inner cells of the neck disintegrate when the archegonium is mature, leaving a liquid-filled passageway to the egg. It is suggested by studies of other organisms that substances secreted in the moss archegonium chemically attract sperm. When a minute, biflagellate sperm, composed largely of nuclear material, swims down the canal of the archegonial neck and enters the egg cell, nuclear union (*fertilization*) follows and a zygote is formed.

As in certain algae (see page 20) and liverworts, the moss zygote does not undergo meiosis, but gives rise to an alternate spore-producing structure, the *sporophyte*. Again, as in the liverworts and *Anthoceros*, and unlike the algae (which have free-living, independent sporophytes), the moss sporophyte is retained permanently on the parent gametophyte; during its early development it remains within the enlarging archegonium (Figure 4.13*d*). These circumstances, no doubt, have exerted a profound effect on the form of the moss (and liverwort) sporophyte. Its incipient growth and nutrition certainly are based on metabolites from the archegonium (here, too, called the *calyptra* as it enlarges after fertilization) and the leafy axis, but very soon the cells of the developing sporophyte become chlorophyllous, an indication that this sporophyte is at least partially photoautotrophic. Still, the nitrogen and other elements that come from the soil necessarily must diffuse into the sporophyte from the gametophyte, which has first absorbed them from the soil.

Development of the sporophyte from the zygote is very rapid in mosses, and the needlelike sporophyte appears above the apex of the leafy plant after the calyptra has ruptured following fertilization. Part of the calyptra is carried upward at the summit of the sporophyte (Figures 4.10*b* and 4.14*e,f*). When the sporophyte has reached the length characteristic of the species, its tip enlarges to form a spore-bearing region called the *capsule,* or sporangium (Figures 4.10 and 4.14*a,e*). The capsule is connected to the leafy gametophyte by a stalk, or *seta,* and a basal *foot* buried in the stem apex of the leafy shoot.

The moss capsule is quite complex and varies in structure among

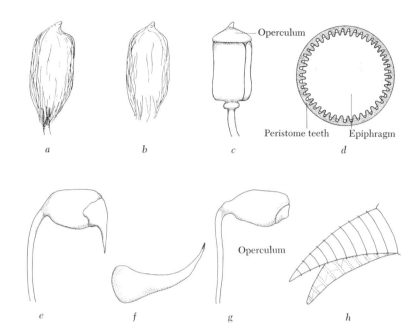

Figure 4.14   Moss capsule structure.
(a–d) Polytrichum sp. (a) Capsule
covered by calyptra. (b) Calyptra. (c)
Capsule with calyptra removed showing operculum. (d) Mouth of capsule
with peristome teeth and membranous
epiphragm. (e–h) Funaria sp. (e)
Capsule with calyptra. (f) Calyptra. (g)
Capsule with calyptra removed showing operculum. (h) Portion of outer
(above) and inner peristome.

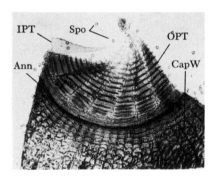

Figure 4.15   Funaria sp. Portion of
capsule wall and peristome, somewhat
flattened; note spores, Spo. Ann, region of the annulus; IPT, inner peristome segment; OPT, outer peristome
tooth; CapW, capsule or sporangium
wall.

the numerous genera. It is significant that only a small fraction of the
component tissues are sporogenous; the remainder are photosynthetic
and vegetative in function until late in development, when the surface
layers thicken and become hard and brown. The cells of the sporogenous
layers undergo meiosis in two successive nuclear and cell divisions.
Each cell undergoing meiosis produces a group of four spores, called a
tetrad. As in all land plants, the cell undergoing meiosis to form a tetrad
of spores is called a sporocyte, or spore mother cell.

The mechanisms of spore liberation and dissemination are fascinat-
ing aspects of mosses and well worthy of study. In most mosses, the
shedding of the calyptra and capsule apex (the *operculum*) after the
spores have formed reveals a structure known as the *peristome*. This
is a single or double ring of toothlike segments around the mouth of
the capsule (Figures 4.14*d* and 4.15). Two types of peristomal "teeth"
are illustrated in Figure 4.14*d,h*. Peristomal movements, which are
triggered by slight changes in humidity, result in gradual and continuous
spore dissemination under favorable (dry) conditions. The life cycle
of a typical moss is summarized in the accompanying diagram on the
following page.

Mosses have not been studied widely in the laboratory because they
seem to be difficult to grow to maturity in laboratory cultures. As a
result, we are inadequately informed about their physiological processes

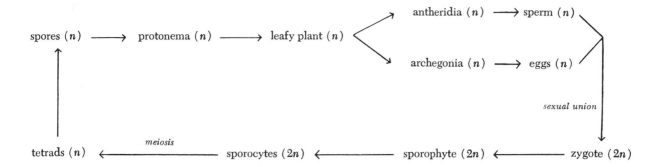

spores (n) $\longrightarrow$ protonema (n) $\longrightarrow$ leafy plant (n) $\Big\langle$ antheridia (n) $\longrightarrow$ sperm (n)

archegonia (n) $\longrightarrow$ eggs (n)

sexual union

tetrads (n) $\xleftarrow{\hspace{1cm}\text{\textit{meiosis}}\hspace{1cm}}$ sporocytes ($2n$) $\longleftarrow$ sporophyte ($2n$) $\longleftarrow$ zygote ($2n$)

and their growth and nutritional requirements. Polyploid° races of certain genera of mosses have been obtained by cutting up their setae and planting the pieces on moist substrates, as well as by wounding the base of the capsule. Since these tissues are diploid, they form diploid protonemata and, subsequently, diploid leafy shoots. The chromosome number (n or $2n$) does not of itself determine whether cells are sporophytic or gametophytic. The diploid cells from the regenerating seta form a gametophytic protonema, not a sporophyte as one might expect, even though they are diploid.

In conclusion, the gametophytic and sporophytic phases of liverworts, hornworts, mosses, and other plants should not be considered as two different, almost opposed entities, for both are manifestations of the same organism in its complete reproductive cycle. This is strikingly illustrated by the remarkable regenerative capacity of mosses: rhizoids, leaves, and stems and their fragments, the various parts of the sporophyte, and even the antheridia and archegonia† may regenerate new protonemata, from which follow all the later stages of the complete life cycle.

SPHAGNUM   The genus *Sphagnum* (Figure 4.16), known as "peat" or "bog moss," is of commercial value in horticulture because of its capacity to hold water and, along with other plant remains, to increase the acidity of soils even when it is dead and pulverized. *Sphagnum*

° The term *polyploid* is used to designate an organism (or a nucleus, cell, or tissue) that has a multiple of the basic number of chromosomes characteristic of the phase or organism. Thus, gametophytes normally are n and sporophytes $2n$ in chromosomal constitution, but naturally occurring and experimentally produced gametophytes may have chromosomal constitutions of n, $2n$, $3n$, and so on. Similarly, sporophytes may be $2n$, $3n$, $4n$, and so forth.

† Formation of protonema from antheridia and archegonia has been demonstrated in the author's laboratory by Dr. James H. Monroe.

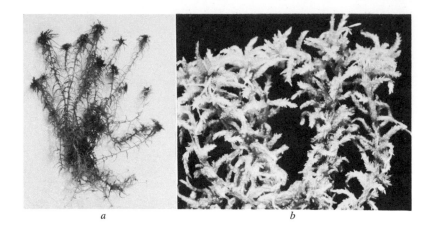

Figure 4.16   *Sphagnum, peat moss: two different species.*

a   b

Figure 4.17   *Sphagnum sp.: portion of leaf showing large, colorless, water-storage cells alternating with smaller cells with chloroplasts.*

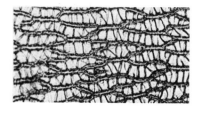

often invades bodies of water and forms extensive surface mats, or "quaking bogs."

This genus differs in a number of respects from most other mosses. The mature plants lack rhizoids and are pale green because of the alternation in the leaves of small, chloroplast-containing cells with larger, nonliving, water-storage cells (Figure 4.17); the latter are also present in the weak stems. The antheridia of *Sphagnum* are long-stalked and globose, and are borne in the axils of the leaves of conelike branches (Figure 4.18*a*); the archegonia are massive (Figure 4.18*b*).

The sporophyte of *Sphagnum* (Figure 4.19) differs from those of most mosses in lacking a peristome and in its domelike area of sporo-

Figure 4.18   *Sphagnum sp. (a) Apex of plant with antheridial branches. (b) Apex of female branch, magnified, showing massive archegonia.*

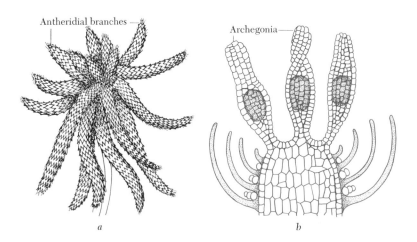

Antheridial branches

Archegonia

a   b

Figure 4.19

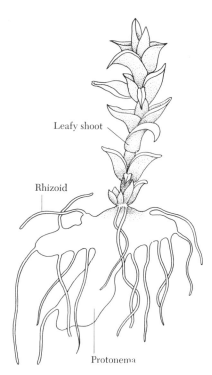

Leafy shoot

Rhizoid

Protonema

Figure 4.20 Sphagnum sp.: protonema with single leafy shoot.

genous tissue. Furthermore, its seta does not elongate, but the entire
sporophyte is elevated at maturity by a gametophytic stalk, the *pseudopodium*. The protonema of *Sphagnum* is spatulate and bears but a
single leafy shoot (Figure 4.20) in contrast to those of most mosses.

Because of the extremely acid conditions in bogs, which prevent the
growth of most microorganisms that would cause decay, *Sphagnum* and
associated plants often accumulate in the form of deep deposits called
peat. The lower strata of such deposits may be of considerable age;
for example, some bogs in the United States are 16,000 years old.
Careful sampling and analysis of the pollen and spores from successively
older strata provide us with a history of vegetation in a given locality
and, indirectly, with evidences of climatic changes (especially temperature and rainfall).

Peat is of economic importance in improving the texture and water-
holding capacity of soils and in providing nutriment to cultivated plants.
In some parts of the world, where other forms of fuel are in limited
supply, peat is compressed, dried, and burned. It is of interest that the
flavor of Scotch whiskeys is in part due to peat smoke.

NONVASCULAR LAND PLANTS:
LIVERWORTS, HORNWORTS,
AND MOSSES

Of greater interest are the bodies of human beings that have been uncovered in peat excavations in Ireland, Denmark, and adjacent parts of Germany. These include clothed bodies from the Bronze Age and among others, the body of a man who had been hung with a leather rope about 2,000 years ago in what is now Jutland, in western Denmark.

EVOLUTION OF NONVASCULAR
LAND PLANTS

Concluding this brief account of relatively simple, haploid land plants —the liverworts, hornworts, and mosses—provides a basis for considering their origin, ancestry, and possible relationships with each other. With respect to interrelationships, once again the fossil record is not helpful. Relatively few (as compared with vascular plants) fossil liverworts and mosses are known, and these resemble our living types. Liverworts occur in Devonian strata (see Table 6.1 on page 98), while fossilized mosses appear in Pennsylvanian strata. There is no evidence from the fossil record, however, that mosses evolved from liverworts. Comparative morphology of living mosses and liverworts reveals some radially symmetrical, erect, leafy liverworts that suggest mosses in their organization. However, the sexual reproductive organs and sporophytes of such liverworts are different from those of the mosses. Both plant groups have similar patterns of alternation of generations: the dominant phase is the haploid gametophyte, which bears the parasitic (*Riccio-carpus* and *Riccia*) or partially parasitic (other liverworts, hornworts, and mosses) sporophyte upon it.

Apparently the algae were the only chlorophyllous plants on earth from Precambrian to Silurian and Devonian times (see Table 6.1 on page 98), if the fossil record is at all complete. The divergence of algal progenitors into liverworts, hornworts, mosses, and the several groups of seedless vascular plants (see Chapters 6 and 7) must accordingly have been very rapid.

IN BEGINNING OUR DISCUSSION OF THE LAND PLANTS* IN THE PRECEDING chapter, we stated that they include two major groups. The members of the first group, the liverworts, hornworts, and mosses, lack vascular tissue (xylem and phloem) and are, without exception, gametophytes with physically attached sporophytes. The second group is by far the larger; normally its members are diploid, spore-producing plants with well-developed vascular tissue. The haploid sexual alternate (gametophyte) in their life cycle may be either free-living and photoautrophic or heterotrophic; in the latter case, the gametophyte is either saprophytic or parasitic upon the sporophyte. It has been suggested that in some of the earliest land plants, the sporophytes became more complex while the gametophytes (the sexual phase), in contrast, became smaller, shorter-lived, and less active in somatic or vegetative functions. In other organisms, however, such as mosses and liverworts, the gametophyte remained dominant, while the sporophytic phase became reduced and

* Nature mocks at human categories! Most liverworts, mosses, and vascular plants are terrestrial, but some of each are aquatic. Furthermore, both aquatic and terrestrial algae and fungi are known.

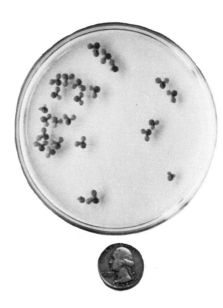

Figure 5.1 Lemna perpusilla, a floating, aquatic seed plant. [Courtesy of Drs. William Hillman and John H. Miller.]

physically attached to it. Another theory holds that the mosses and liverworts are descended from gametophytic algae that "migrated" to the land and, in contrast, the vascular plants are derived from migrant algal sporophytes. The fossil record has not contributed materially to the resolution of these conflicting viewpoints.

Whatever their origin, the vascular plants display a degree of complexity that is unmatched by nonvascular plants. Accordingly, this chapter will present a brief, general introduction to the gross and microscopic structure of the vascular plants in general. In the following four chapters we shall be concerned primarily with a more specific description of the vegetative organs and the reproductive process in representative vascular plants.

A wide range of morphological form and complexity exists among vascular plants. Among the smallest of these is the duckweed, *Lemna* (Figure 5.1), a minute, floating aquatic flowering plant. At the other extreme are woody vines, shrubs, and trees, climaxed by such long-lived giants as the redwood tree *Sequoiadendron gigantea,* and certain species of *Eucalyptus.* Between these extremes occurs a vast assemblage of species intermediate in size. These may be *annual,* their maturity, reproduction, and death occurring in one growing season, or *perennial,* the individual plant persisting for more than one season. In spite of their tremendous variety, all individual vascular plants begin their existence as single-celled zygotes* and achieve their final size by successive nuclear and cytoplasmic divisions of the zygote and its cellular descendants.

Growth involves an increase in volume; it is accomplished most frequently by an increase in cell number and cell size and is usually accompanied by *differentiation* (the modification of individual cells or tissues in accordance with function). Explaining the mechanism of growth and differentiation that forms a complex organism from the cellular progeny of a single zygote is one of the most challenging problems of current biological investigations.

Growth in plants may be either *generalized* or *localized.* The axes of vascular plants, usually composed of *stems* and *roots,* develop from *apical meristems* (Figures 5.6 and 5.14), which are stem and root tips where cells are actively dividing. In some axes, in addition, intercalary regions of dividing cells persist, localized between base and apex like those at the joints of grass stems. Such intercalary meristems frequently give rise to roots when stem cuttings are placed in either moist sand or soil.

* Exceptions are organisms propagated vegetatively—that is, from cuttings, buds, or grafts—or those that reproduce without union of gametes, such as *Cyrtomium* (the holly fern), the common dandelion, and certain grasses.

The following sections offer a more detailed discussion of the processes of growth and differentiation in the vegetative organs of vascular plants—namely, stems, roots, and leaves.

In the following discussion, the external and internal features of stems and roots will be covered separately in four sections.

EXTERNAL MORPHOLOGY OF THE STEM   That portion of the axis which bears leaves is known as the *stem*. Leaves arise from the stem at *nodes;* the regions of the stem between successive nodes are the *internodes*. In most plants, stems seem to be the most obvious, dominant portion of the axis; exceptions are bulbous plants (such as onions and lilies) and ferns other than tree ferns. In these exceptional types the leaves appear to be dominant.

Growth of stems is apical; the extreme growing tip is hidden within a terminal *bud* (Figure 5.2). A bud is a stem with short internodes, bearing early developmental stages of leaves (*leaf primordia*), or in some cases, flowers, or both leaves and flowers. Lateral or *axillary buds* occur between the leaf axil and the stem (Figure 5.6). Buds may be

Figure 5.2   Syringa vulgaris, lilac: successive stages in opening of a terminal bud.

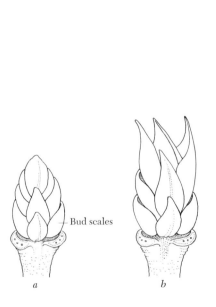

a   b   c   d

Figure 5.3 Twig of buckeye, Aesculus sp., dormant condition.

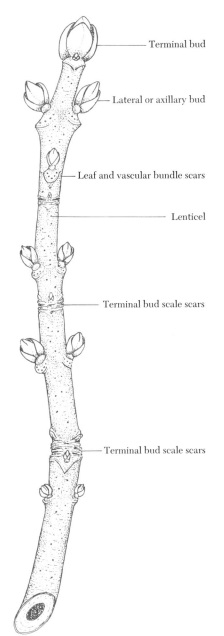

- Terminal bud
- Lateral or axillary bud
- Leaf and vascular bundle scars
- Lenticel
- Terminal bud scale scars
- Terminal bud scale scars

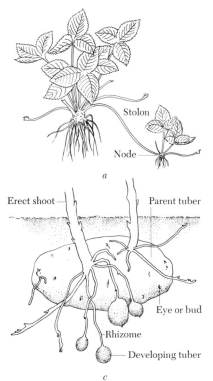

Stolon

Node

a

Erect shoot

Parent tuber

Eye or bud

Rhizome

Developing tuber

c

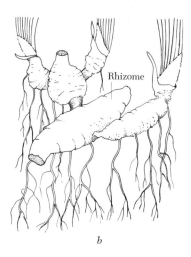

Rhizome

b

Figure 5.4   **Modified stems.** *(a) Stolons of strawberry, Fragaria sp. (Note elongate, horizontal stems that have rooted at a node, forming a plantlet.) (b) Rhizome of Iris sp. (c) Stages in development of a potato tuber (Solanum tuberosum).*

Figure 5.5   **Modified stems.** *(a) Bisection of corm of Gladiolus sp. (b) Bisection of a bulb of onion (Allium cepa).*

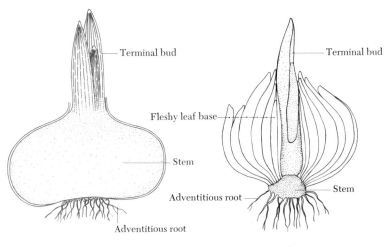

Terminal bud

Terminal bud

Fleshy leaf base

Stem

Stem

Adventitious root

Adventitious root

a

b

closed (*covered*) or *open,* that is, undergoing continuous development and unfolding, as in many herbaceous plants (for example, the geranium *Pelargonium*). Closed buds occur on woody plants of the temperate zone and are protected by variously thickened and gummy outer leaves called *bud scales* (Figure 5.2). The bud scales are shed as spring growth is initiated, leaving behind *bud scale scars* (Figure 5.3). The age and the extent of growth of younger branches may be ascertained by examination of successive groups of bud scale scars.

Woody stems exhibit other characteristic structures during their dormant period (Figure 5.3), in addition to terminal and axillary buds and bud scale scars. *Leaf scars* and *vascular bundle scars* are often evident, as are *lenticels.*

Stems may be self-supporting and erect, or they may require support, as in the case of various types of vines; they vary from the pendulous to the horizontal. Certain modified stem types are illustrated in Figures 5.4 and 5.5, and explained in the figure captions.

DEVELOPMENT OF THE STEM   The *apical meristem* is usually concealed (Figures 5.2 and 5.6) by the numerous, minute leaf primordia that it bears. The cells of the apical meristem divide rapidly, thus increasing in number. Three meristematic regions, the *primary meristems,* are distinguishable just below the apical meristem: (1) the superficial *protoderm;* (2) the *provascular tissue* or *procambium,* in the form of a cylinder or discrete strands; and (3) the *ground meristem* (Figure 5.6). When the apex has grown a certain distance beyond a given region of cells, cell multiplication ceases in this region, and the cells enlarge and differentiate into functional *primary tissues.* In many *herbaceous* (soft-textured, green-stemmed) plants, only these primary tissues function in the plant's normal metabolic processes throughout the existence of the organism.

As the increase in cell size and the change in form of a given region in the developing axis both decelerate, deposition of cell walls in specialized patterns completes the process of differentiation of the primary meristems into three types of primary tissue: (1) the vascular tissues, composed of *xylem* and *phloem* (Figure 5.7) (and sometimes the *cambium layer;* see page 84), deriving from the procambium; (2) the superficial *epidermal layer,* deriving from the protoderm; and (3) the remainder, *cortex* (and *pith,* if present), deriving from the ground meristem (Figure 5.7). The primary vascular tissues of stems and roots are connected with each other; the veins of leaves and reproductive organs are connected to the stem by branches of vascular tissue that are called *traces* (see Figure 5.17).

Xylem cells are often elongate, and their walls are thickened in one of several different patterns with a mixture of lignin and cellulose; it is

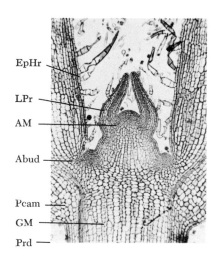

Figure 5.6   Coleus blumei: median longitudinal section of the stem apex. Abud, axillary bud; AM, apical meristem; GM, ground meristem; EpHr, epidermal hair; LPr, leaf primordium or precursor; Prd, protoderm (precursor of epidermis); Pcam, procambium; apical meristem and procambium are precursors of vascular tissue and cambium.

Figure 5.7 Aristolochia sp. (a) Transection of stem in region of primary permanent tissues, low magnification. (b) One vascular bundle and adjacent tissues. Cam, cambium; Co, cortex; Epd, epidermis; Fi, supporting fibers; Phl, phloem; VB, vascular bundle containing primary xylem within, separated by cambium from the primary phloem without; Ves, vessel of xylem; Xy, xylem. Note parenchyma and tracheids in region of xylem label line.

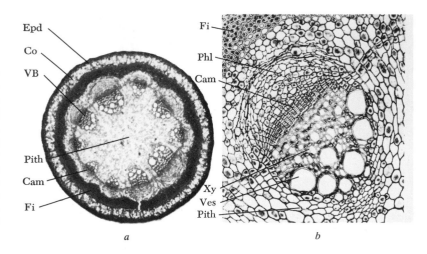

a

b

because of this *lignification* that they are hard. Xylem is a complex tissue consisting of several components. The lignified conducting cells, *tracheids* and *vessels*, together with the *fibers*, are dead at maturity (Figures 5.7 and 5.8); some cells of the xylem, the *parenchyma*, remain alive for a longer time and may have storage functions. The major functions of xylem are the support of the plant and the transport of water and dissolved substances.

Phloem, usually located close to the xylem, may contain lignified fibers, but its other components are living cells with cellulose walls (Figures 5.7b and 5.8). Most important of these are the *sieve cells*—often united end to end in a pipelike series, the *sieve tube*—and the *companion cells,* if present. Phloem serves in the conduction of the complex substances manufactured in metabolism. In stems, the primary xylem and phloem are positioned concentrically, collaterally (opposite each other; Figure 5.7), or bicollaterally (with phloem on both sides of the xylem); in roots, they alternate in a radial pattern (see Figure 5.15).

In some stems the center is occupied by a pith composed of parenchyma cells with thin, cellulose walls; these cells may function in storage (Figure 5.7). The tissue layers lying between the vascular tissues and the epidermis vary in extent and complexity. In general, the cortex is a storage region, although it is photosynthetic in young stems (and in aerial roots). The epidermis is interrupted by minute pores, the *stomata* (singular, *stoma*) surrounded by *guard cells* (see Figure 5.20); it is also cutinized—covered by the *cuticle*, composed of a waxy substance (*cutin*) secreted by the epidermal cells as an outer covering.

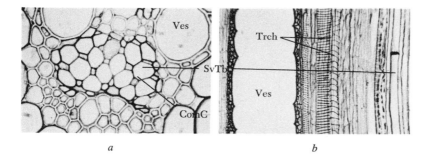

a   b

Figure 5.8 **Vascular tissue.** (a) *Transection of portion of vascular bundle from stem of maize, Zea mays (note sieve plate in one sieve tube). (b) Longitudinal section of vascular tissue of squash, Cucurbita sp. (note remains of dissolved transverse walls in xylem vessel. ComC, companion cell; SvTb, sieve tube of phloem; Trch, xylem tracheid with helical lignification; Ves, xylem vessel.*

Stomata are the main pathways for gaseous interchange, although this also occurs to a limited extent through the cuticle. Various glandular and nonglandular hairs (Figure 5.9) occur on the epidermis of stems and leaves.

The preceding paragraphs have summarized the development and structure of primary tissue, the origin of which may be traced to the apical meristem. In some herbaceous and all woody plants, *secondary tissues* are added to the primary tissues after elongation of the axis (at a certain distance from the meristem) has ceased (Figure 5.10). The extent and the duration of this secondary growth process vary with the species. Thus, in some individuals of such long-lived trees as *Sequoia*-

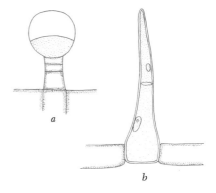

a

b

Figure 5.9 **Epidermal hairs.** (a) *Multicellular glandular and* (b) *nonglandular hair of geranium (Pelargonium).*

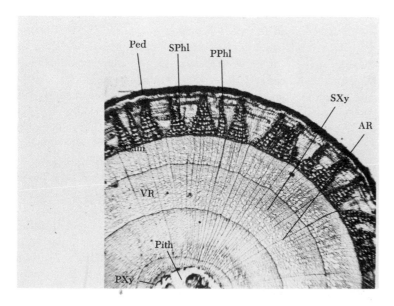

Figure 5.10 **Basswood, Tilia americana.** *Sector of transection of 5-year-old stem. AR, annual ring of secondary xylem; Cam, cambium; Ped, corky periderm that has replaced epidermis; PPhl, primary phloem; PXy, primary xylem covered by secondary xylem, SXy, added by cambium; SPhl, secondary phloem; VR, vascular ray; AR, annual ring.*

83

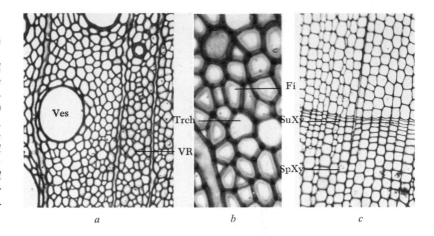

Figure 5.11   Xylem or wood. (a) Oak (Quercus velutina), transection. (b) Portion of oak transection enlarged (note fibers and tracheids). (c) White pine (Pinus strobus), at left in transection, at right in longitudinal (radial) section showing pitted tracheids. VR, vascular ray; Ves, vessel; Fi, fibers; Trch, tracheids; SpXy, large-celled xylem formed early in growing season; SuXy, small-celled xylem formed at end of growing season. Spring and summer xylem of one growing season constitute an annual ring.

dendron gigantea and Pinus aristata (bristlecone pine), secondary growth has been occurring for several thousand years. Were it not for this process, lumber as we know it would not exist.

Secondary growth depends on the active division of a particular layer of cells, the *cambium* (Figures 5.7a,b and 5.10), which lies between the primary xylem and the primary phloem. Most of the cells formed by the cambium differentiate into secondary xylem between the cambium and primary xylem (Figure 5.10), but some become secondary phloem between the cambium and primary phloem. The activity of the cambium is seasonal, and in perennial woody plants this is reflected in the deposition of the secondary xylem as *annual rings,* or cylinders (Figures 5.10 and 5.11). Increased growth in the internal portion of the stem by cambial activity ruptures the epidermis and cortex, which are unable to expand; these outer layers are gradually replaced by corky layers, the *periderm.* As secondary growth continues, the cracks in the outer tissue cut more deeply and additional layers of periderm form. Accordingly, the *bark* of woody plants may become quite complex, consisting of strips of periderm and other tissues such as cortex and phloem.

Secondary xylem is known as *wood* (Figure 5.11). The hardness of wood is caused basically by the lignin that thickens the cell walls, the degree of hardness depending on the amount of lignification and the percentage of thick-walled cells present. When wood is cut, the grain and markings depend on the way in which the annual rings and rays have been exposed.

The patterns of primary vascular organization have been summarized in the concept of the *stele,* a term often used collectively for the vascular tissue of axes. Various types of steles are illustrated in

Figure 5.12 and explained in its caption. Some botanists refer to siphonosteles as *medullated protosteles* and look upon the pith either as an evolutionary invasion of cortical tissue through the *leaf gaps* that are associated with leaf traces (Figure 5.17) or as parenchyma tissue which has developed instead of xylem. *Protosteles,* which in this text are considered to be central cores of xylem surrounded by phloem, may be circular, ridged, or elliptical in transection; in some cases, the phloem occurs in segments among the xylem cells. Protosteles are present in many roots and in stems of many vascular cryptogams, in which they develop almost without exception in the juvenile stages. *Amphiphloic siphonosteles* that are dissected by leaf gaps into seemingly discrete strands of xylem surrounded by phloem and endodermis are known as *dictyosteles.* These occur in a number of fern rhizomes having short internodes.

Discrete vascular bundles, not all of which are separated by leaf gaps (for example, those in *eusteles* and *atactosteles* are not), characterize the stems of many angiosperms (flowering plants).

EXTERNAL MORPHOLOGY OF THE ROOT   Roots differ from stems in lacking leaves (and hence, nodes, internodes, and axillary buds), in possessing an apical root cap (Figure 5.14) and in having an alternate or radial arrangement of their primary xylem and phloem.

Roots are designated according to origin as primary, secondary, or adventitious. A *primary root* is the emergent root of an embryonic plant such as that within a seed (Figure 5.13); branches from it are *secondary roots* (Figures 9.12 and 9.13). By contrast, *adventitious roots* are not of

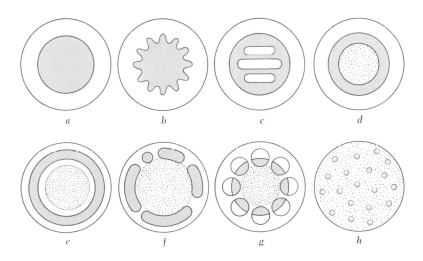

Figure 5.12   *Types of steles, diagrammatic transections. (a) Haplostele. (b) Actinostele. (c) Plectostele. (d) Ectophloic siphonostele. (e) Amphiphloic siphonostele or solenostele. (f) Dictyostele. (g) Eustele. (h) Atactostele (a–c are all protosteles). Xylem, color; phloem, white; pith, stippled.* [From H. C. Bold, *Morphology of Plants,* 2nd ed. (New York: Harper and Row, Publishers, 1967).]

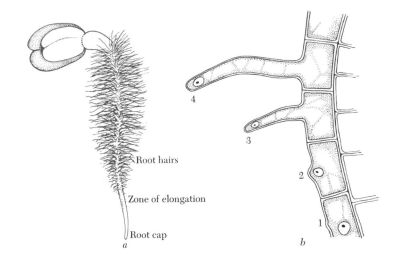

Root hairs

Zone of elongation

Root cap

4

3

2

1

a   *b*

Figure 5.13 *Radish, Raphanus sp. (a) Germinating seed (note root hair zone). (b) Successive stages in root hair formation (numbered).*

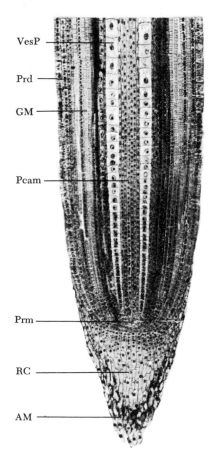

VesP

Prd

GM

Pcam

Prm

RC

AM

embryonic origin but may develop from superficial tissues of stems or leaves, as is the case with rhizomes, stolons, corms, bulbs (Figures 5.4 and 5.5), and cuttings.

When the emergent primary root continues to develop in length and to function throughout the life of the plant, a *tap root* system is present. Some tap roots become woody and others become fleshy (for example, beets, carrots, and turnips). When the primary root is not conspicuous and when adventitious roots comprise the absorbing organs, the root system is said to be *fibrous*.

Externally, roots are simpler than stems. Seedlings grown in a moist chamber illustrate (see Figure 5.13a) the root cap region, the zone of elongation, and the root hair zone. The root hair zone corresponds internally to the region of differentiation into the specialized primary tissues.

DEVELOPMENT OF THE ROOT   The ontogeny of a root is illustrated in Figures 5.14 and 5.15. The apical meristem is protected by a *root cap*, the cells of which are slimy and thus seemingly provide protection as the root elongates through the soil. In most roots, the provascular tissue or procambium matures into a solid core of primary xylem and

Figure 5.14 *Maize, Zea mays: median longitudinal section of a root cap. GM, ground meristem; Prd, protoderm; Prm, promeristem; AM, apical meristem; Pcam, procambium; VesP, xylem vessel precursors; RC, root cap.* [Courtesy of Drs. J. H. Leech and W. G. Whaley.]

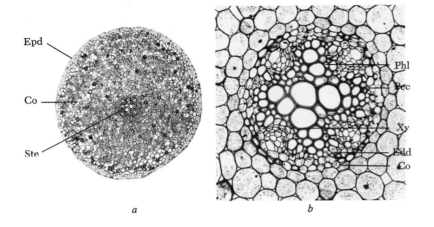

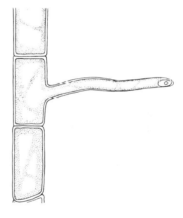

Figure 5.15 *Transection of root of buttercup, Ranunculus. (a) Low magnification. (b) Enlarged view of stele and adjacent regions.* Co, cortex; Epd, epidermis; Ste, stele (xylem and phloem); Edd, endodermis; Phl, phloem; Pec, pericycle; Xy, xylem.

phloem (Figure 5.15), a protostele. The vascular tissue in roots is usually surrounded by a *pericycle,* from which branch roots arise endogenously; the pericycle, in turn, is surrounded by the *endodermis.* The walls of the endodermis are notable for their *suberin* (cork) thickenings of various patterns. A pericycle and endodermis are sometimes present in the stems of vascular cryptogams (seedless vascular plants) and in rhizomes.

The primary xylem and phloem of roots are alternately arranged (Figure 5.15), and a pith is frequently absent. The cortex is an extensive layer used for storage; an extreme of this is seen in fleshy roots like sweet potatoes. The epidermal cells of roots project as *root hairs* (Figure 5.16), which function in absorption; more root hairs are constantly being added as increasingly distal regions of the root mature. The root epidermis, obviously, is not cutinized.

Like their stems, the roots of woody plants also undergo secondary thickening through the activity of both vascular and cork cambium.

Figure 5.16 *Epidermal cell with root hair.*

Leaves arise from the apical meristem as localized mounds of tissue called *leaf primordia* (Figure 5.6). In contrast to axes, most leaves have a simple structure, but there is some evidence that the simplicity may be a deceptive result of secondary simplification from more complex beginnings, a phenomenon known as *reduction.* At one extreme, true leaves (those with vascular tissue) approach moss leaves in size (see Figures 6.9 and 6.13); at the other extreme are the enormous leaves of tree ferns, palms, and bananas. Large leaves (Figure 5.17a) with

ORGANIZATION OF VASCULAR PLANTS

87

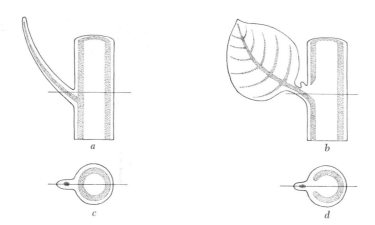

Figure 5.17 **Stems.** *(a,b) Segments of longitudinal bisections of stems: (a) stem with macrophyllous leaf; (b) stem with microphyllous leaf. (c,d) Transections at levels of a and b indicated by dotted lines. Steles, traces and veins indicated in heavy black. Note leaf gaps in a and c and their absence in b and d.* [From H. C. Bold, *Morphology of Plants,* 2nd ed. (New York: Harper and Row, Publishers, 1967).]

branching veins (vascular tissues) generally are thought to be derived from axial branches that have become flattened during the course of evolution, the cortical and epidermal tissues having extended between the branches as a sort of webbing. Certain small leaves (Figure 5.17*b*) with unbranched veins are thought to be fundamentally different: they are assumed to have developed as localized surface outgrowths that later became vascular. However, their simplicity has also been considered a manifestation of evolutionary reduction from more complex types.

Figure 5.18 **Leaf structure.** *(a) Simple leaf, Euonymus sp. (b) Pinnately compound leaf, Sophora sp. (c) Palmately compound leaves, Scheffeleria.*

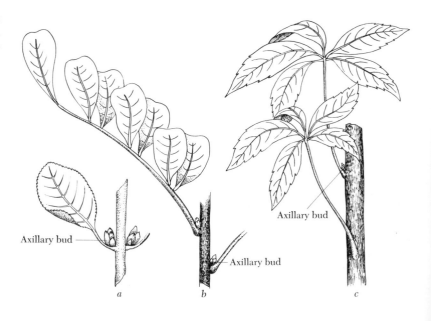

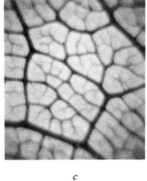

b   c

Figure 5.19 **Venation patterns.** (a) Dichotomous venation in Ginkgo biloba, maidenhair tree. [Courtesy of Professor H. J. Arnott.] (b) Parallel or striate venation in Cyperus sp. (c) Netted venation in Sophora sp. [(b) and (c) courtesy of Professors H. W. Bischoff and D. A. Larson.]

a

In external form, leaves may have whole or divided blades (Figure 5.18); the former are *simple* and the latter *compound* leaves. The *petiole* (leaf stalk) of compound leaves thus bears a number of leaflets, which are shed as a unit with the petiole. Buds occur only at the base of the petiole in both simple and compound leaves, not at the bases of the leaflet stalks. Various types of compound leaves occur, the commonest ones being either palmately or pinnately compound (Figure 5.18b,c).

Leaf blades are traversed by an extensive system of *veins,* which are the ultimate branches of the vascular traces. Several patterns of venation are common, among them the *dichotomous, striated,* and *netted* types (Figure 5.19). Two patterns of netted venation, namely *pinnate* and *palmate,* are widespread.

As compared with axes, most leaves are relatively simple internally. Secondary growth is limited, if it occurs, and affects only the vascular tissues. The leaf surfaces are covered by a cutinized, more or less waxy and impervious epidermis that is interspersed with stomata and guard cells (Figures 5.20 and 5.21). The intervening tissues (Figure 5.21), known as *mesophyll,* are frequently differentiated into an upper series of columnar cells, the *palisade mesophyll,* and a lower series of loosely contiguous cells, the *spongy mesophyll;* however, in some leaves

ORGANIZATION OF VASCULAR PLANTS

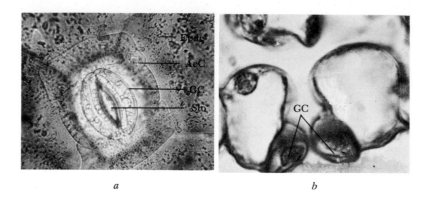

a   *b*

Figure 5.20   Stomata. (a) Surface view of stoma and associated cells of leaf of Rhoeo discolor. (b) Transection of stoma and guard cells of privet leaf, Ligustrum sp. (see Figure 5.21). AcC, accessory cell; EpdC, epidermal cell; GC, guard cell; Sto, stoma.

the mesophyll is essentially a homogeneous region. The mesophyll cells are rich in chloroplasts and thus active in photosynthesis. None of these cells is far from a vein; hence, active transfer of substances to and away from the photosynthesizing mesophyll cells is possible.

Leaves differ in texture, in degree of cutinization, and in the amount of supporting tissue present; they vary also in their pattern of attachment to the stem and in their arrangement in the bud, known as *phyllotaxy*. Leaves may be attached to the stem in *opposite, alternate* (spiral), or *whorled* patterns. The general pattern of arrangement is genetically determined; it is already evident in the bud phyllotaxy, but it may change somewhat during development. Inasmuch as buds, which may give rise to branches, are present in the leaf axils, the arrangement of stem branches is related to that of leaves. Whorled phyllotaxy is rarer than the other types. Phyllotaxy of alternate leaves may be expressed by fractions such as ½, ⅓, and ⅖, the denominator indicating the number of vertical rows of leaves between two vertically aligned leaves, the numerator the number of turns about the stem between two such leaves.

Figure 5.21   Privet, Ligustrum sp.: sector of transection of a leaf. LEpd, lower epidermis; Vlos, longisection of a vein; PaMp, palisade mesophyll; Sto, stoma in section; SpMp, spongy mesophyll; UEpd, upper epidermis; Vtra, transection of a vein.

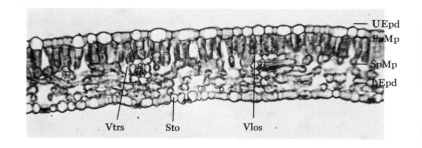

With respect to leaves, plants may be *evergreen* (never completely without leaves) or *deciduous*. In the latter case, all the leaves are shed periodically. Leaf fall is accomplished usually by the formation of a special separating layer, the *abscission layer*, which severs the leaf at its base or at the base of the petiole. In certain geographical regions, especially northeastern America and Scandinavia, the leaf fall of deciduous trees is preceded by the phenomenon of autumnal coloration. The chlorophyll of the leaves disintegrates, leaving the yellow-orange pigments (carotenes and xanthophylls), which then increase in amount. Scarlet coloration often reflects development of the pigment anthocyanin in the cell vacuoles.

Although nonvascular chlorophyllous plants (some algae, most liverworts, hornworts, and mosses) are terrestrial in habitat, it is the vascular plants which comprise the major vegetation of the land. The explanation for this resides in the capacity of vascular plants, through morphological and physiological adaptations, to live under more rigorous and inhospitable conditions, especially with respect to availability of water. Of great adaptive significance in this connection are the cuticle, stomata, and vascular tissue, described earlier in this chapter. These make possible efficient conservation and translocation of water and its solutes, at the same time providing a pathway for gaseous interchange. There is little doubt that the greater size of most vascular green plants, as compared with nonvascular ones, is correlated with these adaptations as well as with the presence of a root system, which is absent in only two or three kinds of living vascular plants.

The development of the extensive, vascularized, subterranean system that we call a root, for anchorage and absorption, must have been of tremendous significance in the evolution of land plants. The origin and course of evolution of the root are unknown. It is probable that certain branches of rhizomes became modified with respect to the functions of anchorage and absorption. Organs of anchorage and absorption are, of course, present in certain algae, liverworts, and mosses, but these lack vascular tissue. It has been suggested that the alternate arrangement of xylem and phloem in roots (in contrast to their commonly collateral arrangement in stems, including rhizomes) facilitates the absorption and conduction of water; if the arrangement were collateral, water would have to pass through the phloem before reaching the xylem. It has also been suggested that the root cap is an adaptation that protects the root's apical meristem, which penetrates the soil more rapidly than does the tip of a rhizome.

6 SEEDLESS
VASCULAR PLANTS: I

VASCULAR PLANTS INCLUDE TWO MAJOR TYPES, SEEDLESS AND SEED-bearing. The fossil remains of seedless vascular plants have been identified with certainty in rock strata as ancient as early Silurian (Table 6.1). Both seedless and seed-bearing types have persisted to the present day.

The presence of vascular tissue in the diploid sporophytic phase of all of the vascular plants has often been interpreted as evidence of kinship through descent from a common precursor. Accordingly, these plants are frequently classified in a single division, the Tracheophyta (see Table 1.1), a name that emphasizes the presence of vascular tissue. The significance thus attached to vascular tissue has not been universally accepted, however; some students of plant relationships (*phylogeny*) consider the widespread occurrence of vascular tissue to be a manifestation of parallel evolution. Proponents of this interpretation classify the vascular plants in a number of separate groups, the ranks of which vary with the classifier (see Table 1.1).

Whatever rank may be assigned them, there is almost unanimous agreement that the seedless vascular plants include four major groups:

(1) the leafless psilophytes; (2) the club and spike "mosses"; (3) the arthrophytes; and (4) the ferns. We shall discuss the first three of these groups in the present chapter and the fourth group in the following one.

In the extinct Devonian (Table 6.1) floras, there were several kinds of vascular plants without leaves and roots. These are known to us through such examples as well-preserved specimens of *Rhynia* (Figure 6.1). The subterranean stems (rhizomes) of these plants bore unicellular rhizoids. Sections of these fossilized axes reveal that the vascular tissues were entirely primary in origin. Some branches of *Rhynia* bore terminal sporangia; the presence of tetrads in these sporangia indicates that the spores arose through meiosis and that the organisms which produced them were sporophytes.

Among extant plants, *Psilotum* (the whisk fern; Figure 6.2a) is one of the very few that display somewhat similar organization. The plant is tropical and subtropical in habitat. Sometimes it is epiphytic, that is, it grows upon other plants, presumably using them only for support. *Psilotum* occurs in the United States in Hawaii, Florida, Louisiana, and Texas.

PSILOTUM   *Psilotum nudum* is an herbaceous, dichotomously branching plant approximately 2 ft in height. Its ridged axes (both the erect ones and the rhizomes) contain vascular tissue (Figure 6.4). The erect stems are the photosynthetic organs, as they are in such plants as cacti and the horsetail, *Equisetum* (see Figure 6.23). The outermost portion of the cortex is composed of cells rich in chloroplasts, and the heavily cutinized epidermis is interrupted by stomata and guard cells (Figure 6.4). The rhizome bears unicellular rhizoids and its cortical cells may contain fungi, the role of which is obscure. Such an association of fungi with the subterranean roots and stems of a vascular plant is called a *mycorrhiza*.

In mature plants, many of the axes become fertile and produce trilobed sporangia on very short lateral branches (Figures 6.2b and 6.3) suggestive of the fertile branches of *Rhynia* (Figure 6.1). Meiosis in *Psilotum*, as in mosses, liverworts, and all vascular plants, occurs when the spores arise in groups of four from the diploid sporocytes or spore mother cells in the sporangia. When the spores have matured, the sporangia crack open and the smooth-walled spores are disseminated. As in all plants with sporic meiosis and morphological alternation of generations (see page 20), the spores in further development produce the sexual gametophytic phase.

Figure 6.1 *Rhynia gwynne-vaughani,* *a middle Devonian (see Table 6.1)* *fossil vascular plant. Spg, sporangium.* [Courtesy of Chicago Natural History Museum.]

a

b

Figure 6.2 *Psilotum nudum. (a) Potted plant. (b) Longitudinal section of stem and branch with sporangium. Dark cells in sporangium are spore mother cells or sporocytes, Spc.*

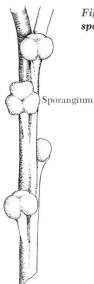

Sporangium

Figure 6.3 *Psilotum nudum: portion of branch with sporangia, enlarged.*

Figure 6.4 *Psilotum nudum: tran-section of stem. Co, cortex; Epd, epidermis; Edd, endodermis; Sto, stoma; VT, vascular tissue, a ridged protostele (actinostele).*

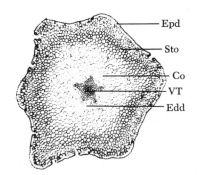

Epd

Sto

Co

VT

Edd

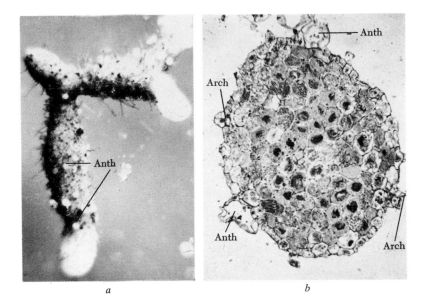

a   *b*

Figure 6.5   *Psilotum nudum. (a) Enlarged view of cylindrical gametophyte. (b) Transection of gametophyte.
Anth, antheridia; Arch, archegonia.*
[Courtesy of Professor David Bierhorst.]

The gametophyte of *Psilotum* is a minute, subterranean, cylindrical
structure (Figure 6.5a) devoid of chlorophyll and, therefore, saprophytic. In some instances, only the antheridia and archegonia (Figure
6.5a,b) enable one to distinguish the gametophyte with certainty from
the juvenile sporophytic axis. The gametophyte, like the rhizome, contains mycorrhizal fungi.

After fertilization is effected by multiflagellate sperms, the zygote
undergoes nuclear and cell division to form a young sporophyte, which
at first is attached to the gametophyte (Figure 6.6). Development of
the gametophyte from the spore and of the sporophyte from the zygote
are both rather slow processes in *Psilotum.*

Psilotum and certain extinct fossil psilophytes that are similar in
organization (Figure 6.1) are unique among vascular plants in lacking
both roots and leaves. Until recently, most botanists have interpreted
them as primitive plants, not greatly modified from their hypothetical,
sporophytic, algal progenitors (see, however, page 96 for a different
viewpoint).

It is of interest that two races of *Psilotum* occur, one diploid with
haploid gametophytes ($n = 52$ to 54 chromosomes) and one tetraploid
with diploid gametophytes. In some of the latter, a vascular strand surrounded by an endodermis is present. The presence of vascular tissue
in both gametophyte and sporophyte suggests the fundamental similarity
between the alternating generations. Furthermore, it is again clear that

Figure 6.6   *Psilotum nudum: young
sporophyte still attached to gametophyte.*

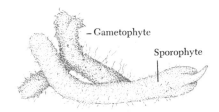

95

*Figure 6.7 **Tmesipteris sp.: living plant from the Philippines.*** [Courtesy of Don Reynolds.]

the chromosome number of itself does not determine whether sporophytic or gametophytic characters prevail. The mechanism that controls this is still obscure.

TMESIPTERIS   The superficially leafy genus *Tmesipteris* * (Figure 6.7) is fundamentally similar in organization to *Psilotum. Tmesipteris* occurs natively in New Caledonia, Australia, and New Zealand, Depending on the species, the plants may be either erect or pendulous epiphytes. The flattened, leaflike appendages are usually interpreted as stem branches. Associated with some of these appendages are bilobed sporangia, the spores of which develop into cylindrical subterranean gametophytes much like those of *Psilotum.*

The cylindrical, subterranean, saprophytic, mycorrhizal gametophytes of *Tmesipteris* and *Psilotum* were considered to be almost unique, but Dr. D. W. Bierhorst has recently found similar ones in certain ferns, namely, *Schizaea melanesica* and *Stromatopteris moniliformis.* Furthermore, the embryology and the subterranean and erect axes of these ferns are similar to those of *Psilotum* and *Tmesipteris,* at the same time showing such fernlike attributes as circinate vernation (see page 95) and frondlike organization. In light of these and other similarities, Bierhorst has recommended that *Psilotum* and *Tmesipteris* be classified as primitive members of the Pterophyta (ferns) rather than as the Psilophyta; the latter category would then contain only extinct plants.

CLUB AND SPIKE MOSSES

A second line of seedless vascular plants with Devonian (Table 6.1) precursors are the club and spike "mosses." They have been called mosses because living species are for the most part small-leaved, herbaceous plants. The "club" and "spike" portions of their names refer to the localization of spore-bearing structures, called *sporophylls,* at the tips of certain branches with short internodes; such branches are known as *strobili* (Figure 6.9a).

Three living genera, *Lycopodium* (Figure 6.9), *Selaginella* (Figure 6.13), and *Isoetes* (Figure 6.20), which belong to this group, are rather widely distributed in both temperate and tropical habitats. A fourth, *Stylites* (similar to *Isoetes*), grows in the Andes mountains of Peru, and a fifth, *Phylloglossum* (Figure 6.8), is native to New Zealand and Australia.

LYCOPODIUM   Species of *Lycopodium,* commonly known as "ground pine" and "trailing evergreen," are abundant on the floor of coniferous forests, though some species are tropical epiphytes.

* The first "t" is silent.

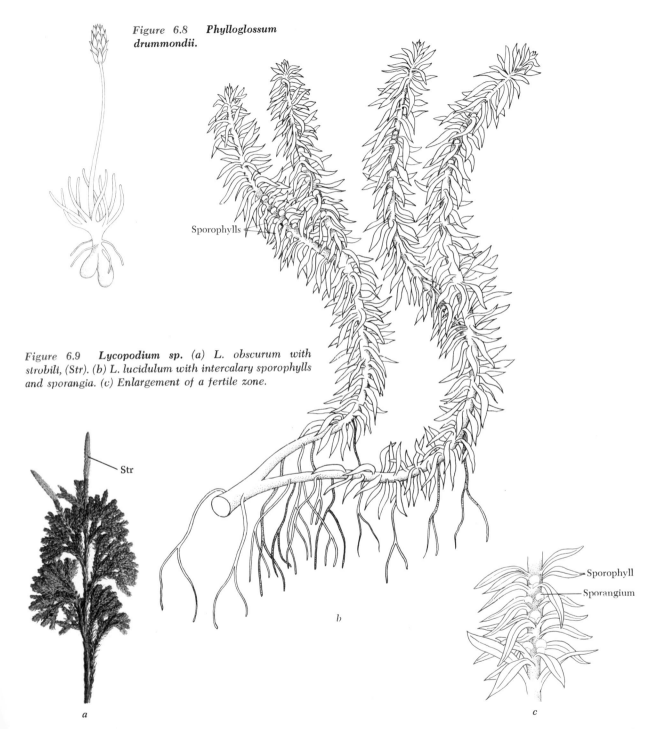

Figure 6.8 **Phylloglossum drummondii.**

Figure 6.9 **Lycopodium sp.** *(a) L. obscurum with strobili, (Str). (b) L. lucidulum with intercalary sporophylls and sporangia. (c) Enlargement of a fertile zone.*

Sporophylls

Str

Sporophyll

Sporangium

a

b

c

Table 6.1   Geologic time as related to occurrence of major plant groups

			ESTIMATED TIME, IN 10^6 YEARS, FROM BEGINNING OF EPOCH	PROBABLE TIME OF ORIGIN OF EXISTING PLANT GROUPS
Cenozoic	Quaternary	Recent		
		Pleistocene		
	Tertiary	Pliocene	1.5–2	
		Miocene	7	
		Oligocene	26	
		Eocene	37–38	
		Paleocene	53–54	
			65	
Mesozoic	Cretaceous	Upper (Late)	————	Angiosperms
		Lower (Early)		
			136	
	Jurassic	Upper (Late)		
		Middle (Middle)		
		Lower (Early)		
			190–195	
	Triassic	Upper (Late)		
		Middle (Middle)		
		Lower (Early)		
			225	
Paleozoic	Permian		————	Gymnosperms
			280	
	Carboniferous			
	Pennsylvanian	Upper (Late)		
		Middle (Middle)		
		Lower (Early)	———	Mosses
			325	
	Mississippian	Upper (Late)		
		Lower (Early)		
			345	
	Devonian	Upper (Late)	————	Liverworts
		Middle (Middle)	——/—	Arthrophytes
		Lower (Early)	————	Pterophytes
			395 —/—	Lycopods
	Silurian	Upper (Late)		Psilophytes
		Middle (Middle)		
		Lower (Early)		
			430–440	
	Ordovician	Upper (Late)		
		Middle (Middle)		
		Lower (Early)		
			500	
	Cambrian	Upper (Late)		
		Middle (Middle)		
		Lower (Early)		
			570	
Precambrian			(3,100) ————	Algae, bacteria, and fungi
			4,500	

A comparison of the plant body of *Lycopodium* (Figure 6.9) and other club mosses with that of the psilophytes at once reveals two striking differences: unlike the psilophytes, the club mosses have both vascularized leaves and roots. The axes elongate by growth of the apexes and produce a profusion of small, mosslike leaves, each with a single unbranched vein. Leaves such as these (with single, unbranched veins), the traces of which do not leave marked gaps (Figures 5.17*b* and 6.10) as they leave the vascular system of the stem, are called *microphylls*. The stem in most species of *Lycopodium* contains some type of protostele (Figure 6.10).

The sporangia of *Lycopodium* are borne at or near the bases of certain leaves and on their upper (adaxial) surfaces (Figure 6.11). Such fertile leaves are known as *sporophylls*. In some species of *Lycopodium*, there is evidence that every leaf potentially is a sporophyll (Figure 6.9*b*). In many others, only the apical leaves of certain branches are fertile; they are associated in strobili (Figure 6.9*a*). Each sporangium produces a number of fertile, sporogenous cells; these enlarge, often separate from one another, become spherical, and function as sporocytes. They then undergo meiosis and give rise to tetrads of haploid spores. When the spores have matured, each sporangium develops a fissure through which the spores are disseminated.

The spores, under suitable conditions, develop into the haploid, sexual, gametophytic stage of the organism, during which gametic union and zygote production proceed to initiate a new sporophytic generation. The bisexual gametophytes of *Lycopodium* (Figure 6.12*a*) are rather fleshy structures. In some species, they are subterranean, devoid of chlorophyll, and saprophytic; in others, they are at the soil surface and have some chlorophyll.

After fertilization of an egg by a biflagellate sperm, the zygote develops into an embryonic sporophyte (Figure 6.12*b*). The early leaves of this sporophyte lack vascular tissue, although typical microphylls develop later. The gametophytes of a number of species are quite persistent, and are recognizable long after the embryonic sporophytes have become established.

SELAGINELLA Many of the species of *Selaginella* require a more hydric (abundantly moist) habitat than *Lycopodium,* but a few, like the familiar "resurrection plant" (Figure 6.13*b,c*), normally live in arid soils. A majority of the species are tropical. The plants may be either prostrate (Figure 6.13*a*), covering the surface of the soil, or ascending and frondlike (Figure 6.14*a*).

In some species of *Selaginella*, the microphyllous leaves are spirally arranged and all of similar size. In others, the leaves are borne in four rows on the stem, two dorsal and two ventral, the dorsal leaves being smaller than the ventral.

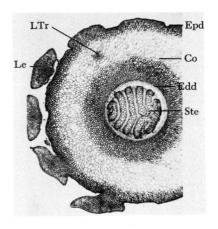

Figure 6.10   Lycopodium clavatum: transection of stem. Co, cortex; Epd, epidermis; Edd, endodermis; Le, leaf; LTr, leaf trace; Ste, stele (plectostele; see Figure 5.12).

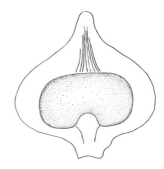

Figure 6.11   Lycopodium obscurum: adaxial view of sporophyll and sporangium.

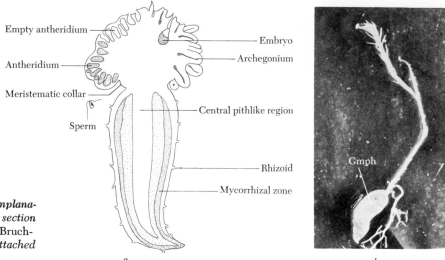

Empty antheridium

Embryo

Antheridium

Archegonium

Meristematic collar

Central pithlike region

Sperm

Rhizoid

Mycorrhizal zone

Gmph

Figure 6.12   Lycopodium complanatum. (a) Median longitudinal section of gametophyte. [After H. Bruchmann.] (b) Young sporophyte attached to gametophyte, Gmph.

a

b

Prominent, leafless branches, the *rhizophores*, which bear delicate, dichotomously branching roots as they enter the soil, are present in many species. There is increasing evidence that the rhizophore itself is a root that branches just before it approaches the soil.

Figure 6.13   Selaginella sp. (a) S. kraussiana, a creeping species, (b, c) Selaginella lepidophylla, the "resurrection plant," (b) in dry state, and (c) in moist state.

a

b

c

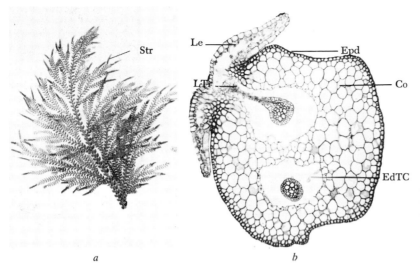

Le ─── Epd

Str

LTr

Co

EdTC

Figure 6.14 Selaginella sp. (a) S. pallescens, a frondose species, branching in one plant. (b) S. caulescens, transection of stem. Str, strobilus; Co, cortex; Epd, epidermis; EdTC, endodermal trabecular cell; Le, leaf; LTr, leaf trace.

a   b

The stems contain one or more branching protosteles that are often separated from the cortex by a cavity (Figure 6.14b) traversed by elongate endodermal cells.

The sporophylls in all species of *Selaginella* occur in more or less compact strobili, and are equal in size (Figure 6.15).

Figure 6.15 Selaginella pallescens. (a) Strobilus, enlarged. (b) Adaxial view of microsporophyll. (c) Adaxial view of megasporophyll.

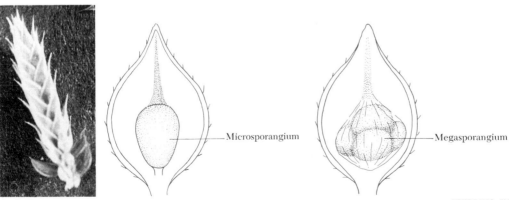

─── Microsporangium

─── Megasporangium

a   b   c

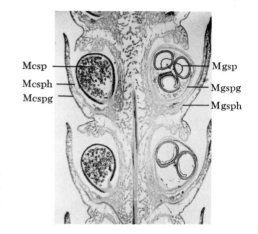

Figure 6.16   *Selaginella* sp.: *portion of a longitudinal section of the* strobilus. *Mgspg, megasporangium; Mgsp, megaspore; Mgsph, megasporophyll; Mcspg, microsporangium; Mcsp, microspore; Mcsph, microsporophyll.*

Figure 6.17   *Selaginella* sp. *(a–c) Development of the male, and (d,e) female gametophytes (e in apical view). (f) Embryo.*

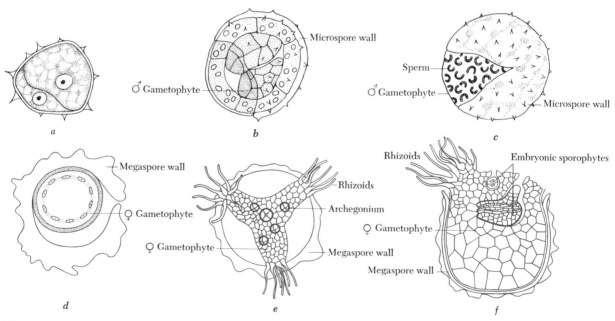

Sporogenesis in *Selaginella* is especially significant and instructive. The sporophylls of a particular strobilus produce some sporangia that develop essentially like those of *Psilotum* and *Lycopodium*, resulting in the production of a large number of spores [Figures 6.15 and 6.16 (left)] by the meiotic division of the sporocytes. In other sporangia in the strobili of *Selaginella*, however, development of most of the sporocytes is arrested before meiosis; in most cases, only one sporocyte in such a sporangium completes the meiotic process while the remainder degenerate. As the single spore tetrad forms, there is available a vast amount of nutritive material originally incorporated within the aborted sporocytes. The members of the single tetrad apparently absorb this material, enlarging enormously until they actually distend the sporangial wall [Figures 6.15c and 6.16 (right)]. These large spores are called *megaspores;* the cells from which they arise are *megasporocytes*. In contrast, the ordinary-sized spores have come to be called *microspores,* although they are about the same size as the spores of many other plants that lack this spore dimorphism or *heterospory*. The sporangia that bear megaspores are *megasporangia* (on *megasporophylls*), while the microspores arise in *microsporangia* (on *microsporophylls*). *Selaginella*, with its two kinds of spores, is *heterosporous* (Figure 6.16), whereas *Phylloglossum, Isoetes, Lycopodium, Psilotum,* mosses, liverworts, and hornworts are *homosporous.*

In all heterosporous plants, microspores develop into male gametophytes and megaspores into female gametophytes. Development of the male and female gametophytes of *Selaginella* takes place largely within the spores (Figure 6.17) and sporangia, and only in the later stages are the gametophyte-containing spores shed; such development is *endosporic*. The male and female gametophytes of *Selaginella* are reduced in size and amount of vegetative tissue, as compared with the sexual phases of *Psilotum* (Figure 6.5a), *Equisetum* (Figure 6.27a), and ferns (see Figure 7.6b).

The male gametophyte consists largely of an antheridium that contains biflagellate sperms (Figure 6.17a–c); the female gametophyte has some sterile cells and rhizoids and a cluster of archegonia (Figure 6.17d–f). Both the male and female gametophytes are achlorophyllous and saprophytic; their nutrition is based on substances stored within the microspores and megaspores by the parent sporophyte. As a result of fertilization, which is reported to occur in two species before the megaspores have been shed from their sporangia, one zygote of a given female gametophyte usually gives rise to a juvenile sporophyte (Figure 6.18), thus completing the life cycle.

A number of phenomena that occur in *Selaginella* characterize both

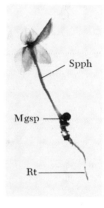

Figure 6.18   Selaginella sp.: young sporophyte, Spph, attached to ♀ gametophyte within megaspore, Mgsp; Rt, root.

Figure 6.19   Reconstruction of a coal age (Pennsylvanian) forest. C., Calamites sp., a giant arthrophytan plant; Le, Lepidodendron, a treelike form reminiscent of Lycopodium and Selaginella; S, Sphenophyllum sp., an herbaceous genus; SF, an unidentified seed fern; Si, Sigillaria, a treelike form also
reminiscent of Lycopodium and Selaginella and related to Lepidodendron.
[Courtesy of Illinois State Museum.]

extinct fossil seedless vascular plants and extant seedbearing plants.
These include (1) localization of sporangium-bearing appendages in
strobili; (2) heterospory; (3) endosporic and intrasporangial development of the gametophytes; and (4) unisexual gametophytes.

   Although extant club mosses such as *Lycopodium* and *Selaginella*
are small herbaceous plants, some of their extinct fossil relatives
achieved treelike proportions. This is true of such genera as *Lepido-*

THE PLANT KINGDOM

104

dendron and *Sigillaria* (Figure 6.19), which rested on huge branching bases and approached forest trees in height. These plants were perennial and had active cambia.

ISOETES   Although the leaves of the quillwort, *Isoetes* (Figure 6.20), are much larger than those of *Lycopodium* or *Selaginella*, these leaves are considered to be microphylls because they have single, unbranched veins, and their traces do not leave gaps as they pass out from the stem stele. The various species of *Isoetes* are either submerged aquatics, or terrestrial, living in marshy areas.

The quill-like leaves arise spirally from an extremely short, fleshy, cormlike stem; from a groove in the base of this stem the numerous, dichotomously branching roots emerge. Every leaf of an *Isoetes* plant is potentially a fertile sporophyll; like *Selaginella, Isoetes* is heterosporous (Figure 6.21). The massive sporangia are partially partitioned by septa. Each megasporangium produces several hundred megaspores, while the microsporangium produces up to a million microspores. The leaves and sporophylls of both *Selaginella* and *Isoetes* have at their bases small appendages, the *ligules*, the function of which is unknown (Figure 6.22).

Unlike those of *Selaginella*, the spores of *Isoetes* do not germinate until after they have been set free by decay of their sporangia. The endosporic gametophytes (Figure 6.22a,b) are much like those of *Selaginella* (Figure 6.17), but the sperms of *Isoetes* are multiflagellate. An embryonic sporophyte, emergent from the female gametophyte and megaspore, is illustrated in Figure 6.22c.

It is sometimes maintained that *Isoetes*, with multiflagellate sperms, stems with pith, persistent leaf bases, and secondary growth in the stem, is too different from *Lycopodium* and *Selaginella* to be included in the Microphyllophyta.

Figure 6.20   ***Isoetes melanopoda.***

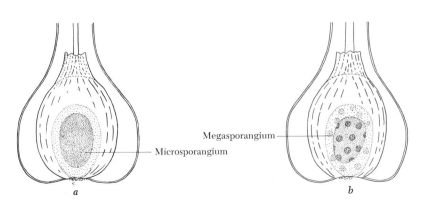

Megasporangium ———

——— Microsporangium

a

b

Figure 6.21   ***Isoetes sp.*** *(a) Adaxial view of microsporophyll and microsporangium. (b) Adaxial view of megasporophyll and megasporangium.*

SEEDLESS VASCULAR PLANTS: I

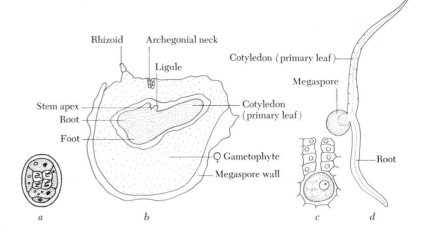

Figure 6.22 **Isoetes sp.** *(a) Isoetes lacustris L. Section of microspore containing mature ♂ gametophyte; note prothallial cell, jacket cells, and four spermatogenous cells. [After J. Liebig.] (b) Isoetes lithophila Pfeiffer. Sectional view of megaspore with mature ♀ gametophyte and young embryo. (c) Single archegonium, median longitudinal section. [(b,c) after C. Lamotte.] (d) Juvenile sporophyte attached to gametophyte within megaspore.*

Labels in figure: Rhizoid, Archegonial neck, Ligule, Stem apex, Root, Foot, Cotyledon (primary leaf), ♀ Gametophyte, Megaspore wall, Cotyledon (primary leaf), Megaspore, Root

a   b   c   d

ARTHROPHYTES

Both woody and herbaceous arthrophytes inhabited the earth in Pennsylvanian times (Figure 6.19). Their fossil remains are at once recognizable by the whorled arrangement of their branches and fertile appendages (Figures 6.19, 6.23, 6.24, and 6.25), and in many cases by their ridged stems. The clearly defined nodes and internodes give the plants a jointed appearance, and have suggested the name arthrophytes. As in the treelike fossil relatives of the club mosses, cambial activity added secondary xylem over the primary vascular skeleton of some arthrophytes; in other words, their axes were quite woody.

Figure 6.23 **Equisetum.** *(a, b) E. arvense: (a) vegetative plants; (b) fertile branches with strobili. (c) E. hyemale: vegetative axils with terminal strobili.*

a   b   c

This third group of seedless vascular plants, far more widespread and abundant in Pennsylvanian times (see Table 6.1) than at present, is represented in our living flora only by *Equisetum* (Figure 6.23). Species of this genus are known as "horsetails," "pipes," and "scouring rushes," the last name being inspired by the siliceous texture of some of the species.

EQUISETUM The whorled habit of growth of arthrophytes is well illustrated by branching species of *Equisetum* (Figure 6.23). In these, a circle of branches arises at a given node. The nodes are marked by a leaf sheath composed of a number of minute, toothlike leaves joined at their bases (Figure 6.24*a*). The photosynthetic activity of the leaves is negligible; the bulk of photosynthesis occurs in the vertical, ribbed stems, as in *Psilotum*. These erect stems arise from deeply subterranean rhizomes that bear whorls of wiry roots. The roots and stems of *Equisetum* develop from apical meristems in which single, prominent apical cells are present.

Figure 6.25*a* illustrates the transection of an internode of an *Equisetum* stem. The vascular tissue forms a circle of discrete strands, a *eustele*. At maturity the vascular tissue of each strand is associated with a canal (Figure 6.25*b*) that lies on the same radius as a surface ridge. The central part of the pith is absent. A prominent *endodermis*

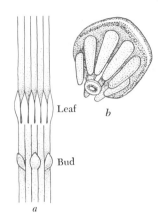

Figure 6.24 **Equisetum.** *(a) E. hyemale; detail of node and two adjacent internodes. (b) E. arvense; sporangiophore and sporangia.*

Figure 6.25 **Equisetum arvense, transection of erect stem.** *(a) Low magnification. (b) Area of one carinal canal, enlarged. Co, cortex; CrCa, carinal canal; CeCa, central canal; Epd, epidermis; Edd, endodermis; Phl, phloem; Xy, xylem; VCa, vallecular canal.*

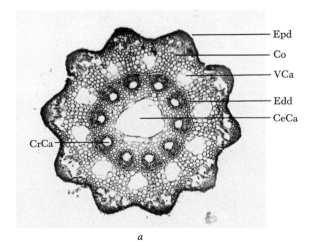

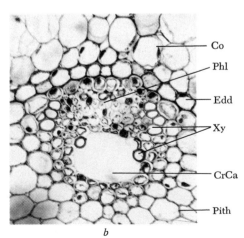

is present outside the circle of vascular bundles and, in some species, inside this circle as well. The cortex also has canals; these correspond in position to the valleys of the ridged stem surface. The epidermal cells are silicified, and numerous stomata and guard cells occur on the flanks of the ridges (Figure 6.25*a*).

As in many club mosses, the sporangia of *Equisetum* are localized in strobili (Figures 6.23*b,c* and 6.26). In the common *Equisetum arvense,* the strobiliferous branches (Figure 6.26*a*), which appear early in the spring, usually lack chlorophyll. As they shed their spores, green vegetative shoots develop from other buds on the same rhizome. In such evergreen species as *Equisetum hyemale,* by contrast, the strobili arise at the tips of the vegetative shoots as these shoots mature (Figure 6.23*c*). The appendages that bear the sporangia in *Equisetum* are known as *sporangiophores,* rather than sporophylls, inasmuch as good evidence from the study of fossils indicates that these appendages are not leaflike. Each sporangiophore bears from five to ten cylindrical sporangia on its adaxial surface (Figure 6.24*b*). These sporangia contain sporogenous tissues that give rise successively during the stages of maturation to sporocytes, tetrads, and mature spores as the meiotic process takes place.

The spores of the homosporous arthrophyte *Equisetum* are re-

Figure 6.26   ***Equisetum sp.*** *(a) E. arvense: enlarged view of strobilus, the one at left ready to shed spores and showing sporangia. (b, c) Equisetum hyemale: (b) spore and elaters; (c) young gametophyte.*

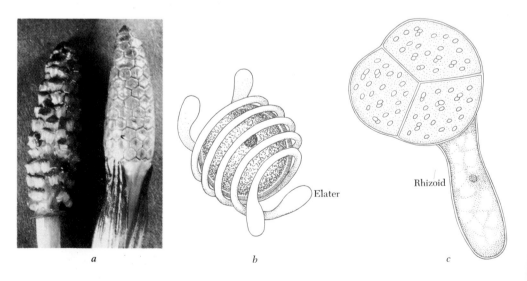

_a_   _b_   _c_

Figure 6.27 **Equisetum hyemale.** (a) Living gametophyte. (b) Gametophyte with young sporophytes attached.

markable because of their appendages, the *elaters*, which arise by the cracking of the outermost layer of the spore wall (Figure 6.26b). These appendages are exceedingly sensitive to moisture, contracting and expanding with slight variations in relative humidity. The thin-walled green spores are liberated from the strobili by elongation of the internodes, curvature of the sporangiophore stalks, and bursting of the sporangia; they germinate rapidly (Figure 6.26c).

The richly chlorophyllous spores of *Equisetum* develop on moist soil into minute, moundlike, green gametophytes* (Figure 6.27a). These grow from their margins and produce dorsal, membranous outgrowths upon and between which the antheridia and archegonia are borne. Rhizoids penetrate the substratum. Following fertilization by one of the multiflagellate sperms, one or more zygotes of a given gametophyte initiate development of the sporophytic (Figure 6.27b) stage, thus completing the life cycle.

SUMMARY

The Psilophyta, Microphyllophyta, and Arthrophyta represent ancient lines of plant life with few present survivors. These three groups can be traced back in the fossil record through the Devonian (see Table 6.1). Although living members of these groups are herbaceous, relatively small, inconspicuous plants, woody, treelike members (especially of the

* These gametophytes are of two types. Some are strictly male, while others are bisexual, first producing archegonia and later developing antheridia.

SEEDLESS VASCULAR PLANTS: II

Microphyllophyta and Arthrophyta) were abundant during the Carboniferous (see Table 6.1 and Figure 6.19).

Generally, the living representatives are either leafless (Psilophyta) or microphyllous (Microphyllophyta), although the leaves of *Equisetum* may be much-reduced macrophylls. The sporangia of these plants are borne either at the tips of stem branches (as in Psilophyta and *Equisetum*) or in association with leaves (as in Microphyllophyta). The sporangium-bearing appendages of *Equisetum, Selaginella* and most species of *Lycopodium* are grouped in strobili.

All the living genera alternate a dominant, free-living sporophytic phase with a less conspicuous gametophytic phase. *Selaginella*, however, exhibits extreme reduction of the gametophytic phase along with a tendency to retain the gametophytes upon the sporophyte, both of which are characteristic of seed plants (see Chapters 8 and 9).

OF THE SEEDLESS VASCULAR PLANTS, THE PSILOPHYTA, MICROPHYL-
lophyta and Arthrophyta have few representatives in our present flora.
By contrast, the Pterophyta (ferns), although probably equally ancient
in origin (see Table 6.1), have been more successful in competing for
survival. This chapter includes both an account of the Pterophyta and a
comparative summary of the seedless vascular plants.

Because of the aesthetic appeal of their foliage ferns are widely cultivated and appreciated. They are often used as ornamental plants in
temperate and tropical gardens as well as in conservatories. The species
with large, finely divided leaves are highly prized by connoisseurs of
foliage plants. The wiry root mass of tree ferns is sometimes used as a
substrate for growing epiphytic orchids.

The representatives of the three groups of seedless vascular plants
discussed in the preceding chapter were leafless (psilophytes), microphyllous (club and spike mosses), or characterized by much-reduced

FERNS

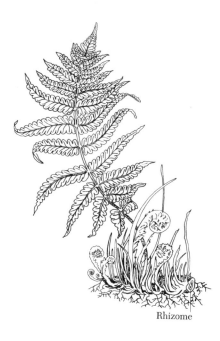

Rhizome

leaves (arthrophytes). In striking contrast to these are the ferns (Figures 7.1 and 7.2), which, like the seed plants, are *macrophyllous*. Leaves of such plants have branching veins and the emergence of their traces leaves gaps in the vascular tissue of the stem (see Figure 5.17*a*), except in the few genera where there is a protostele in the stems of the mature plant. Even in the mind of the layman, the leaf is the dominant organ of the fern plant, and this impression has a sound scientific foundation.

The ferns exhibit considerable diversity of habitat and growth habit. At one extreme are the erect-stemmed, large-leaved tree ferns that grow in tropical rain forests (Figure 7.3); at the other are small aquatic organisms such as *Salvinia* and *Azolla* (see Figure 7.10). A large group of ferns that are intermediate in size includes the familiar cultivated varieties and the natives of shady ravines and woodlands in both the temperate zones and the tropics. As a group, ferns thrive best in moist, shady environments, although a few inhabit rock fissures in bright sunlight (the latter ferns are subject to periodic desiccation, however). Ferns are, with the rarest of exceptions, perennials. In the temperate zone, they survive from year to year by means of fleshy, often subterranean rhizomes. The portions of the leaves above the soil die at the end of each growing season; a new set of leaves, already developed near the rhizome apex during this growing season, is elevated the following spring.

The fern leaf is the dominant organ of the plant, except perhaps in the tree ferns, in which the leaf is challenged by the trunklike stem. In most ferns, the leaves have a unique arrangement in the bud known as *circinate vernation:* the lower or abaxial surface of the leaf during early development consistently grows more rapidly than the upper surface, resulting in the coiling of the leaf (Figure 7.1 and 7.2). The large, circinate leaves of certain ferns have suggested the name "fiddle head." Fern leaves may be either simple, with undivided blades, or compound in various forms, with the divided blades (leaflets) attached to a *rachis,* a prolongation of the petiole (Figure 7.1). Stomata and guard cells occur predominantly in the lower epidermal layer; the upper and lower epidermal layers are cutinized, and enclose a *mesophyll* region rich in chloroplasts. The mesophyll is traversed by strands of xylem and phloem, which form the veins.

Rhizome

Figure 7.2 *Adiantum capillus-veneris,* "Venus maidenhair fern."

The stems of most ferns other than tree ferns are prostrate and fleshy, at the surface of, or under, the soil. The wiry roots originate among the leaf bases (Figures 7.1 and 7.2). The addition of secondary tissues by cambial activity does not occur in most ferns, and even the stems of tree ferns are entirely primary in origin.

With few exceptions, conduction in the xylem of most fern stems is via single-celled tracheids; vessels (multicellular, perforated tubes) do occur, however, in the xylem of the bracken fern, *Pteridium,* and in *Marsilea,* as they do sparingly in *Selaginella* and *Equisetum,* discussed in the preceding chapter.

Figure 7.3 **Cyathea sp., a tree fern, from the West Indies.** [Courtesy of Dr. W. H. Hodge.]

SEEDLESS VASCULAR PLANTS: II

a

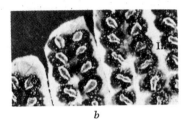

b

c

Spg

d

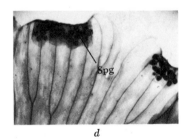

Spg

e

As in all vascular plants, the plant itself is the sporophytic generation, and, accordingly, at maturity it develops sporogenous tissue. In the ferns, this tissue may be borne on a special spike (Figures 7.11 and 7.12), on modified segments of leaves, or on the abaxial (lower) surfaces of the vegetative leaves themselves (Figure 7.4). The fertile regions on fern leaves that bear sporangia are known as *receptacles,* and the group of sporangia upon a single receptacle is called a *sorus.* In many species, but by no means in all, the sorus of sporangia is covered during development by a flap of tissue (*a true indusium;* Figure 7*a,b*) or by the inrolled margin of the leaf (*a false indusium;* Figure 7.4 *c,d*). The sporangia of some (mostly tropical) ferns are rather massive and thick-walled, and produce numerous spores (Figures 7.11 and 7.12) as do those of the club and spike mosses and *Equisetum.* A few genera are heterosporous. In the more familiar ferns, such as *Adiantum,* the maidenhair fern, and *Dryopteris,* the shield fern, the numerous sporangia, grouped in sori on the backs or margins of the leaves, are comparatively small, thin-walled, and long-stalked (Figure 7.5*a*); these sporangia produce only from 48 to 64 spores. Such spores arise by meiosis from sporocytes, and at maturity their walls thicken with a dark brown, impervious substance, resulting in the brown color of the mature sori.

Indusia ultimately shrivel when the spores have matured, exposing the sporangia (Figure 7.4*b,e*). The spores are ejected from the sporangia, which crack open (Figure 7.5*b*) in the region of the delicate lip cells as the thickened cells of the annulus, a ringlike layer of cells, contract and then expand suddenly. Tremendous numbers of spores are produced by ferns, but the special requirements of most species for moisture and shade effectively reduce the number of gametophytes that develop from these spores.

Spores that are deposited by air currents upon suitably moist soil and rocks germinate within 5 to 6 days (Figure 7.6*a*) and commence developing into the sexual phase, the gametophyte. This stage begins as a small, algalike chain of cells, each filled with chloroplasts; often, there is a colorless rhizoid emerging from the basal cell of the chain. As growth continues, a membranous structure develops; this has an apical notch in which the apical meristem is situated (Figure 7.6*b*).

Figure 7.4 **Spore production in ferns.** *(a,b) Dryopteris: (a) immature and (b) mature sori. (c–e) Lower leaf surface of Adiantum. (c) Immature and (d) mature stages; the leaf margin covers the sporangia in c and d (cleared preparation) while the sporangia, Spg, are exposed in e. In, indusium shrivelled, exposing sporangia.*

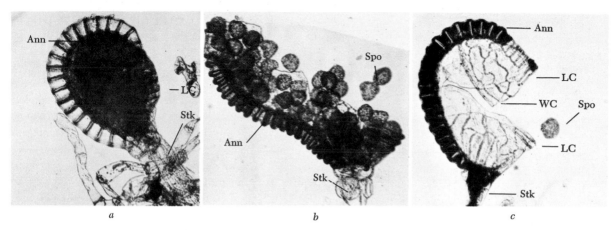

Figure 7.5   *Dryopteris dentata.* (a) *Mature, intact sporangium.* (b) *Sporangium after contraction of annulus.* (c) *Empty sporangium. Ann, annulus; LC, lip cells; Spo, spore; Stk, stalk; WC, wall cells.*

The central portion of the developing gametophyte is several cell layers thick, but the wings have only one layer. Additional rhizoids emerge from the cells of the ventral surface and penetrate the substrate. When the germinating spores are well separated, the resulting gameto-

Figure 7.6   *Dryopteris dentata.* (a) *Spore germination.* (b) *Gametophyte (prothallus) 41 days old.* (c) *Ventral view of portion of mature gametophyte showing sex organs. Anth, antheridium; Arch, archegonium; SpoW, spore wall.*

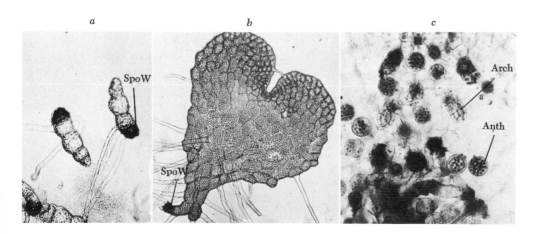

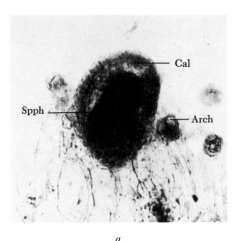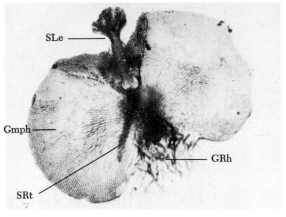

a   b

Figure 7.7   *Dryopteris dentata: early development of the sporophyte. (a)*
Embryonic sporophyte before emergence from calyptra. (b) Leaf and root
of sporophyte emergent from gametophyte. Arch, infertile archegonium; Cal,
calyptra; Spph, embryonic sporophyte; Gmph, gametophyte; Sle, leaf of
sporophyte; SRt, root of sporophyte; GRh, rhizoids of gametophyte.

phytes are heart-shaped and may in some species approach 0.5 in. in
diameter. The fern gametophyte was long ago designated the *prothallus*
or *prothallium*, as it was known to be the precursor of the fern plant
even before its sexual function was clearly understood.

As well-nourished, bisexual gametophytes mature—about 40 to 60
days after the spores have been planted in laboratory cultures—they
develop antheridia and archegonia on their ventral surfaces (Figure
7.6c). Slight accumulations of moisture between the substrate and the
ventral surface of the gametophyte suffice to open both the antheridia,
which discharge the multiflagellate sperm, and the necks of mature
archegonia. The cells inside the necks of the mature archegonia dissolve
and are extruded; thus, a moist passageway develops through which the
sperms swim to the mature eggs. The eggs of several archegonia may
be fertilized, but usually only one of the zygotes develops into a juvenile
sporophyte (Figure 7.7).

The sporophyte development, which is very rapid in the common
garden and woodland ferns, is initiated by three successive nuclear and
cell divisions of the zygote within the archegonium, forming what is
called an octant. By further cell divisions, an embryonic *root, leaf, stem,*
and *foot* are organized. The foot seemingly functions in nutrient absorp-

tion from the gametophyte. In many ferns, the primary or embryonic leaf (Figure 7.7b) emerges through the apical notch. The stem develops slowly, but ultimately it produces additional leaves. The first few leaves of juvenile ferns differ from those of the mature sporophyte. As growth continues, the later-produced leaves finally come to resemble those typical of the adult species. When the minute sporophyte has become established, the membranous gametophyte dies. The gametophyte generation, then, in the ferns, as in other seedless vascular plants, is relatively short-lived and simple in structure. The sporophytic phase is dominant in the life cycle. The fern life cycle is summarized in the accompanying diagram.

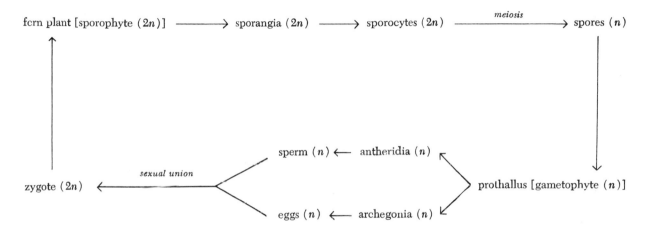

In a number of species of ferns, the gametophyte stage either fails to develop any sex organs at all, or lacks archegonia or antheridia. In such cases, the vegetative tissue of the gametophyte, below its apical notch, develops without fertilization into a juvenile sporophyte that then matures. This is the phenomenon of *apogamy*, the development of an embryo without union of gametes. In such ferns, sporophyte and gametophyte have the same chromosomal constitution, further evidence that, as we noted in the mosses, sporophytes and gametophytes are not merely the expression of diploid and haploid chromosome complements.

The preceding paragraphs have emphasized the organization and reproduction of ferns like *Adiantum* and *Dryopteris,* which are abundant and conspicuous representatives of the fern flora of the temperate zone.

Two additional series of somewhat different ferns remain to be described, namely, the heterosporous water ferns and a small, seemingly relict group of ancient, primitive ferns.

THE HETEROSPOROUS WATER FERNS   The heterosporous water ferns

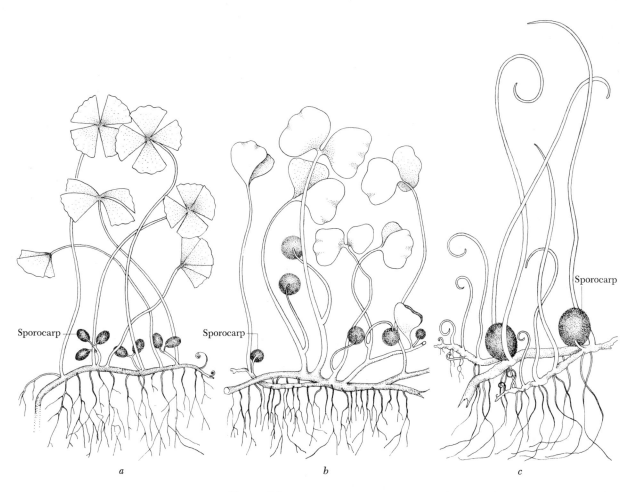

Sporocarp

Sporocarp

Sporocarp

a   *b*   *c*

Figure 7.8   **Heterosporous water ferns.** *(a) Marsilea sp. (b) Regnellidium diphyllum. (c) Pilularia americana. Note the sporocarps containing micro- and megasporangia.*

include the amphibious genera *Marsilea, Regnellidium,* and *Pilularia* (Figure 7.8), and the strictly aquatic genera *Salvinia* and *Azolla* (Figure 7.10).

Marsilea is often mistaken for wood sorrel (sour grass) or for four-leaved clover by the layman. This genus grows in or at the margins of shallow bodies of water, the cloverlike leaves arising alternately from prostrate stolons (Figure 7.8*a*) that are rooted at the nodes. The young leaves are circinate and the two pairs of leaflets are dichotomously veined. The stomata of the floating leaflets occur only on the upper surface.

The sporangia, which are small like those of *Adiantum* and *Dryopteris*, lack annuli and lip cells. They develop within *sporocarps* (Figure 7.8a) that are probably modified leaflets, brown, hard, and nutlike at maturity. Two kinds of sporangia—megasporangia and microsporangia—are present within the sporocarp, each megasporangium containing only one ovoid megaspore at maturity.

Unlike those of *Selaginella,* the megaspores and microspores of *Marsilea* do not germinate until they have been shed into the water by disintegration of the sporocarp wall. Germination can be hastened by cutting or filing away a segment of this wall. When such has been done, the gelatinous contents of the sporocarp become hydrated and swell; in expanding, they carry the sori of microsporangia and megasporangia out into the water (Figure 7.9a). The megaspores and microspores (Figure 7.9b) then germinate rapidly to form small ephemeral male and female gametophytes. After fertilization by a large, multiflagellate sperm, the single zygote of each female gametophyte develops into an embryonic sporophyte.

The male gametophyte is colorless and saprophytic, as is the female during early development; however, the latter develops photosynthetic tissue and rhizoids after fertilization.

Marsilea and the related *Regnellidium* and *Pilularia* provide evidence

Figure 7.9 **Marsilea vestita.** (a) Germinating sporocarp. (b) Megaspores and microspores. Note sorus of sporangia enclosed in indusium.

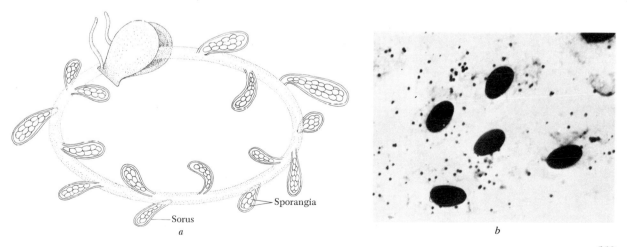

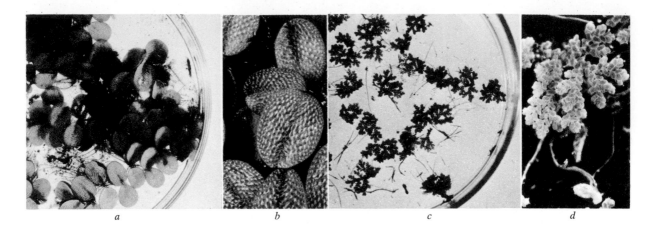

a   b   c   d

Figure 7.10 **Heterosporous ferns.** (a,b) Salvinia natans. (c,d) Azolla caroliniana (b and d are considerably enlarged).

Figure 7.11 **Ophioglossum engelmannii, the adder's tongue fern.**

that heterospory apparently evolved more than once in different vascular plants [recall *Selaginella* and *Isoetes* (pages 102 to 105) and see *Salvinia* and *Azolla* (below)].

Salvinia and *Azolla* (Figure 7.10) are minute floating aquatics that, although heterosporous, are not closely related to *Marsilea, Regnellidium,* or *Pilularia.* Like these three genera, *Salvinia* and *Azolla* bear their sporangia in sporocarps; however, their sporocarps are enclosed in a hardened indusium. Their heterospores also produce minute, colorless gametophytes after being shed from the sporocarps.

THE PRIMITIVE OR ANCIENT FERNS   In the ferns so far described, the sporangia are small, delicate, thin-walled structures containing few spores (up to 64). About six genera of mostly tropical ferns differ in having massive, thick-walled sporangia that each produce a large number of spores (up to 15,000).

Two genera of the ancient ferns [so-called because their fossil record extends back to the Carboniferous (see Table 6.1)] occur in the temperate zone. These are *Ophioglossum,* the "adder's tongue fern" (Figure 7.11), and *Botrychium* the "grape fern" or "moonwort" (Figure 7.12). In both, the large sporangia occur on axes that arise at the junction of blade and petiole.

Unlike those of almost all other ferns, the gametophytes of *Ophioglossum* and *Botrychium* are subterranean, fleshy, achlorophyllous structures containing fungi in some of their cells. The nutrition of these gametophytes is saprophytic, like that of *Psilotum.*

THE FOSSIL RECORD OF FERNS   The earliest clearly fernlike plants are recognizable in middle Devonian strata (see Table 6.1). In some of these plants the plant body consisted of branching axes, some of which terminated in circinate tips that developed into pinnate branches. *Cladoxylon scoparium* (Figure 7.13) illustrates another type, in which the plant consisted of an irregularly branched primary axis with dichotomously branching, flattened, leaflike appendages (Figure 7.13*b*). Certain of the flattened appendages of *Cladoxylon* bore terminal sporangia at their apexes (Figure 7.13*c*).

In the early fossil ferns, the leaves were not clearly distinct from the branches of the axis, which grew out in many planes. Later, in the Carboniferous and Permian (see Table 6.1), certain branches of the fossil fern axes became flattened and more frondlike; eventually they all grew one plane (Figure 7.14), as in modern ferns. The fern leaf is thought by most botanists to have evolved from a system of branches in an ancestral type that became planate and developed a webbing of tissue between the branches. This, it has been suggested, is the method of evolution of all macrophyllous leaves. Such leaves, then, are considered to be fundamentally different from microphyllous leaves (see Figure 5.17), which are thought to be localized surface outgrowths that later developed xylem and phloem.

The occurrence of fernlike leaves with seeds, belonging to the extinct seed ferns of the Carboniferous, has cast some doubt upon the earlier designation of that period as "the age of ferns," for many of the putative ferns may then have been seed plants.

Figure 7.12 Botrychium virginianum, the rattlesnake fern.

Figure 7.13 Cladoxylon scoparium, a middle Devonian fern. (a) Reconstruction of growth habit. (b) Sterile leaf. (c) Fertile leaf, enlarged, showing terminal sporangia. [After R. Krausel and H. Weyland.]

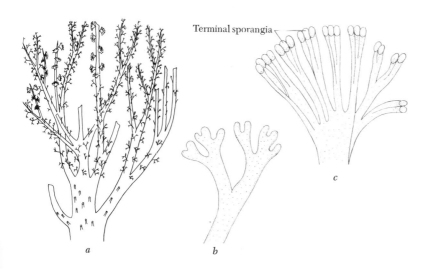

Terminal sporangia

a   *b*   *c*

Figure 7.14   Psaronius sp., an extinct arborescent fern from Carboniferous and Permian strata. [After J. Morgan, from H. N. Andrews.]

SUMMARY OF SEEDLESS
VASCULAR PLANTS

With this brief account of the structure and reproduction of ferns, we have considered all of the four groups of seedless vascular plants: the psilophytes (Figure 6.1 to 6.7: *Psilotum, Tmesipteris,* and the extinct *Rhynia* and *Psilophyton*); the club mosses (Figures 6.8 to 6.22: *Lycopodium, Selaginella, Isoetes,* and such fossil types as *Lepidodendron* and *Sigillaria*); the arthrophytes (Figures 6.23 to 6.27: *Equisetum* and the extinct *Calamites, Sphenophyllum,* and *Calamophyton*); and, finally, the ferns (Figures 7.1 to 7.14).

These plants have in common the dominance of their sporophytic phase over the gametophytic phase, and presence of vascular tissue (attributes shared also by seed plants). In the past, the four groups of seedless vascular plants were classified as a single division of the plant kingdom (see Table 1.1) designated Pteridophyta, which was freely translated as "the ferns and their allies." The fossil record does not provide compelling evidence of alliance or common origin; instead, it indicates that these four series all extend back into Devonian times (see Figure 6.1) and probably earlier.

The ferns differ from other seedless vascular plants in having large, complex leaves that are interpreted as modified branching axes. Such axes are thought to have undergone branching in only one plane, forming flattened and webbed branch systems. The microphyllous leaves of other seedless vascular plants (except, perhaps those of *Equisetum*), on the contrary, have been looked upon as merely localized emergences of the axes, similar to thorns or the spines of psilophytes, although the leaves have vascular tissue; less frequently, microphyllous leaves have been interpreted as branch systems, reduced in extent. When we consider, in retrospect, the leaves of certain seaweeds (algae), mosses, liverworts, club mosses, arthrophytes, ferns, and seed plants, we might well pause to reflect whether all leaves are strictly *homologous*—that is, fundamentally similar in structure—just because we call them "leaves."

As noted above, the seedless vascular plants all have the same type of life cycle, characterized by a prominent sporophyte and a less complex gametophyte. In light of their many diversities, however, the similarity of life cycle may be interpreted as an example of convergent or parallel evolution.

8 GYMNOSPERMS

WE NOTED EARLIER THAT PLANTS MAY BE DIVIDED INTO TWO GREAT categories on the basis of whether or not they produce seeds. None of the plants discussed in the preceding chapters produces seeds. Algae, fungi, liverworts, and mosses are nonvascular, seedless plants, whereas the psilophytes, club mosses, arthrophytes, and ferns are vascular in that they develop xylem and phloem, as do the members of the second great group, the seed-bearing plants.

Among the seed plants themselves, two types are clearly distinguishable; the distinctions relate primarily to the location of the seeds, but are also based on other attributes. In one type, the seeds are commonly borne within structures known as *fruits* (Figure 8.1*a,b,c*); these may open at maturity, exposing and shedding seeds, but at least in the early stages of development, the seeds are enclosed. Plants that bear their seeds in this manner are known as *angiosperms,* or "flowering plants" (see Table 1.1). In the other group, the *gymnosperms,** the seeds develop on the surface or tip (Figur 8.14) of an appendage

* Although "Gymnospermae" has been abandoned by many as a formal taxon (see Table 1.1), "gymnosperm" remains a useful descriptive term.

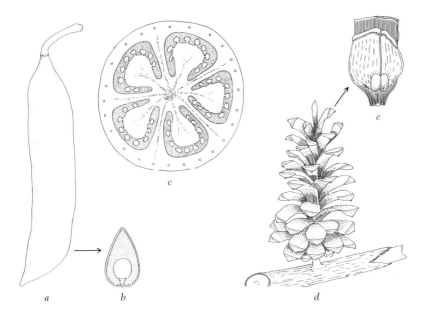

Figure 8.1 **Methods of bearing seeds.** (a–c) Angiospermy: pod (fruit) of garden pea; (b) the same in transection showing enclosed seed. (c) Transection of tomato fruit with enclosed seeds. (d,e) Gymnospermy: (d) seed cone, or strobilus, of pine; (e) portion of one of segments of d showing unenclosed, winged seeds.

(which has various names), and are not enclosed in it (Figure 8.1d,e). Although the seed-bearing structures of gymnosperms may occur in cones or strobili (Figures 8.1d,e and 8.2) that hide the seeds from view, the seeds are not enclosed within the structures that bear them, but are merely concealed by the grouping and overlapping of those structures.

Gymnospermous plants may be woody trees, shrubs, or vines. Familiar examples of these include the pine, hemlock, spruce, fir, juniper, cypress, and maidenhair tree, *Ginkgo biloba* (Figure 8.14); other gymnosperms are somewhat fleshy like the less familiar fernlike and palmlike *cycads* (Figures 8.9 and 8.10). Among the flowering plants, in contrast, both woody and herbaceous types are abundant, but the herbaceous outnumber the woody in genera, species, and individuals. Stems of herbaceous plants are green and soft in texture because very little (if any) secondary xylem is added by the vascular cambium if, indeed, this cambium is present at all (see Chapter 5). In woody plants, of course, the vascular cambium adds annual increments of secondary xylem (see page 84). Oaks, elms, maples, lilacs, roses, and grapes are woody angiosperms that are familiar to most people; iris, grasses, daisies, tomatoes, and morning glories are common examples of herbaceous angiosperms.

The classification of seed-bearing plants, like that of other organisms, varies with the classifier (see Table 1.1). The discovery in Carboniferous rocks of fossil fernlike leaves with attached seeds, representative of a group of extinct plants known as "seed ferns," suggested that seed-bearing plants and ferns evolved from a common ancestor. This discovery, and the fact that seed ferns and other seed plants are macrophyllous, inspired the classification of both ferns and seed plants in a single taxon, the Pteropsida. Other classifiers, including the author, look upon the ferns, seed plants, and even the gymnosperms and angiosperms, as separate lines of evolutionary development, and accordingly, classify them in several separate divisions of the plant kingdom.

The remainder of the present chapter presents and discusses reproduction in gymnosperms and considers certain representative types. In Chapter 9 we shall continue to discuss the angiosperms in further detail.

Before proceeding to an examination of reproduction in gymnosperms, let us consider in general terms the reproductive process that results in the production of seeds. All seed plants, like all seedless vascular plants, are sporophytes. Accordingly, at maturity, certain portions of the vegetative organism become fertile, that is, reproductive, and produce spores. In most gymnosperms, as in the club mosses and *Equisetum*, the spore-bearing appendages are aggregated in localized regions of the axes to form cones or strobili (Figures 8.1*d* and 8.2). As noted earlier, the spores produced by the sporophytes of all land plants arise by meiosis in sporocytes, eventually developing into the sexual, gametophytic phase of the plant's life cycle.

In connection with the present discussion, several phenomena that occur in *Selaginella* (see page 104) are especially noteworthy. The spores of *Selaginella* are of two sizes, and differ in both origin and in subsequent development. The spores of ordinary size, the *microspores*, produced in large numbers in their sporangia, develop into *male gametophytes*. Other spores, the *megaspores*, of which only four are typically produced in a given sporangium, become filled with stored foods, enlarge tremendously, and upon germination produce *female gametophytes*. The production of two types of spores, it will be recalled, is known as *heterospory*. A further significant feature of *Selaginella* is that the early stages of both the male and female gametophytes develop within the microspores and megaspores, respectively, so that the gametophytes are dependent for nutrition on materials stored in the spores; this is called *endospory*. Under certain conditions, the spores may be retained within their sporangia until they have completed developing into mature gametophytes, and reportedly, in two species of *Selaginella* the spores are retained until after fertilization has occurred. In summary, then, we observe in *Selaginella* the presence of (1) heterospory (involving tremendous size differences between the microspores and megaspores); (2) the inevitable corollary of heterospory, unisexual gametophytes; (3) dependence of the developing gametophytes on nutrients from the sporophyte; (4) endosporal development of the gametophytes; and (5) prolonged retention of the spores and their contained gametophytes within the sporangia. With certain modifications and innovations, these same phenomena occur in reproduction leading to the formation of seeds.

All seed plants produce two kinds of spores in different sporangia: those spores that grow into male gametophytes are usually called *microspores;* those that grow into female gametophytes are usually called *megaspores* (although they do not differ markedly in size*). These spores of seed plants and the sporangia that produce them differ from those of *Selaginella* in several important aspects; these can be briefly summarized.

1   The megasporangia in seed plants are surrounded by several layers (sometimes a double layer) of cells called the *integument;* these covered megasporangia are called *ovules* (Figures 8.3c and 8.4a).

2   Of the four potential spores formed in the megasporangium at meiosis, only one, the *functional megaspore,* survives (Figure 8.4b).

3   The surviving megaspore at maturity approximates the size of the microspore, and in most cases, lacks a markedly thickened wall and stored foods, although it may enlarge considerably during the development of the female gametophyte.

4   The microspores are shed ultimately as *pollen grains,* which contain the male gametophyte; these grains are transferred, by various mechanisms, from the microsporangium to a point more or less closely proximate to the ovule containing the megaspore (and later, containing the female gametophyte). This transfer is called *pollination.*

5   The functional megaspore is *never* shed from its megasporangium and integument, that is, from the ovule.

6   This megaspore completes its development in the megasporangium into a mature female gametophyte (Figure 8.6a), using

* The megaspores of seed plants are not very different in terms of size from the microspores. Can we say, then, that the seed plants are heterosporous in the sense that seedless vascular plants are? The terms microspore and megaspore have been applied to the male-gametophyte-producing and female-gametophyte-producing spores of seed plants, respectively, in spite of their similarity in size. A suggested explanation of the similarity is that permanent retention of the megaspores within the megasporangium has reduced the size of the megaspore.

metabolites transferred to it from the surrounding tissues of the megasporangium and sporophyte; the functional megaspore may thicken its wall during this process.

7   The sperms are brought into the vicinity of the egg directly or indirectly by means of an outgrowth of the male gametophyte, called the *pollen tube*.

8   Fertilization and development of an embryonic sporophyte regularly take place within the female gametophyte, still within the megaspore, and in turn, within the megasporangium (thus within the ovule). When the embryo within the female gametophyte has developed, the ovule is called a *seed*, the end-product of these correlated phenomena.

The structures and activities summarized in *1* to *8* above are, of course, only an outline of a rather complicated process resulting in the production of seeds, but this summary will be useful for repeated reference as the details of the reproductive process in the several types of seed plants are described.

One further point is noteworthy. In gymnosperms the ovule does not increase much in size after fertilization. In angiosperms, by contrast, fertilization stimulates rapid growth of the ovule as it matures into the seed.

Three types of gymnospermous seed plants are commonly seen in nature or in cultivation, namely, the cycads (Figures 8.9 and 8.10), the *Ginkgo* (Figure 8.14), and the conifers (Figures 8.2 and 8.8); a fourth type, exemplified by *Ephedra* (Figure 8.15), occurs in the southwestern and far western parts of the United States. In the following paragraphs, *Pinus* (pine), a conifer, will be treated in some detail as a basis for comparison with other gymnospermous types.

PINES AND OTHER CONIFERS   Pines and associated conifers form extensive forests in various parts of the world; they are highly important commercially as sources of lumber, wood pulp for the manufacture of paper, and naval stores (a general term for the products of coniferous gums or resins). Like many woody plants, the apical growth of *Pinus* is seasonal. During dormant periods, the delicate tips of the branches are covered by relatively impervious scales, forming *covered buds*. During the growing season, these buds unfold by division and elongation of the stem cells within the bud (Figure 8.2). Pine leaves, familiarly known as needles, have little surface area (Figure 8.2). Within the leaves and throughout the plant are numerous canals filled

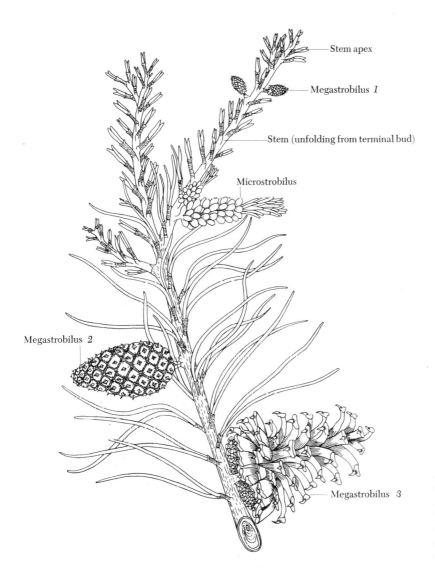

Stem apex

Megastrobilus *1*

Stem (unfolding from terminal bud)

Microstrobilus

Megastrobilus *2*

Megastrobilus *3*

Figure 8.2   Pine: composite sketch of branch in springtime. Megastrobilus 1 is at pollination; 2 was pollinated 1 year earlier; 3 was pollinated 2 years earlier, and is mature and shedding seeds. Note spur shoots bearing clusters of needles.

with a secretion known as *resin*. In most species, the needles are borne in clusters on minute lateral branches of the main axes, called *spur shoots* (Figure 8.2). The stems and roots of pine contain active, vascular cambial layers that add secondary xylem, thus increasing the woodiness and diameter of the axes. The wood of pine is homogeneous, consisting largely of conducting cells (called *tracheids*) and associated living parenchyma cells (see Figure 5.7*c*).

After a number of years of purely vegetative growth, young trees begin to bear spores. Unlike *Selaginella,* the microspores and megaspores of *Pinus* occur in separate strobili, accordingly called *microstrobili* and *megastrobili.* Both are produced on the same individual, which is therefore said to be *monoecious.* The microstrobili occur in subterminal clusters (Figure 8.2) as the buds unfold at the beginning of the growing season, while the minute, light green (or red, in some species) megastrobili are borne on short lateral branches of the expanding axes of terminal buds (Figure 8.2). The microstrobilus is composed of an axis bearing microsporophylls, each with two elongate microsporangia on its abaxial surface (Figure 8.3*a*). Early in the spring, the microsporocytes produce tetrads of haploid microspores as a result of meiosis; these separate into individual microspores with inflated ("winged") cell walls (Figure 8.3*b*).

The megastrobili are more complex in structure; their appendages, which seemingly represent fertile spur shoots, each bear two ovules (Figure 8.3*c*). An ovule, as we saw, is a megasporangium covered with an integument (Figure 8.4*a*); the passageway through the integument is known as the *micropyle.* A single megasporocyte in each ovule forms a row of four megaspores by meiosis; of these, the three nearest the micropyle degenerate, leaving one functional megaspore (Figure 8.4*b*). This is approximately the same size as the microspore and lacks a thickened wall; it is intimately associated with the surrounding cells of the megasporangium, from which it no doubt draws nutriment, instead of being free from the sporangial wall as are the megaspores of *Selaginella.* With the formation of microspores and megaspores by meiosis, sporogenesis is complete, and the development of the sexual phase follows.

The microspores begin their endosporic production of male gametophytes before they are shed from the microsporangia; they are shed when they have produced a four-celled, immature male gametophyte (Figure 8.5*a*). These microspores, containing the male gametophyte, are known familiarly as *pollen grains.*[*] The opening of the microsporangia releases large clouds of these sulfur-colored, dustlike pollen grains (with their contained male gametophytes), which are transported great distances by air currents. At the same time in the spring that the pollen is being shed, the internodes of the axes of the megastrobili elongate slightly, causing fissures to form between successive ovule-bearing appendages. Some of the airborne pollen grains sift into these

[*] The term "microspore" is usually restricted to the spore before it has undergone nuclear division to form the male gametophyte; after the nucleus has divided, the microspore is called a pollen grain.

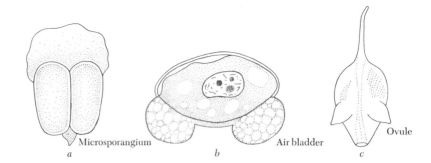

Figure 8.3 **Pinus sp.** (a) Microsporophyll with two microsporangia.
(b) Magnified aspect of single microspore with air bladders. (c) Appendage
of megastrobilus with two ovules.

Microsporangium   Air bladder   Ovule

a   b   c

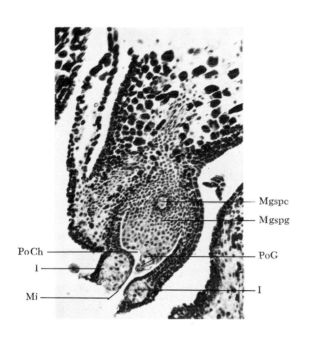

Figure 8.4 **Pinus virginiana.** (a)
Ovule and its appendages in longitudinal section soon after pollination.
(b) Functional megaspore with degenerating products of meiosis. I,
integument; Mgspc, megasporocyte;
Mgspg, megasporangium; Mi, micropyle; PoCh, pollen chamber; PoG,
pollen grain.

Mgspc

Mgspg

PoCh

PoG

I

Mi

I

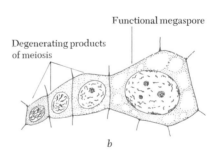

Functional megaspore

Degenerating products
of meiosis

b

Figure 8.5 **Pinus virginiana:** development of the ♂ gametophyte. (a)
Microspore containing immature ♂
gametophyte. (b) Mature ♂ gametophyte (note pollen tube and two sperm
nuclei, just after division).

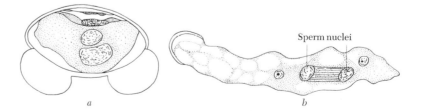

Sperm nuclei

a   b

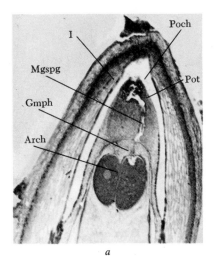

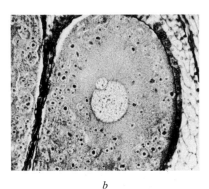

Figure 8.6 *Pinus virginiana.* (a) Longitudinal section of upper half of ovule at fertilization. (b) Fertilization, union of small male with egg nucleus. Arch, archegonium, egg, and nucleus; ♀ Gmph, female gametophyte; I, integument; Mgspg, megasporangium; PoCh, pollen chamber; PoT, pollen tube, or male gametophyte.

fissures and come into contact with the tips of the ovules, which at this time have secreted a so-called *pollination droplet* through the micropyle. Upon contact with this droplet, the pollen grains float through it, or are drawn by its contraction, into the *pollen chamber* (Figure 8.4*a*), a slight depression in the apex of the megasporangium. The transfer of pollen from the microsporangium to the micropyle of the ovule is known as *pollination.*

After pollination, the functional megaspore in each ovule initiates the development of a female gametophyte by a series of nuclear divisions followed by synthesis of cytoplasm, which proceeds at first without wall formation; later, wall formation does occur. The ovules and all the tissues of the megastrobilus enlarge during this process. The mature female gametophyte finally differentiates two or three archegonia at its micropylar pole (Figure 8.6*a*). The interval between pollination and maturation of the male and female gametophytes of pine is about 13 to 14 months.

Meanwhile, the pollen grains, stranded on the surface of the pollen chamber (megasporangial apex) when the pollination droplet disappears, germinate to form pollen tubes (Figures 8.5 and 8.6*a*), which parasitically digest the tissues of the megasporangium and convey the sperm to the mature archegonia. The pollen grain and tube with their component cells represent the mature male gametophyte. Union of one of the sperm nuclei with the egg nucleus at fertilization transforms the egg nucleus into a zygote nucleus. The second sperm nucleus degenerates.

Development of embryonic sporophytes is initiated by all the zygotes, but one of the embryos of each archegonium outstrips the others, which may then abort; if they survive, they are poorly developed and suppressed at germination. As the embryo develops, it grows out of the base of the egg cell (Figure 8.7*a,b*) into the vegetative tissues of the female gametophyte, a good deal of which it absorbs before it becomes dormant, several months after fertilization. During embryogeny, the cells of the integument harden by thickening their cell walls.

Similarly, soon after pollination, the appendages that bear the ovules begin to enlarge (Figure 8.3) and harden so that by the time the embryos have become dormant, the megastrobilus is extremely hard. The ovule with its embryo composes the *seed.* Strictly speaking, a gymnospermous seed (Figure 8.7*c*) is an embryonic sporophyte, surrounded, in turn, by the female gametophyte, the megaspore wall, and remains of the megasporangium, all of which are surrounded by the hardened integument, now called the *seed coat.*

As the seeds mature, the appendages of the megastrobilus that bear them spread apart, and the winged seeds (Figure 8.1*d,e*) are shed.

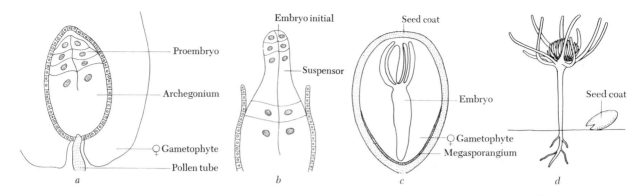

Figure 8.7 **Pinus sp.: development of embryo and seed, and germination.**
(a) Section of archegonium with proembryo soon after fertilization. (b) Elongation of suspensor, which pushes embryo-forming cells out of archegonium into female gametophyte. (c) Median longitudinal section of seed. (d) Seedling.

The embryos of those seeds that fall in suitable environments renew growth through *seed germination* (Figure 8.7d). The embryonic leaves of seed plants are called *cotyledons*.

The seed, then, is in a sense a prefabricated miniature of the mature seed plant, in this case, the pine; the "germ" of a seed is its embryo. The seed develops as the result of the series of correlated morphological and physiological processes we have just summarized.

Pinus is but one of about 40 to 50 genera of conifers, including more than 500 species, distributed in both hemispheres. This group includes cedars, larches, cypresses, spruce, and yew, among others. The reproductive process in all these plants is similar, in general, to that of pine, except for certain variations in detail.

Although the term *conifer* is sometimes considered to be synonymous with *evergreen*, several genera, such as cypress (*Taxodium*), larch (*Larix*) and dawn redwood (*Metasequoia*) are deciduous. The true cedar (*Cedrus*) is widely cultivated as an ornamental in the United States, where the native species of juniper (*Juniperus*), from the wood of which pencils and cedar chests are made, is often called "red cedar."

The conifers include some of the largest and longest-lived trees. Among them are the California redwood (*Sequoiadendron gigantea*), certain individuals of which may exceed 300 ft in height. Some living individuals of the California bristlecone pine, *Pinus aristata*, are more than 4,000 years old.

Among conifers native to the Southern Hemisphere, two, *Podocarpus* (Figure 8.8a) and *Araucaria* (Figure 8.8b), are widely cultivated as

a

b

Figure 8.8   Southern hemisphere conifers. (a) Podocarpus sp., branch. (b) Araucaria imbricata in cultivation at Seattle, Washington.

Figure 8.9   Zamia floridana, plant with ovulate strobilus.

ornamentals in this country and Europe. In the southern United States *Podocarpus* is called "yew," a vernacular name used for *Taxus* in some other parts of the world. Two species of *Araucaria*—*A. araucana,* the "monkey puzzle tree," and *A. heterophylla,* the "Norfolk Island Pine" —are widespread in cultivation.

CYCADS   Members of this small group of ten tropical, strobilate genera (Cycadophyta: see Table 1.1), are reminiscent of the tree ferns because of their fleshy, trunklike stems and pinnately compound leaves; the leaflets of some, like *Cycas,* have circinate vernation. The leaves also suggest palms, which are, however, angiosperms. Cycads are limited to the tropics and subtropics of both hemispheres. In the United States, only *Zamia* (Figure 8.9) occurs natively, in Florida. In addition, the genera *Cycas* (Figure 8.10a) and *Dioon* (Figure 8.10b) are widely cultivated for their stately, palmlike foliage. The stems of cycads are

a   b

Figure 8.10 Cycads. (a) Cycas
revoluta. [Courtesy of Professor Elsie
Quarterman.] (b) Dioon edule.

mostly unbranched, slow-growing (both in height and in girth), and
covered by the leaf bases of preceding seasons. Although a cambium
layer is present in the stems, additions of secondary tissues are composed in large part of thin-walled parenchyma cells; thus, the stems
are not very woody. Abundant mucilage canals occur in cycads.

The ovulate (megaspore-producing) and microsporangiate cones of
cycads are borne on separate individuals, unlike those of pine; cycads
are, therefore, said to be *dioecious. Cycas* differs from other cycads
in that its ovules are borne in a loosely arranged crown of fernlike
megasporophylls and not in a strobilus. The gigantic strobili of *Dioon*
are rather striking (Figure 8.11).

As in *Pinus*, the immature male gametophytes (pollen grains) are
transferred to the megastrobili and their ovules in the process of pollination, and pollination drops are present at the micropyles. Also as in
Pinus, there is an interval between pollination and fertilization, although
it is shorter in *Zamia* (about 5 months) than in *Pinus* (14 months).

The female gametophytes and archegonia, and especially the egg
cells, are readily visible to the naked eye; they are the largest among
those of the seed plants (Figure 8.12). The sperms of cycads are the
largest in the plant kingdom, often more than 300 μm° in diameter,
and are motile through the beating of numerous short flagella often
called *cilia* (Figure 8.13).

° One *micrometer* (formerly called a micron) equals 0.001 mm.

Figure 8.11   Dioon edule: megastrobilus.

Micropyle

Integument

Pollen chamber
Pollen tube
Archegonial chamber

Megasporangium

Archegonium and egg

♀ Gametophyte

Figure 8.12 **Zamia sp.: median longitudinal section of ovule (diagrammatic) made near the time of fertilization.** *Note pollen grains attached to megasporangium in pollen chamber.*

Figure 8.13 **Cycas sp.: sperm in (a) lateral and (b) apical aspects.** *Note many small flagella or cilia.*

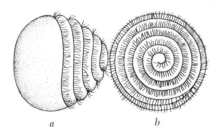

a   b

Figure 8.14 **Ginkgo biloba, maidenhair tree.** *(a) Spur shoot with microstrobili. (b) Spur shoot with ovules. (c) One pair of ovules, enlarged.*

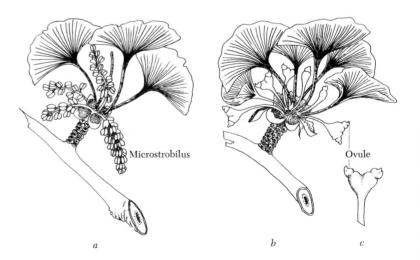

Microstrobilus

Ovule

a   b   c

The seeds of cycads have brightly colored, fleshy coats and their embryos emerge, although very slowly, without requiring a period of dormancy.

GINKGO   The Ginkgophyta (see Table 1.1) are represented in our extant flora only by the maidenhair tree, *Ginkgo biloba* (Figure 8.14), which, like the pine and most conifers, is a many-branched tree. As in pines, the clusters of leaves arise from lateral spur shoots. The plant takes its common name from the resemblance of its thin, deciduous leaves to the leaflets of the maidenhair fern.

Like the conifers, *Ginkgo* is extremely woody because of the activity of a cambium layer that adds cylinders of secondary xylem each growing season. Mucilage canals, like those of the cycads, are present in the stem and the other organs of *Ginkgo*. The microspores occur in lax, pendulous strobili, whereas the ovules are borne in pairs at the tips of delicate stalks on different trees; hence, *Ginkgo* is dioecious. The microstrobili and ovules emerge in spur shoots with the young leaves each spring.

In *Ginkgo*, as in the cycads, several months elapse between pollination and fertilization, and during this period the ovules enlarge greatly. They are abscised and fall to the ground in late August and September; hence, fertilization and embryogeny may occur after the ovules have been shed. The motile, ciliate sperms of *Ginkgo* are not quite as large as those of the cycads. As *Ginkgo* seeds ripen, the outer layer of the integument gets fleshy, the seeds having the appearance of mottled plums. The fleshy layers of the mature seed may cause nausea, if smelled, and superficial skin lesions in some individuals, if touched. Although *Ginkgo* grows rapidly and is cultivated widely in the temperate zone, it almost seems to have disappeared in nature, though it is reported to be native to eastern China. The reasons for its near extinction are unknown. In the United States, *Ginkgo* flourishes as an ornamental tree in the parks and on the streets of many cities, such as New York and Washington, D.C. *Ginkgo* is widely cultivated all over the world, especially in Asian temple grounds. The graceful trees take on a brilliant golden-yellow hue in the autumn.

EPHEDRA, GNETUM, AND WELWITSCHIA   *Ephedra*, *Gnetum*, and *Welwitschia*, often classified in either the same order or the same division, are seemingly not very closely related, certainly insofar as their vegetative organization is concerned. They are restricted in distribution and not widely cultivated; accordingly, they are probably less familiar than other gymnosperms.

Only *Ephedra* (Figure 8.15) is native to the United States, where it grows as a shrub or vine in Texas, New Mexico, Arizona, California, and Nevada, although it can survive in cultivation out-of-doors in such northern latitudes as Boston and Marburg, Germany. In vegetative appearance, *Ephedra* suggests *Equisetum*, as both have green stems with minute leaves.

Gnetum (Figure 8.16), a vine or small tree, is pantropic and has broad, deciduous leaves, like a dicotyledonous angiosperm.

The third genus, *Welwitschia* (Figure 8.17), grows natively in Angola (Portuguese West Africa) under extremely arid conditions. *Welwitschia* is unique, the slow-growing toplike, concave stem ending in a deeply growing tap root. The first pair of true (postcotyledonary) leaves persist in their basal growth throughout the life of this gymnospermous plant.

Figure 8.15 (left) Ephedra anti-syphilitica.

Figure 8.16 (right) Gnetum gne-mon: greenhouse-grown seedling.

In contrast to other gymnosperms, these three genera have some multicellular vessels in their xylem, in addition to the unicellular tracheids. All are dioecious, with relatively reduced gametophytes. The female gametophytes of *Gnetum* and *Welwitschia* are angiospermlike in producing eggs rather than archegonia. The sperms of all three genera lack flagella. In discussions of the evolutionary origin of the angiosperms, these gymnosperms have often been suggested as possible precursors.

We should emphasize that the extant gymnosperms are vegetatively quite diverse, although all have a generally similar pattern of reproduction in which the manner of seed production especially differentiates them from angiosperms. As compared with angiosperms, gymnosperms are decidedly a minority group in our present flora.

Figure 8.17   Welwitschia mirabilis.

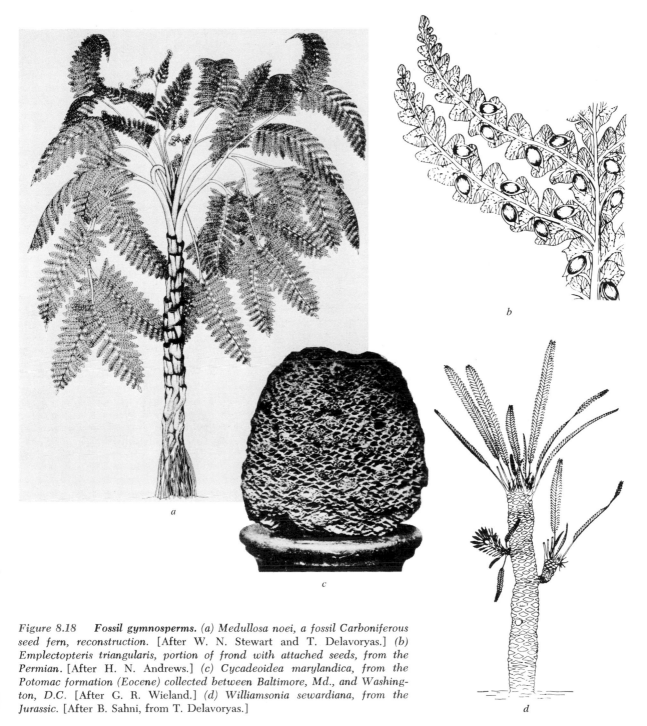

Figure 8.18 **Fossil gymnosperms.** *(a) Medullosa noei, a fossil Carboniferous seed fern, reconstruction.* [After W. N. Stewart and T. Delavoryas.] *(b) Emplectopteris triangularis, portion of frond with attached seeds, from the Permian.* [After H. N. Andrews.] *(c) Cycadeoidea marylandica, from the Potomac formation (Eocene) collected between Baltimore, Md., and Washington, D.C.* [After G. R. Wieland.] *(d) Williamsonia sewardiana, from the Jurassic.* [After B. Sahni, from T. Delavoryas.]

139

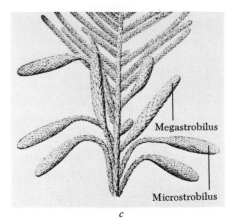

a   *b*   *c*

Megastrobilus

Microstrobilus

Figure 8.19   **Fossil gymnosperms.** *(a,b) Fossil Ginkgophyta leaves: (a) Baiera gracilis, from the Jurassic; (b) Ginkgoites digitata, from the Jurassic. [a,b after A. C. Seward.] (c) Lebachia piniformis var. solmsii, a fossil conifer from the Upper Carboniferous, reconstruction. [After R. Florin, from T. Delevoryas.]*

FOSSIL GYMNOSPERMS

Indisputable precursors of *Ephedra, Gnetum,* and *Welwitschia* have not yet been found in the fossil record, but fossilized remains of several groups of gymnospermous plants have been found, including: (1) cycads; (2) cycadeoids; (3) seed ferns; (4) precursors of *Ginkgo;* (5) and conifers. The cycadeoids and the seed ferns are both extinct, and neither has any known living descendants.

Coniferous fossils and seed ferns are known from the Carboniferous (see Table 6.1) and *Ginkgo* precursors are known from the Permian. Although cycads and cycadeoids have been considered to be present only from the Mesozoic (see Table 6.1), a cycadlike fossil has recently been reported in Carboniferous strata. Several fossil gymnosperms are illustrated in Figures 8.18 and 8.19.

THE SECOND GREAT GROUP OF SEED-PRODUCING PLANTS, THE ANGIO-
sperms—commonly known as flowering plants (see Table 1.1)—is
both the largest group in number of genera, species, and individuals,
and the most recent to develop on the earth (see Table 6.1). The
angiosperms differ from gymnospermous seed plants in that their ovules
and seeds are enclosed within the pistil,* or megasporophyll (see Figure
8.1a–c), which later becomes a seed-bearing *fruit*. The structure of the
pistil in certain primitive angiosperms suggests that the enclosure of
the seeds may have come about by the evolutionary folding of a leaflike,
ovule-bearing megasporophyll. Other important differences between
the reproduction of gymnosperms and angiosperms are summarized on
page 158.

The angiosperms exceed all other vascular plants in range of

---

* A simple pistil is composed of one ovule-bearing megasporophyll, or
carpel; the carpel, therefore, is the equivalent of the megasporophyll. Compound pistils are composed of several simple pistils (or carpels or megasporophylls) that have become united during evolution and may become
further united in development.

diversity of the plant body and habitat, and in their utility to mankind. Both woody and herbaceous angiosperms exist, and among the latter, especially, there is considerable diversity of vegetative structure, exemplified by bulbous hyacinths, onions, lilies, rhizomatous *Iris,* and many grasses. Diversity of habitat is demonstrated by such aquatics as water lilies, *Elodea,* and duckweed, or *Lemna* (see Figure 5.1); such xerophytic genera as cacti; and such epiphytes as "Spanish moss," orchids, and bromeliads. In mature cacti, the leaves are either much reduced or absent.

Woody angiosperms are used extensively as lumber and fuel and as the source of commercial cork, while herbaceous types are important sources of food, beverages, textiles, drugs, and vegetable oils. Both the vegetative and reproductive portions of angiosperms are used as foods. Sweet potatoes, carrots, turnips, beets, and parsnips are examples of fleshy roots that are important foods; white, or "Irish," potatoes and asparagus are stems. Various greens, such as spinach, turnips, chard, and lettuce are leaves. One eats the immense terminal buds of cabbages and head lettuce, whereas the fleshy petioles of rhubarb and celery are also eaten.

Examples of the reproductive organs of angiosperms—flowers, fruits, and seeds—used as food are even more abundant. In both cauliflower and broccoli, we eat groups of flowers, called *inflorescences.* National cultures and economies are based on the use for food of such fruits as the grains of corn, rice, wheat, and rye. Indeed, fruits used as food are too numerous to list completely, but among them we may cite citrus fruits, squashes and melons, tomatoes, grapes, bananas, apples, pears, and various berries. The preceding list contains examples, such as tomatoes and squash, of fruits that laymen frequently classify as "vegetables." However, structures are truly fruits if they are derived at least in part, from the pistil(s) or megasporophyll(s) of the flower; vegetative organs and vegetables, strictly speaking, are nonreproductive parts of plants; the term vegetable is much more loosely used otherwise in common idiom.

After the angiosperm seed germinates, there follows an extensive period of somatic or vegetative development of the sporophyte. This may be terminated by flowering, as in annuals (for example, corn), or may continue during and after flowering, as in woody perennials (for example, magnolia or maple). Since 1920 it has been known that in many plants the change from the vegetative to the reproductive state is dependent on the daily balance between duration of daylight and darkness, that is, the photoperiod. More recently, it has been demonstrated that the initiation of flowering involves a hormonal mechanism. Flowering, therefore, is triggered by chemical changes under the influence of light.*

The *flower* is the reproductive structure of the angiosperms, but it is a difficult structure to define in precise enough terms to distinguish it from aggregations of microsporophylls and megasporophylls, which we have called strobili or cones in gymnosperms. A schematic section of a flower is illustrated in Figure 9.1, and the parts mentioned in the following discussion of the flower may be located either in this figure or in Figure 9.2.

Flowers, like strobili, are stems in which the apical meristems have differentiated completely, so that the meristem, in a sense, is "used

* See in this series A. W. Galston, *The Life of the Green Plant* (2nd ed.) (Englewood Cliffs, N.J.: Prentice-Hall, Inc., 1964), Chap. 4.

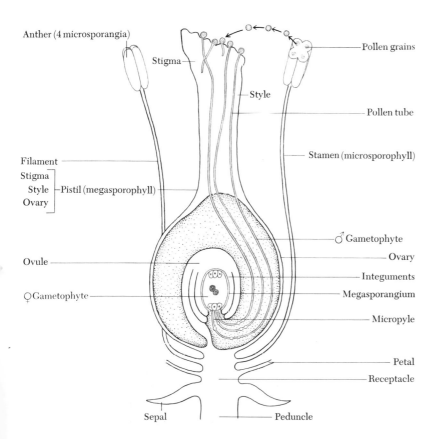

Figure 9.1 Schematized longisection of a flower, parts labeled.

Anther (4 microsporangia)

Stigma

Pollen grains

Style

Pollen tube

Filament

Stamen (microsporophyll)

Stigma
Style ⎤Pistil (megasporophyll)
Ovary ⎦

♂ Gametophyte

Ovary

Ovule

Integuments

♀ Gametophyte

Megasporangium

Micropyle

Petal

Receptacle

Sepal

Peduncle

Figure 9.2 *Ranunculus macranthus floral structure. (a) Single flower. Note numerous petals, stamens, and pistils; at right, receptacle with numerous single-ovule simple pistils (carpels) enlarging after pollination and fertilization. (b) Bisection of flower. Note massive, elongate receptacle to which are attached, from base to apex: sepals, petals, stamens, and pistils. (c) Single pistil with ovary bisected longitudinally. Note parietal placentation of single ovule.* [From H. C. Bold, *Morphology of Plants,* 2nd ed. (New York: Harper & Row, Publishers).]

up." In flowers, as in strobili, the axis, or *receptacle,* that bears the sporophylls has short internodes, so that the sporophylls are borne either in a tight spiral or in a seemingly whorled and cyclic arrangement. In the latter case, three, four, or five sporophylls usually arise at a given level of the axis. In addition to the sporophylls, floral axes usually bear sterile appendages called *sepals* (collectively, the *calyx*), which are generally green (but sometimes other colors), and *petals* (collectively, the *corolla*). The sepals and the petals or corolla together comprise the *perianth.*

The essential parts of the flower are the sporophylls themselves. In angiosperms, the microsporophylls are known as *stamens* and the megasporophylls, or fused groups of them, are known as *pistils.* Stamens produce microspores, and pistils produce megaspores (within their ovules). Stamens and pistils of angiosperms probably correspond especially in function to the microsporophylls and megasporophylls, respectively, of both gymnosperms and certain seedless vascular plants; this correspondence will facilitate our understanding of the reproductive process in angiosperms, described below.

Pistils (Figures 9.1, 9.2, and 9.13) usually consist of an enlarged basal portion, the *ovary,* which contains one or more ovules, and a receptive surface for pollen, the *stigma;* the stigma and ovary are connected by a more or less elongated *style.* Pistils may be either simple or compound. Simple pistils (see Figures 8.1a,b and 9.1) usually have but one cavity containing ovules, whereas many compound pistils have ovaries partitioned into two or more chambers (see Figures 8.1c and 9.13b).*

In the vast majority of angiosperms, both stamens and pistils occur on the same individual sporophyte and are usually borne together in single flowers. In some species, however, *staminate flowers* bear microsporophylls alone, while *pistillate flowers* have only megasporophylls on their receptacles. Such staminate and pistillate flowers are said to be imperfect. Corn (Figure 9.3) is a good example of a *monoecious* plant with imperfect flowers, since both types of flowers are borne on the same individual. In other angiosperms, the staminate and pistillate flowers occur upon different individuals, as in the willow, poplar (cottonwood), and mulberry, among others (Figure 9.4); such plants are, accordingly, *dioecious.*

Flowers may be large, conspicuous, and borne singly, or they may arise on the same axis in various types of inflorescences in which the individual flowers are smaller and less striking. Of the various types of

* However, some compound pistils, like those in the grass, sedge, and composite families, have only one chamber, lacking partitions between the parts.

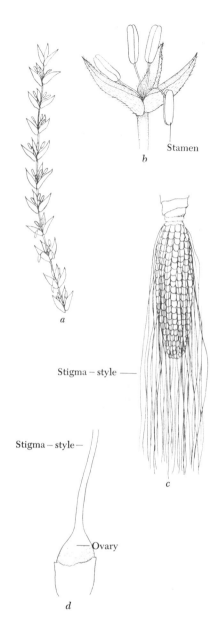

Figure 9.3 **Flowers of corn.** *(a) Portion of staminate inflorescence. (b) Single staminate flower. (c) Pistillate inflorescence or young "ear" of corn. (d) Single pistillate flower with stigma-style.*

inflorescences, the head, or *capitulum* (Figure 9.5*a*), is especially frequent. In the type of capitulum illustrated in Figure 9.5, two types of flowers are present: the minute, bell-like, central *disc flowers* (Figure 9.5*b*) and the larger, peripheral *ray flowers* (Figure 9.5*c*). The disc flowers are perfect and complete, with stamens, a pistil, a calyx, and a corolla. In the ray flowers, the corolla is split open near the base, and stamens are absent.

Figure 9.4 **Willow inflorescences and flowers.** *(a) Staminate, with single staminate flower. (b) The same, enlarged. (c) Pistillate, with single flower. (d) The same enlarged.*

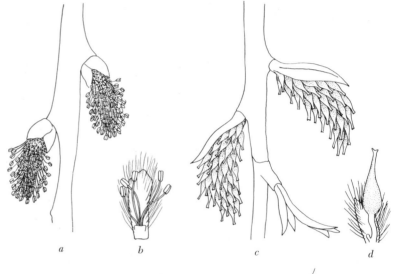

Figure 9.5 **Helianthus sp.** *(a) Capitulum, or inflorescence. (b) Detail of disc flower. (c) Detail of ray flower (corolla only partially shown).*

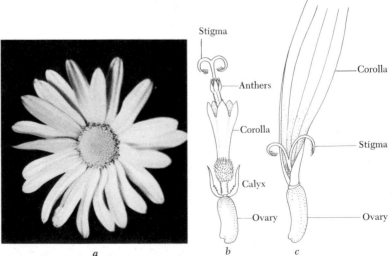

To anyone who has mastered the essential features of reproduction in gymnosperms described in the preceding chapter, the reproductive process in angiosperms will not seem unduly complicated. However, attempts to abbreviate an account of this process often result in inaccuracies and confusion, so we shall proceed to discuss it in some detail in the following.

Reproduction in angiosperms includes the following phenomena: (1) sporogenesis; (2) development of the gametophytes and gametogenesis; (3) pollination; (4) fertilization; and (5) embryogeny and development of the seed and fruit.

SPOROGENESIS   The production of the flowers with their sporophylls marks the maturation of the angiosperm sporophyte. In all annuals and in many perennials, the flowers, seeds, and fruit are produced during the first growing season; however, in many other perennials, a number of years of purely vegetative growth precede the appearance of flowers.

Microsporogenesis does not differ in any important way in angiosperms and gymnosperms. Microspores are produced in groups of four from microsporocytes (microspore mother cells) undergoing meiosis within the microsporangia of the stamen (Figures 9.6 and 9.7). The microsporangia are collectively called the *anther;* the stalk that elevates them is the *filament.* Like the microspores and pollen grains of gymnosperms, those of angiosperms have walls that are variously sculptured and ornamented in ways that are highly characteristic of a given species; this marking may be quite elaborate (Figure 9.7*d*). In any case, the spores of individuals plants can be identified and assigned with great accuracy to their species; this, in part, is the division of botany known as *palynology.* Identification of pollen grains is important in the diagnosis and treatment of such allergies as hay fever, rose fever, and so forth. Furthermore, through the examination of peat and other deposits containing spores and pollen grains, it has been possible to ascertain the composition of ancient floras and to determine past changes of climate in locations where such deposits occur.

Megasporogenesis in flowering plants is also like that in gymnosperms. You will recall that the megasporangia of seed plants are permanently enclosed in integuments and are called *ovules* (Figures 9.1 and 9.8*a–c*). Recall, too, that in gymnosperms, the ovules are produced on the surface of appendages of strobili (as in most cycads and conifers; see Figure 8.1*d,e*), or at the ends of stalks (as in *Ginkgo;* see Figure 8.14). In the angiosperms, the ovules always occur within the

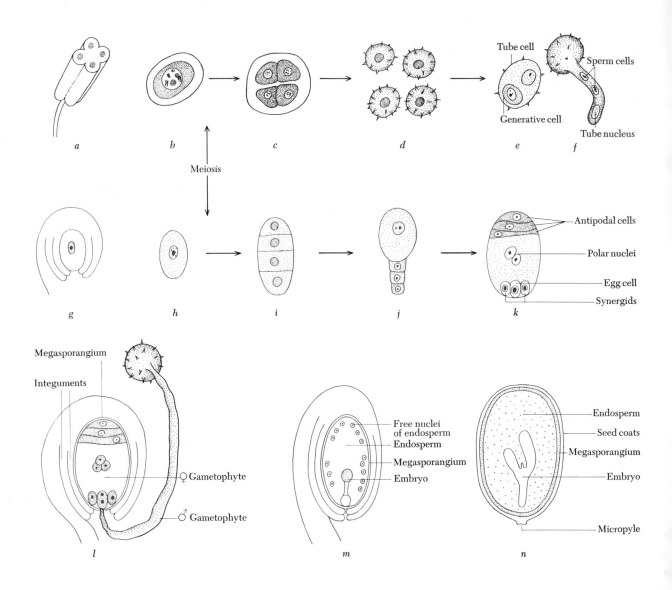

Meiosis

Tube cell

Sperm cells

Generative cell

Tube nucleus

Antipodal cells

Polar nuclei

Egg cell

Synergids

Megasporangium

Integuments

♀ Gametophyte

♂ Gametophyte

Free nuclei
of endosperm

Endosperm

Megasporangium

Embryo

Endosperm

Seed coats

Megasporangium

Embryo

Micropyle

a   *b*   *c*   *d*   *e*   *f*

g   *h*   *i*   *j*   *k*

l   *m*   *n*

*Figure 9.6   **Summary of the reproductive process in angiosperms.** (a) Lower portion of an anther (four microsporangia). (b) Microsporocyte. (c) Tetrad of microspores. (d) Mature microspores. (e–f) Maturation of male gametophyte and formation of pollen tube. (g) Median longitudinal section of an ovule containing a megasporocyte. (h) Megasporocyte enlarged. (i) Linear tetrad of megaspores. (j) Functional and three degenerating megaspores. (k) Mature female gametophyte developed by functional megaspore. (l) M.l.s. of an ovule at moment of double fertilization. (m) M.l.s. of an ovule soon after fertilization. (n) Dormant seed with dicotyledonous embryo.*

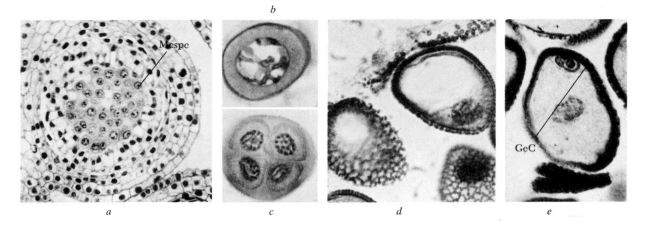

Figure 9.7   Lily, Lilium. (a) Transection, anther lobe or microsporangium (Mcspc, microsporocytes). (b) Microsporocyte, prophase of meiosis. (c) Tetrad of microspores. (d) Microspore with sculptured wall. (e) Pollen grain containing immature male gametophyte consisting of large tube cell and generative cell, GeC.

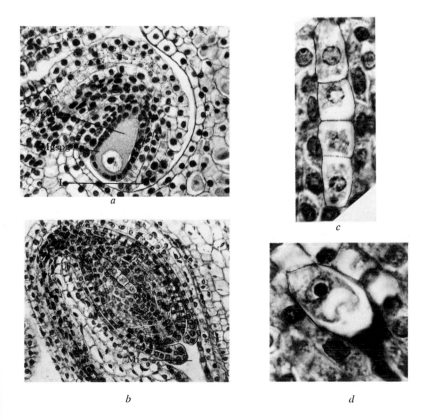

Figure 9.8   Sporogenesis. (a) Median longitudinal section of young ovule of lily, Lilium; (b–d) Oenothera sp. (b) M.l.s. of ovule with linear tetrad of megaspores. (c) The same, enlarged. (d) Functional and degenerated megaspores. I, integuments, Mgspc, megasporocyte; Mgspg, megasporangium; Mi, micropyle.

more or less enlarged base of the pistil or megasporophyll, known as the *ovary* (see Figures 8.1*a–c,* 9.1, and 9.13). The number of ovules within an ovary varies from one to many, as does the place of their attachment, or type of *placentation;* the ovules may occur either on a central axis or on the ovary wall. The remainder of the megasporophyll is composed of the style and stigma (Figures 9.1, 9.2, and 9.13*a*); the stigma is a specialized receptive surface to which the pollen grains adhere at pollination. As in the gymnosperms, each ovule usually produces only a single megasporocyte; this undergoes meiosis to form a linear tetrad of megaspores (Figures 9.6*i* and 9.8*b–d*), while the flower is in the bud stage. In angiosperms, as in all other seed plants, only a single functional megaspore normally survives (Figure 9.8*d*). Thus, megasporogenesis in angiosperms is not essentially different from that in gymnosperms.

GAMETOGENESIS AND DEVELOPMENT OF GAMETOPHYTES   Compared with the time required for the development of the gametophytes in many gymnosperms, the process in most angiosperms is rapid. This is correlated with the fact that the gametophytes themselves are smaller and less complex in angiosperms. As usual in seed plants, the development of the male gametophyte from the microspore is at first endosporic and is initiated soon after microsporogenesis has been completed (Figures 9.7*e* and 9.9*a*). Except for the formation of the pollen tube after pollination, development of the male gametophyte may be completed within the microspore wall before the pollen has been shed from the anther. In some species, on the other hand, the nuclear division in which the generative cell (Figure 9.9*a*) produces the two sperm nuclei occurs in the pollen tube during germination. The mature male gametophyte (Figures 9.6*f* and 9.9*b*) contains only three nuclei, the *tube nucleus* and two *sperm nuclei;* the latter probably are surrounded by

Figure 9.9   ***The gametophytic phase in flowering plants.*** *(a) Immature male gametophyte within pollen grain consisting of generative cell and tube cell. (b) Pollen germination and mature male gametophyte. (c) Median longitudinal section of ovule with mature female gametophyte. (d) Double fertilization in lily.*

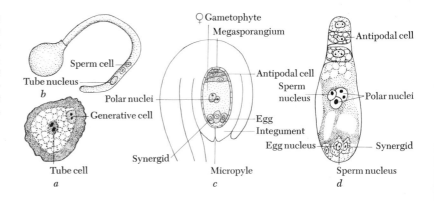

delicate sheaths of specialized cytoplasm delimited from that of the pollen tube.

In most angiosperms, the nucleus of the functional megaspore undergoes three successive divisions to form eight haploid nuclei that become somewhat differentiated and characteristically arranged within the mature female gametophyte, which has developed from the functional megaspore (Figures 9.1, 9.6*l*, and 9.9*c,d*). The megaspore wall does not thicken. Of the three nuclei nearest the micropylar pole of the female gametophyte, one functions as the *egg nucleus* and the other two are known as *synergids*. These three nuclei are delimited from the common cytoplasm by delicate membranes. At the opposite pole, three *antipodal cells* are formed. The remaining two nuclei, having previously migrated from the poles to the center of the female gametophyte are, because of their migration, called *polar nuclei*. Compared with the female gametophyte of most gymnosperms, the female gametophyte of angiosperms has a short existence and little internal differentiation. A female gametangium, or archegonium, is absent and represented only by an egg cell. As the flower opens, and as the stigmas become receptive, the ovule(s) within the ovary contain(s) mature or maturing female gametophytes. Angiosperm gametophytes, like those of gymnosperms, are parasitic on the sporophyte.

POLLINATION AND FERTILIZATION　When the flowers open and afterwards, the microsporangia, often called "pollen sacs" in angiosperms, open by fissures or pores and begin to shed the pollen grains and their enclosed male gametophytes. Some of these pollen grains are transferred by various forces, such as gravity, wind, insects and other animals, and even by water (in certain aquatics), to the receptive surface of the stigma (Figure 9.1). A number of special relationships between insects and the pollination of flowers are well-known; they are indicative of close correlations between the evolution of the flowering plants and that of the insects involved. Thus, pollination of the female inflorescence of figs, resulting in the edible fruit, is accomplished by a small wasp, *Blastophaga;* when these wasps are absent, edible fruits do not develop. Long-tongued insects such as certain bees, wasps, and butterflies in search of nectar (which may contain up to 25 percent glucose) and pollen, are the agents of pollination in many plants. One of the most interesting examples of a seemingly obligate relationship is that between the Spanish bayonet. *Yucca,* and the yucca moth, *Pronuba.* This moth lays its eggs in the ovary of the *Yucca* flower and simultaneously pollinates it. The larvae developing from the eggs eat a few of the seeds, but large numbers of seeds survive and maintain the species of *Yucca.*

In the process of pollination, a second great difference between angiospermous and gymnospermous seed plants is apparent. In angiosperms, pollination is the transfer of pollen grains from the microsporangia of the stamen to the stigma of the megasporophyll, but not directly to the micropyle of the ovule (as in gymnosperms). Once on the stigma surface, the pollen grains germinate rapidly to form pollen tubes, which penetrate the tissues of the stigma and style and enter the ovary. If pollination has been heavy enough, there is sufficient pollen for a pollen tube to grow toward the micropyle of each ovule, enter it, and make contact with the female gametophyte. Probably because of differences in turgor pressure, the pollen tubes burst and discharge their nuclei into the cytoplasm of the female gametophyte upon making contact within the ovule.

At this point, a third important difference between angiosperms and gymnosperms becomes apparent, that is, the occurrence of *double fertilization,* a phenomenon known only in flowering plants. This involves two sperms: one sperm nucleus unites with the egg nucleus, and the other with the two polar nuclei ° of the female gametophyte to form a triploid nucleus (Figure 9.9*d*). The functioning of both sperm suggested the term "double fertilization." Here again, although fertilization is accompanied by a number of attendant secondary phenomena, we see that sexual reproduction involves the union of cells and nuclei, and the association of chromosomes—in this case, forming both a zygote nucleus and a triploid nucleus (*the primary endosperm nucleus*). In the postfertilization processes, now to be considered, these two nuclei play leading roles.

EMBRYOGENY AND THE DEVELOPMENT OF THE SEED AND FRUIT   The occurrence of pollination and double fertilization stimulates nuclear and cell division in the ovule and pistil (and often in such closely associated structures as the receptacle); accordingly, these enlarge greatly. Their enlargement is controlled by formation of hormones. It will be recalled that the gymnosperm ovule reaches its maximum size approximately at fertilization, but in angiosperms, ovule enlargement follows fertilization. The stamens and petals gradually disintegrate or are shed. These changes eventually become noticeable to the unaided eye as the ovary enlarges to form the fruit and ovules enlarge to form the seeds.

Soon after double fertilization, the primary endosperm nucleus initiates a series of nuclear divisions to form triploid endosperm nuclei (Figure 9.10*a*) which, in most cases, are sooner or later separated from one another by cell walls. Thus a *cellular endosperm* is formed. This tissue is rich in stored metabolites that have been transported from the parent sporophyte; hence the cellular endosperm serves as a

° These may unite with each other before fertilization.

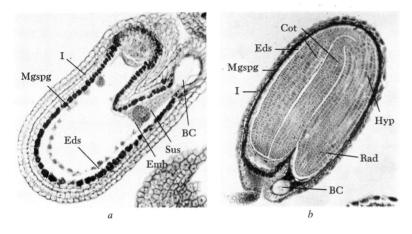

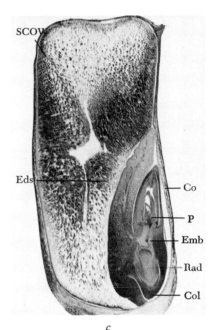

Figure 9.10 Embryogeny of flowering plants. (a,b) Capsella, shepherd's purse. (c) Zea mays, corn. [After J. E. Sass.] Emb, embryo; Eds. endosperm; I, integument; BC, basal cell; Cot, cotyledons; Hyp, hypocotyl; Mgspg, megasporangium; Rad, radicle or embryonic root; Sus, suspensor; SCOW, seed coats and ovary wall.

source of nutrition for the developing embryo. Here we have a fourth difference between the angiosperms and gymnosperms. In angiosperms, the embryonic sporophyte is nourished by a special nutritive tissue, the triploid endosperm, which is formed after fertilization. However, the gymnosperm embryo obtains its metabolites from the haploid vegetative tissues of the female gametophyte (see Figure 8.7c) formed before fertilization.

Sometime after the initiation of endosperm development, the zygote, by a series of nuclear and cell divisions, forms a mass of cells that varies in extent and degree of organization, depending upon the particular genus of flowering plant. This mass of cells is the young embryonic sporophyte of the next generation, the so-called *germ* of the seed. In some angiosperms, such as many orchids, the embryo enters a period of dormancy after only a few cells have developed. In most others, the embryo consists of an axis, the *hypocotyl*, bearing one or two leaves, the *cotyledons*, between which (in dicotyledons) is a terminal bud, the *plumule*, or *epicotyl*, and below which is an embryonic root, the *radicle* (Figure 9.10b,c). As the development of the embryo nears completion, the tissues of the ovule become dehydrated, and the integuments become impervious and dark in color; by this time, the ovules have matured into seeds. As Figure 9.10b,c illustrates, a seed consists of an embryonic sporophyte (a "germ") in a dormant con-

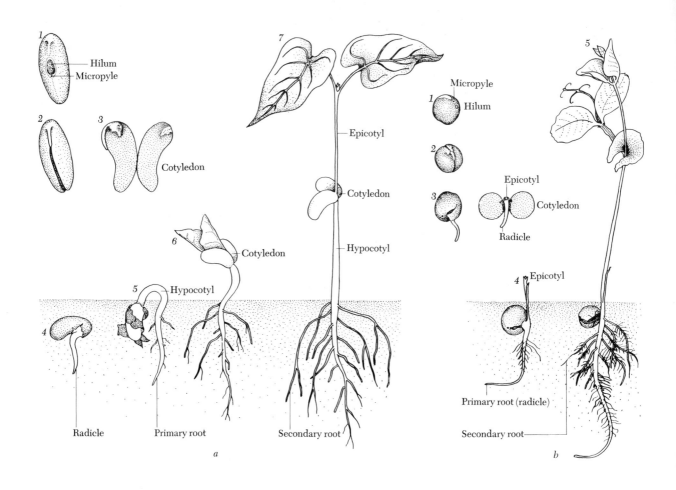

Figure 9.11 *Seeds, germination, and seedlings (successive stages numbered). (a) Phaseolus vulgaris, garden bean. (b) Pisum sativum, pea (seed coats removed in 2 and 3).*

dition; this is embedded within the endosperm and the remaining megasporangial tissues and integuments; these integuments are now called *seed coats*. In some angiosperms, the embryo does not become dormant until it has digested most of the endosperm and absorbed into itself (usually into the fleshy cotyledons) the metabolites stored in the endosperm; as a result, the embryo is massive. Beans (Figure 9.11*a*), peas (Figure 9.11*b*), peanuts, and many other leguminous plants have

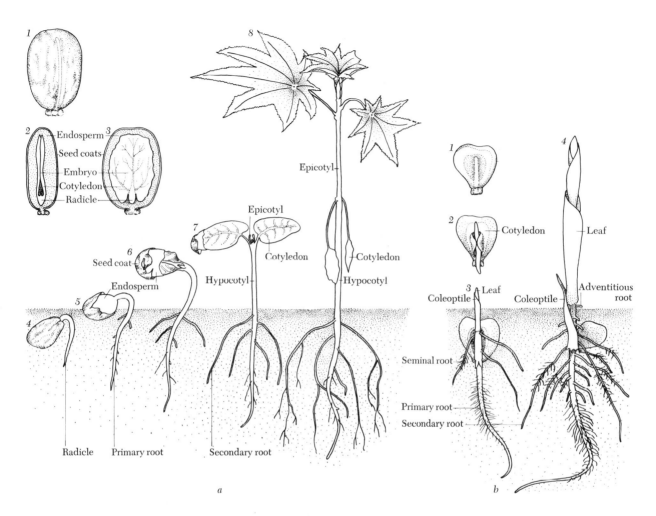

Figure 9.12   **Seeds, germination, and seedlings (successive stages numbered).** *(a) Ricinus communis, castor bean (seed bisected, in two different aspects in 2 and 3). (b) Zea mays, corn.*

seeds of this type. In such seeds as corn (Figure 9.10c), wheat, barley, rye, and the castor bean (Figure 9.12a), an extensive endosperm persists. The starch grains from the endosperm of wheat constitute flour.

In addition to enlarging, the ovary of the flower (and in some cases, associated structures) may undergo considerable change of shape and differentiation of tissues during embryogeny. This is clear in such a familiar example as the tomato (Figures 8.1c and 9.13), in which the

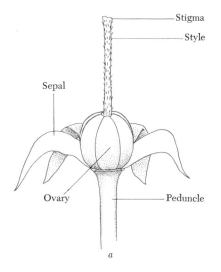

ovary in the flower bud is a minute, rather firm, whitish green structure composed largely of meristematic cells and some vascular tissues. After fertilization, the ovary enlarges tremendously, passing through the familiar "green tomato" stage, until it finally ripens. As the tomato is ripening, the green plastids become yellow-orange, and complex cellular changes occur to form the skinlike, firm, fleshy layer and the juicy layer of the fully ripened fruit. Different changes occur in fruit formation in other angiosperms, giving rise, with various modifications, to the great diversity of fruits characteristic of that group.

The *fruit* is the ripened ovary of one or more flowers, sometimes with accessory components. Fruits are usually classified by origin as simple, aggregate, or multiple. A *simple fruit* (Figure 9.14a) arises from the single ovary of one flower. An *aggregate fruit* arises from a number of separate ovaries attached to the single receptacle of one flower (Figure 9.14b–d). A *multiple fruit* (Figure 9.14e), such as an ear of

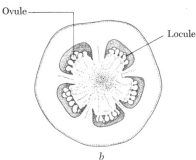

Figure 9.13 Structure of the tomato pistil. *(a) Flower just after pollination, with petals and stamens, and with one sepal removed. (b) Transection of ovary, somewhat enlarged.*

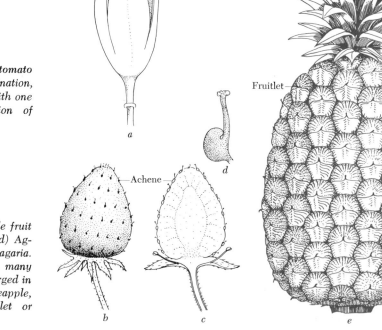

Figure 9.14 Fruits. *(a) Simple fruit (dehiscent capsule) of Iris. (b–d) Aggregate fruit of strawberry, Fragaria. Note enlarged receptacle with many simple fruits (achenes), one enlarged in d. (e) Multiple fruit of pineapple, Ananas sativa, showing fruitlet or single fruit.*

156

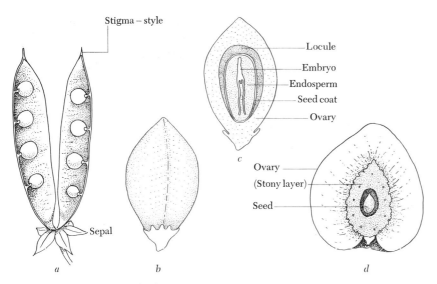

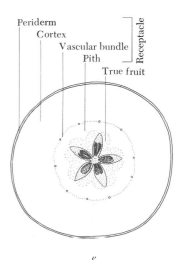

Figure 9.15 **Simple fruits.** *(a) Pea (Pisum sativum), a legume or pod. (b–c) Buckwheat (Fagopyrum esculentum), an achene, showing (b) surface view and (c) bisection. (d) Peach (Prunus armeniaca), a drupe. (e) Apple (Pyrus malus), a pome.*

corn, a mulberry, or a pineapple, develops from a number of ovaries of the flowers of an inflorescence.

Simple fruits may be dry [either dehiscent (Figure 9.15*a*) or indehiscent (Figure 9.15*b,c*)] or fleshy. Examples of fleshy types are berries, such as tomatoes (Figures 8.1*c* and 9.13) and grapes, and stone fruits (Figure 9.15*d*), such as cherries, peaches, and plums. The apple (Figure 9.15*e*), pear, and quince are simple fruits arising from compound ovaries; during development, the receptacle and other accessory parts enlarge and become fleshy.

As the seeds and the fruits mature in various plants, the seeds may be ejected by the splitting of the drying fruits, or they may be freed only after the fleshy and stony layers of the enclosing fruits have rotted. If the seeds are planted, or if they happen to come to rest in a suitable environment, they sooner or later germinate (Figures 9.11 and 9.12). Germination is merely a continuation of embryogenesis involving the emergence of the embryonic sporophyte into an external environment.

The monocotyledonous (Figure 9.12*b*) or dicotyledonous (Figures 9.11 and 9.12*a*) organization of an angiosperm is obvious in its seed and seedling. The single cotyledon of cereal grains, such as corn (Figure 9.12*b*), functions in digestion and absorption of the endosperm and remains within the seed during germination; the engorged, fleshy cotyledons of the pea (Figure 9.12*b*) also remain below the soil. In contrast, the two cotyledons of the garden bean (Figure 9.11*a*) are raised above the ground by the elongation of the *hypocotyl*, as are those of the castor bean (Figure 9.12*a*), after they have digested the nutriments of the endosperm and transferred them into the developing seedling.

Various types of *seed dormancy* occur among angiosperms; they may be morphological, as in the case of the rudimentary embryos alluded to previously, or physiological, involving changes in permeability of seed coats, activation of enzymes, and so forth. In general, seeds germinate when in the presence of adequate moisture and oxygen and within a given range of temperatures; the specific requirements of these conditions vary with the species. Light, too, is necessary for seed germination in some species (some varieties of lettuce are well-known examples). The emergence of the radicle and of the other embryonic organs, the formation of additional leaves, and the increase in axis length sooner or later establish the embryonic sporophyte as an independent organism, and the remains of the seed then disintegrate.

Reproduction of angiosperms, then, although similar in many ways to that of gymnosperms, differs in a number of important respects.

1   The ovules, and hence the seeds, are borne within megasporophylls (*angiospermy*) instead of being exposed on their surfaces (*gymnospermy:* see Figure 8.1).

2   Development of the gametophytes is a much more abbreviated process in angiosperms than it is in gymosperms.

3   The gametophytes themselves are smaller and simpler in angiosperms.

4   Pollination in angiosperms involves the transfer of pollen grains from the microsporangia (anther) to the receptive surface of the megasporophyll (stigma), rather than to the micropyle of the ovule, as in gymnosperms.

5   Double fertilization occurs only in angiosperms.

6   The embryo of angiosperms is nourished by the endosperm, a special tissue that arises after fertilization, rather than by the female gametophyte, as in gymnosperms.

7   The angiosperm ovule does not enlarge to seed size until after fertilization, in contrast to that of gymnosperms.

8   The seeds of angiosperms are enclosed within fruits, which are enlarged megasporophylls (pistils), sometimes with associated parts of the flower; in gymnosperms, fruits of this type are absent, as the megasporophyll does not enclose the seed.

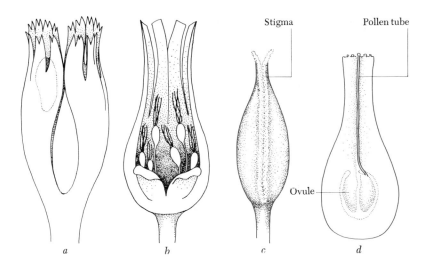

Figure 9.16 *Seed-bearing structures of primitive plants. (a,b) Extinct seed-ferns: (a) Stamnostoma huttonense [After A. G. Long]; (b) Calathospermum sooticum [After J. Walton]. (c,d) Primitive angiosperm carpel (pistil): (c) ventral view showing paired stigmatic areas; (d) transection. [(c,d) After I. W. Bailey and B. G. L. Swamy.]*

The fossil record has not provided conclusive information about the origin of angiosperms. Although absent in earlier Mesozoic strata, diverse and abundant angiosperms first appear in Cretaceous deposits in the form of leaves, flowers, pollen, seeds, and fruits. In these specimens, angiospermy is clearly well established, so that no insight regarding its origin has been supplied by such fossil remains. Various groups of gymnosperms have been suggested as angiosperm precursors, but these hypothetical ancestors have not been universally accepted as authentic. Angiospermy, it has been suggested, may have arisen from cuplike structures (Figure 9.16) that loosely surrounded the seeds of certain seed ferns. An alternate hypothesis, supported by the evidence of ontogeny and the study of certain supposedly primitive living genera, suggests that angiospermy developed by the phylogenetic unfolding and fusion of leaves that bore marginal ovules (Figure 9.17). Charles Darwin's statement,* "The rapid development as far as we can judge of all the higher plants within recent geological times is an abominable mystery," aptly characterizes the present state of our knowledge, or the lack of it, regarding the origin of the angiosperms.

FOSSIL ANGIOSPERMS

Figure 9.17 *Drimys winteri var. chilensis: ontogenetic closure of carpels (pistils) in transection, three with margins appressed and two with margins still open. [Modified from S. Tucker.]*

* The author is grateful to Professor Herbert G. Baker of the University of California at Berkeley for providing him with an accurate quotation from Charles Darwin's letter (395) to J. D. Hooker.

10 CONCLUSION

IT NOW SEEMS APPROPRIATE TO CONSIDER THE VARIOUS TYPES OF ORGA-nisms described in some detail in earlier chapters, for the purpose of consolidating our understanding of the plants themselves and the groups they represent, and to emphasize some of the important principles they illustrate. We are now in a better position than at the outset to consider the diversity of the plant kingdom, the causes for this diversity, and the problems of the relationships and classification of plants. Let us begin by summarizing some of the more important phenomena described in the preceding chapters.

ORGANIZATION OF THE PLANT BODY

Our discussion of the diversity of the plant kingdom has included reference to such groups of organisms as algae, fungi, mosses and liverworts, seedless vascular plants (psilophytes, club mosses, arthrophytes, and ferns), and seed-bearing vascular plants, including gymnosperms and angiosperms. Was there any important reason for studying them in that particular order? Could we have started as well at the other end of the series, or perhaps with any intermediate group, and have proceeded in a different sequence? The order of study is indeed significant for it reflects to a great degree both an increasing complexity and the order of appearance of the earth's flora. There is evidence that this increasing complexity was built up over several billion years, starting from relative simplicity. Diversities of structure and function, both vegetative and reproductive, are best explained as manifestations of gradual change, or *evolution*. We must be cautious, however, in our appraisal of supposed simplicity and complexity. In the first place, *apparent* simplicity, as in the case of the many aquatic plants that have little differentiated xylem, may well be a secondary simplicity through loss of complexity, a phenomenon known as *reduction*. The absence of xylem and phloem from algae (except for the phloemlike tubes in certain kelps), liverworts, and mosses, on the other hand, is usually interpreted as true simplicity and as a *primitive* condition.

Some further words of caution are appropriate here. In spite of their manifest complexity, the so-called higher plants are performing essentially the same biological functions that go on even in unicellular organisms, which are often spoken of as the "lower" or "simple" plants. These manifold chemical and physical processes are elegantly complex, interrelated, and coordinated in all living organisms; thus the terms "higher" and "lower" are often misleading and illusory, as are "simple" and "complex." The following terms might more appropriately be used in some of these comparisons: "alternate" or "different"; "ancient," "less ancient," and "recent"; and "similar" and "dissimilar."

On the other hand, when one considers unicellular, colonial, and multicellular organisms, it is clear that an organism is more than the sum of its individual cells. This is evidenced by the movement through the plant body of organizing substances * that evoke different responses from different descendants of the initial reproductive cell (usually the zygote). The evidence of modern electron microscopy shows clearly that multicellular plants are not made of isolated cells stacked together like bricks or boxes (see Figure 1.2). An extensive, netlike system passes through the walls from cell to cell, so the original unity of the zygote probably is partially preserved as it gives rise to the multicellular organism. Furthermore, development of the multicellular organism involves coordinated responses to the environment. Multicellular plants and animals are considered by some biologists to be *cell republics* that have evolved from the aggregation of unicellular organisms. Others look upon unicellular organisms as complex and acellular, not strictly com-

* See in this series A. W. Galston, *The Life of the Green Plant* (2nd ed.) (Englewood Cliffs, N.J.: Prentice-Hall, Inc., 1964).

parable to single tissue cells. These theorists regard multicellular organisms as having arisen by secondary subdivision of the organisms into cells.

Since all organisms start as single cells, *ontogeny* (the development of an individual organism) suggests that multicellular organisms probably arose by the failure of cells to separate after the completion of cell division. Growth in multicellular plants may be generalized, as in such filamentous blue-green algae as *Oscillatoria* (see Figure 2.9*a*); but in most cases, it is restricted to the tips of stems and roots or to certain other definite regions. Such apical growth occurs in a number of algae and fungi, and is the rule in almost all of the remaining types of plants, although in many plants lateral growth is also pronounced. Some exceptions occur in members of the grass family, in which intercalary meristems are also present.

A survey of the plant kingdom indicates that when the component cells of a plant are essentially uniform in structure and function, as in the sea lettuce, *Ulva* (see Figure 2.15), and a number of other algae and liverworts, the size of the plant is limited, especially when the plants are not aquatic. Although internal differentiation is apparent to a limited degree in such algae as certain kelps, in which phloemlike tissues are present, the stimulus for internal complexity seems to have been the land habitat. This is apparent to some degree in such liverworts as *Ricciocarpus* (see Figure 4.2*b,d*), in the stems and leaves of certain mosses, and, finally, to the greatest degree in the vascular plants.

In the vascular plants, with the exception of the Psilophyta, the plant body consists of an axis composed of stem, root, and leaves. There are two fundamentally different types of leaves. Of these, microphylls (with simple, unbranched veins) characterize only the Microphyllophyta (*Selaginella* and so forth), whereas the remaining vascular plants are macrophyllous. It has been suggested that macrophyllous leaves represent branching axes that have become flattened and bladelike through extension of the nonvascular tissues by a sort of webbing.

REPRODUCTION

We have alluded in earlier chapters to various methods of reproduction, both asexual and sexual, the latter involving cellular and nuclear union, the association of parental chromosomes, and meiosis. The simplest and most direct method of asexual reproduction is by *fragmentation* of a plant itself. This is exemplified by binary fission (cell division) in unicellular organisms, as well as by various cases in which fragments of a plant regenerate complete new individuals: dissociation of such colonial algae as *Merismopedia* (see Figure 2.8), dissociation of such truly multicellular organisms as branching liverworts, mosses, ferns, and other rhizomes, and cuttings of leaves, stems, and roots. Special agents of reproduction (unicellular and multicellular spores such as the air-borne spores of fungi, liverworts, mosses, and ferns, and the zoospores of certain algae and fungi) and gemmae (buds or fragments) are also produced. All of these are asexual in that they develop into new plants individually without uniting with another spore or gemma.

Sexual reproduction throughout the plant kingdom almost always involves a union of cells; it always involves a union of nuclei, the consequent association of chromosomes and, ultimately, meiosis. The origin of sexual reproduction remains unknown, but evidence in unicellular algae suggests that union of cells may have resulted from inadequate supplies of certain metabolites.

Less complex organisms, such as unicellular algae and fungi, are only apparently and deceptively simple, for they carry on both vegetative (somatic) and reproductive functions within a single cell. The gamete of *Chlamydomonas* (see page 19) is merely an immature individual that is sexually active; it is capable of union with another compatible individual as a result of certain chemical changes within it and on its surface. In certain colonial and filamentous algae and fungi, and in all plants of other groups, the vegetative function is more clearly segregated from the reproductive, as indicated by the formation of special fertile areas containing reproductive cells, often in gametangia and sporangia. The gametes of *Chlamydomonas*, on the contrary, are both vegetative and reproductive in function, and are primitive in this respect. This is evidenced by the fact that gametes failing to unite will, under suitable conditions, produce large populations by cell division. In most multicellular organisms, these powers of rejuvenation and asexual reproduction no longer characterize the differentiated reproductive cells, and those reproductive cells that do not unite die.

From the preceding chapters, it is clear that, with respect to the distribution of the compatible gametes (+ and −, male and female), *individuals* may be either bisexual (hermaphroditic) or unisexual. Individuals of a number of species of *Volvox*, liverworts, mosses, and the gametophytes of *Psilotum, Lycopodium, Equisetum,* and of many ferns are bisexual. In contrast, the individuals of *Chlamydomonas* and those of *Pandorina, Achlya ambisexualis, Rhizopus,* and *Polytrichum*, as well as the gametophytes of *Selaginella* and of all the seed plants, are unisexual, either + or −, or male or female.

It should also be apparent that gametes may or may not be differentiated *morphologically*. Thus, we have seen that among the algae and fungi various degrees of gametic differentiation exist, from morphological isogamy (*Chlamydomonas moewusii, Rhizopus*) through heterogamy (*Chlamydomonas* spp.), culminating in oogamy. Oogamy, in which the minute male gametes are called *sperms* and the large female gametes are called *eggs*, occurs in some algae (*Volvox, Fucus*) and fungi (*Achlya*), and in all liverworts, mosses, and vascular plants. It should be evident that in defining isogamy as the condition that produces undifferentiated gametes, we are saying that the lack of difference between uniting gametes is more apparent than real. The term isogamy is founded upon morphology; from ingenious genetical and biochemical experiments, it is clear that even isogametes are physiologically and chemically different from each other, and these differences are apparently the basis for the compatible unions in which zygotes are formed.

From a survey of the various reproductive phenomena in the plant kingdom, we may arrive at a number of generalizations, among them the following.

1 Some plants may be *haploid*, with a single, basic complement of chromosomes in their nuclei, throughout their existence. The *diploid* condition prevails only temporarily in the zygote of such species, which divides meiotically at germination to form a new generation of haploid individuals. This occurs only among algae and fungi and is exemplified by *Chlamydomonas, Rhizopus,* and *Achlya,* among others. Meiosis in such organisms is *zygotic;* that is, it occurs in the germinating zygote.

2 In a few algae (*Fucus,* for one), the individual plant is diploid throughout its existence and only its gametes, which arise by meiosis, are haploid. The gametic union, forming a zygote, initiates a new diploid individual. Meiosis here is *gametic,* occurring during gametogenesis.

3 Certain algae (for example, *Ulva,* the sea lettuce) and fungi, and all the liverworts, mosses, and vascular plants (therefore, the great majority of plants) have both haploid and diploid phases, which are designated as the *gametophytes* and *sporophytes,* respectively. These alternate in regular sequence, so that the haploid, sexual gametophyte forms gametes that unite to produce zygotes, which in turn give rise to diploid sporophytes that undergo meiosis and produce asexual spores. The sporophytes and gametophytes may be physically connected, either sporophyte upon gametophyte (as in mosses) or gametophyte upon sporophyte (as in seed plants), or they may be independent of each other (as in ferns). In the liverworts and mosses, the gametophytic phase is dominant in duration and stature, whereas in vascular plants the sporophyte is dominant and the gametophyte is ephemeral.

It should not be construed that there is a sort of antagonism between sporophyte and gametophyte; both are merely different phases of the same organism. Inasmuch as meiosis, with its reassortment of parental genes, is the culmination of sexual reproduction, spores are "asexual" only in the sense that they undergo further development without union with each other. Actually, since they are products of meiosis, they themselves are an ultimate result of sexual union.

Finally, the land plants may be divided into those that are *homosporous* (producing similar spores) and those that are *heterosporous* (producing dimorphic spores). The most pronounced types of heterospory we have discussed are present in *Selaginella* (in some species of which the megaspores are hundreds of times larger than microspores), and in *Isoetes, Marsilea, Salvinia,* and *Azolla.* The inevitable consequence of heterospory, it will be recalled, is the production of unisexual gametophytes (although these sometimes also arise from homosporous sporophytes, as in *Polytrichum*). The seed plants are usually interpreted as heterosporous; the similar size of microspores and megaspores is regarded as the result of the permanent retention of the megaspore within the megasporangium.

The seed is apparently a highly efficient mechanism for perpetuating and disseminating the species. Furthermore, the habit of producing seeds must account in large part for the dominance of the angiosperms in our present flora.

In Chapter 1, we stated that most current classifications of the plant kingdom are phylogenetic, in that they attempt to group organisms in categories that indicate real, genetic relationships. Now that we have surveyed representative types of plants, we can discuss the possible relationships of currently living plant groups to one another and to extinct members of the plant kingdom that are known to us only through fossils. Phylogenetic systems of classification of higher taxa, such as families, orders, classes, and divisions, necessarily are increasingly speculative regarding real relationships, as one progresses to the higher categories of classification. This is in contrast to evidence of evolutionary change in individuals and species, where experimental procedures are possible. Thus, the changes in individuals that may be transmitted to their offspring, or *mutations*, produced by X rays, chemicals such as nitrogen mustard gas, and other agents, are a direct and incontrovertible indication of change and of relationship by descent, or *evolution.* The occurrence of such mutations in nature and their segregation and recombination in sexual reproduction are undoubtedly responsible for changes in individuals, species, and populations. These changes are effected by natural selection of mutations.

From such evidence, we infer that the operation of mutation and natural selection over millions of years has brought about the diversity now apparent in our flora and fauna. Although the adequacy of such mechanisms in evoking the present manifold diversities among plants and animals has from time to time been questioned, no satisfactory alternative has yet been proposed. No experimental evidence is available to confirm relationships among plants of the past and their supposed descendants now living. Recent identification of amino acids from fossil material, however, suggests that comparative chemical analyses of fossils might well contribute to our knowledge of plant relationships. The evidences that support speculations regarding the origin and putative relationships among the groups of plants in our present flora and those of the past result from studies of comparative morphology of living plants, of their geographical distribution, of their comparative biochemistry, and of extinct plants as revealed in the fossil record. A few examples of these several lines of evidence will be presented in the following paragraphs.

The comparative study of plants (and animals) reveals certain common attributes cited previously. Among these are similarities of cellular organization, metabolism, reproductive phenomena (including sexuality, meiosis, and life cycles), inheritance, and the capacity for adaptation. The occurrence of the same active, photosynthetic pigment, chlorophyll *a*, throughout the plant kingdom (except in fungi) and of the storage product, starch, in a great majority of green plants, provides two examples of a widely distributed characteristic. In a word, there are a number of attributes common to species, genera, families, orders, classes, and, finally, to divisions of plants—both living and fossil—that indicate continuity. These are most satisfactorily explained on the basis of kinship.

The fossil record presents us with important information regarding the course of evolution and the relationships of various forms of plant life. As the original, igneous rocks of the earth's crust weathered, particles were washed away and deposited as sediments in bodies of water. Among these particles, various organic remains were deposited. Later, when compression transformed these mixed sediments into sedimentary rocks, the organic remains sometimes were preserved as fossils. These are of various types and differ in the perfection of their preservation. The most perfectly preserved are *petrifactions* (fossil plant remains themselves embedded in a rocky matrix), in which details of microscopic structure are remarkably clear upon sectioning.

The older strata of sedimentary rocks obviously contain fossil remains of the most ancient organisms, whereas strata deposited subsequently contain increasingly more recent organic remains, culminating in those of extant plants. Although this "rock record of plants" is remarkably long and uninterrupted in such localities as the Grand Canyon, there are few places where such a great series of strata is exposed. Paleobotanists are forced, therefore, to rely on the exposure of fossil-bearing strata by landslides, washouts, road and rail construction, and, especially, mining and drilling operations.

In spite of the incompleteness of the fossil record, considerable information has been obtained about plants of the past (see Table 6.1). Paleobotany has not shed direct light on the earliest forms of life, but indirect evidence of their existence—for example, calcareous sediments (limestones) and iron ores—are available. Algalike organisms have been discovered in Precambrian rocks in Africa over 3 billion years old and in similar rocks in Canada about 1.9 billion years old. The earliest organisms were aquatic—algal, bacterial, and probably fungal. Many calcareous algae occur in the lower Ordovician strata of the Paleozoic era. Rock from the Devonian period of the Paleozoic is strikingly different from earlier strata in that it contains the remains of truly terrestrial plants, including liverworts and representatives of the four lines of seedless vascular plants (see Chapters 6 and 7). The gradual development of terrestrial plants with vascular tissue indicates the correlation between the migration of plant life to land and the evolution of xylem and phloem. In spite of the rise of the land plants, however, aquatic algae, bacteria, and fungi have continued to flourish until the present, apparently with little change.

Sedimentary rocks of nonmarine origin from the late Paleozoic (Mississippian and Pennsylvanian) contain a wealth of fossils, some of which have been referred to briefly in earlier chapters. The occurrence of extensive deposits of coal from the Pennsylvanian is an indirect evidence of the abundance of photosynthetic plants in that period. The Pennsylvanian often is called the "age of ferns" because of the abundance of fossilized fern leaves in its strata. Many of these, however, were seed ferns (now extinct), sometimes considered to be the precursors of the flowering plants. In addition, giant tree-size *Equisetum*-like plants (see Figure 6.19) and others of similar dimensions, somewhat resembling our modern *Lycopodium* and *Selaginella*, flourished in swamps in Pennsylvanian times. Furthermore, fossilized mosses, liverworts, and the remains of treelike gymnosperms (in addition to seed ferns) are preserved in Pennsylvanian strata. Many of these are still well represented as fossils in Mesozoic strata, but in the Jurassic and Cretaceous periods (especially the latter), angiosperms appeared and became dominant as the number and diversity of other plants waned.

CONCLUSION

We can make several important generalizations on the basis of this brief survey of the fossil record and by inspection of Table 6.1.

1 Indirect and direct evidence indicates that algae, fungi, and bacteria are probably among the most ancient plants, their presence on the earth extending back into the Precambrian, 3 billion years ago, and possibly even longer. Similar organisms, with slight modifications, are represented in our flora at the present time; thus, algae have evolved little and slowly.

2 Land plants, probably derived from algae that gradually colonized muddy shores and finally drier habitats, had evolved and become abundant by the Devonian (395 million years ago). The number, complexity, and diversity of fossilized vascular plants in the Devonian strongly suggest that they must have evolved considerably earlier, although unequivocal evidence of this earlier than the Silurian is lacking.

3 The widespread occurrence of vascular tissues (xylem and phloem) probably coincided with colonization of the land. Colonizers that lack vascular tissues, such as mosses and liverworts, have remained small on land.

4 Successively more recent strata reveal an apparent orderliness of development of representative divisions of plants, from ancient to recent: the algae, bacteria, and fungi; seedless vascular plants; and, finally, seed plants. Of the seed plants, the flowering plants are the most recent.

5 A number of organisms prominent in ancient floras are no longer extant. In most cases, the reasons for their extinction are not clear.

Plant fossils, then, indicate that our present flora is changed in composition from floras of earlier periods of the earth's history. Since we know that living organisms are descendants of living precursors, we conclude from the fossil record that our present plants (and animals, of course) are modified descendants of more ancient ones. This, in essence, is what is meant by organic evolution. All modern biologists accept this point of view. It is when individual biologists attempt to outline the course of evolution, and thus to draw up the actual phylogenetic lines of descent (especially among the taxa that are more comprehensive than genera), that they often disagree, because they interpret evidences differently.

Anyone who surveys the comparative morphology of living plants in the light of the paleobotanical record usually becomes convinced that terrestrial plants have evolved from aquatic algal precursors, and that the primitive, spore-bearing, seedless vascular plants growing upon the earth from the Devonian through the late Paleozoic periods have now themselves been crowded into near oblivion by the flowering plants that have been dominant since the Cretaceous. What will occur in plant life in the millions of years ahead is open to speculation. The changes are occurring inexorably at present, but the limited framework of the human life-span clouds our perception of the long-range events yet to transpire in the evolutionary process.

GLOSSARY

ABSCISSION LAYER   A zone of cells at the base of an appendage (petiole, fruit stalk, and so forth) that causes the separation of that appendage from another organ.

ADVENTITIOUS ROOT   A root that is neither primary nor secondary, nor one that arises therefrom.

AGAR   A gel-forming polysaccharide, a polymer of galactose, derived from certain red algae and used in microbiology as a solidifying agent in culture media.

AGGREGATE FRUIT   A receptacle bearing a number of matured pistils (fruits) of a single flower.

AKINETE   A vegetative cell that has been transformed by wall thickening into a nonmotile spore.

ALGINIC ACID   A polyuronic acid located in the middle lamella and the primary walls of brown algae.

AMPHIPHLOIC   Having phloem on both sides of the xylem.

ANGIOSPERM   A seed plant with ovules and seeds enclosed in a carpel, pistil, or fruit.

ANNUAL   A plant that develops, reproduces, and dies in a single growing season, usually within a year.

ANNUAL RING   The cylinder of secondary xylem added to a woody plant stem by the cambium in any one year.

ANNULUS   A specialized or differentiated ringlike layer of cells in the moss capsule or in the sporangial wall of ferns.

ANTHER   The apex of the stamen, composed of microsporangia and containing pollen at maturity.

ANTHERIDIOPHORE   A fertile branch that bears antheridia.

ANTHERIDIUM   In plants other than algae or fungi, a multicellular, sperm-producing organ consisting of spermatogenous tissue and a sterile jacket; in algae and fungi, a unicellular sperm-forming organ.

ANTIPODAL CELL   Any of three cells of the mature female gametophyte of angiosperms that are located at the opposite end from the micropyle and usually degenerate after fertilization.

APICAL MERISTEM   The cells at the apex of a root or stem that are actively dividing.

APOGAMY   Formation of an organism without gametic union.

ARCHECONIOPHORE   A fertile branch that bears archegonia.

ARCHEGONIUM   A multicellular, egg-producing gametangium with a jacket of sterile cells.

ASCOCARP   The ascus-containing body of Ascomycota.

ASCOSPORE   A spore produced by free-cell formation following meiosis in an ascus.

ASCUS   A saclike cell of Ascomycota in which karyogamy is followed immediately by meiosis and in which ascospores of a definite number arise by free-cell formation.

ASEXUAL   Not involving cellular or nuclear union.

ATACTOSTELE   A scattered arrangement of xylem and phloem groups or vascular bundles.

AUTOTROPHIC   Requiring only inorganic compounds for nutrition; see also *heterotrophic*.

AXILLARY BUD   A bud borne in the axil of the leaf.

BACILLUS   A rod-shaped bacterium.

BACTERIOPHAGE   A virus that is parasitic on bacteria.

BASIDIOCARP   The basidiospore-containing structure of certain Basidiomycota.

BASIDIOSPORES   A spore attached to a basidium and arising after meiosis.

BASIDIUM   A nonseptate or septate hypha bearing (usually) four basidiospores exogenously following karyogamy and meiosis.

BUD   A minute stem with short internodes, bearing the primordia of vegetative leaves or sporophylls.

BUDDING   Multiplication by abscission of a cellular protuberance, as in certain yeasts.

BUD SCALE   A modified basal leaf that encloses the more delicate leaf primordia or sporophyll primordia.

BUD SCALE SCAR   A scar on a woody stem that marks the site of attachment of a bud scale.

BULB   A short, vertical, subterranean stem covered by fleshy leaf bases or scales, as in lily and onion.

CALYPTRA   The enlarged and modified archegonium that for a while encloses the embryonic sporophyte of liverworts, mosses, and seedless plants.

CALYX   The collective term for the sepals of a flower.

CAMBIUM   A zone of meristematic cells located between the primary xylem and phloem, the division products of which differentiate into secondary xylem and phloem.

CAPITULUM   A headlike inflorescence of composite flowers, as in daisy.

CAPSULE   (1) The sporangium of liverworts and mosses. (2) The colloidal sheath of algae and bacteria.

CARPEL   The enclosing structure of angiospermous ovules, often considered to represent a folded megasporophyll.

CARPOGONIUM   The female gametangium of red algae.

CARPOSPOROPHYTE   In red algae, a group of carposporangia and carpospores, which arises directly or indirectly from the zygote.

CARRAGEENIN   A substance composed of D-galactose units and sulfate groups, formed by extracting polysaccharides by hot water from certain red algae.

CHEMOAUTOTROPHIC   Using chemical energy to synthesize protoplasm from inorganic sources.

CHLOROPLAST   A membrane-bounded area of cytoplasm, containing photosynthetic lamellae.

CILIUM   A short flagellum.

CIRCINATE VERNATION   The curled arrangement of leaves and leaflets in the bud resulting from their more rapid growth on one surface than on the other.

CLOSED BUD   A bud covered by bud scales and dormant except during the growing season.

COCCUS   A spherical bacterium.

COENOCYTIC   Multinucleate and nonseptate.

COLUMELLA   A sterile region surrounded by spores in certain molds and mosses, as well as in *Anthoceros*.

COMPANION CELL   A small, nucleated cell associated with some sieve cells.

COMPOUND LEAF   A leaf with a divided blade.

CONIFER   A cone-bearing tree or shrub with nonciliate sperms, such as pine, hemlock, and so forth.

CONTRACTILE VACUOLE   A vacuole that dilates as it accumulates liquid, and subsequently contracts to excrete the liquid.

CORM   A short, vertical, fleshy, subterranean stem.

COROLLA   A collective term for petals.

CORTEX   The region between the stele and the epidermis in stems and roots.

COTYLEDON   A primary embryonic leaf.

COVERED BUD   See *closed bud*.

CUTICLE   An impermeable surface layer on the epidermis of plant organs.

CUTIN   A waxy substance composing the cuticle.

CYANOPHYCEAN STARCH   An amylopectin fraction of starch produced by blue-green algae; resembles glycogen.

CYSTOCARP   The carposporangia and its associated sterile covering cells, in red algae.

DECIDUOUS   Shedding all leaves periodically (usually annually).

DIATOMACEOUS EARTH   The siliceous remains (cell walls) of fossilized diatoms.

DICHOTOMOUS   Branching into two equal parts.

DIFFERENTIATION   The change from homogeneous tissue to heterogeneous tissues, for example, from meristem to primary tissues.

DIOECIOUS   Producing microspores and megaspores on separate individuals.

DNA   Deoxyribonucleic acid.

DOUBLE FERTILIZATION   In fertilization of angiosperms, the union of one sperm with the egg and of the other sperm with two polar nuclei or a secondary nucleus.

DIPLOID   Having two complements or sets of haploid chromosomes.

ECTOPHLOIC   Having phloem located external to the xylem.

EGG   A large, nonflagellate female gamete.

ELATER   (1) A sterile, hygroscopic cell in the capsule of certain liverworts. (2) The appendages formed from the outer spore wall in *Equisetum*.

ENDODERMIS   The innermost, differentiated layer of the cortex, present in roots, rhizomes, and certain cryptogamous stems.

ENDOPLASMIC RETICULUM   The lamellar or tubular system of the colorless cytoplasm in a cell.

ENDOSPERM   The nutritive tissue used by the embryo in angiosperms.

EPICOTYL   See *plumule.*

EUKARYOTIC   Having membrane-bounded nuclei, plastids, Golgi apparatus, and mitochondria.

EUSTELE   Arrangement of primary xylem and phloem in discrete strands separated by parenchymatous tissue interspersed with leaf gaps.

EVERGREEN   Never entirely leafless, as in pine or live oak.

FALSE INDUSIUM   An inrolled leaf margin that covers marginal sporangia; see also *true indusium.*

FERMENTATION   The anaerobic respiration of substrates.

FERTILIZATION   The union of an egg and a sperm in oogamous sexual reproduction.

FILAMENT   (1) A chain of cells. (2) The stalk of the angiosperm stamen.

FLAGELLUM   An extension of the protoplasm, the beating of which propels the cell (plural, flagella).

FLORIDEAN STARCH   A substance composed of extraplastid polysaccharides of red algae similar to the branched amylopectin fractions of other plant starches.

FOOT   The absorbing organ of the embryonic sporophyte in liverworts, mosses, and seedless vascular plants.

FRUIT   The matured ovary or ovaries of one or more flowers and their associated structures.

FRUSTULE   The siliceous cell wall of diatoms.

FUNCTIONAL MEGASPORE   The surviving megaspore of the linear tetrad in seed plants, which produces the female gametophyte.

GAMETE   A sex cell which unites with another to form a zygote.

GAMETANGIUM   A structure containing gametes.

GAMETOPHYTE   A plant or phase that produces gametes.

GEMMA   A bud or fragment of an organism that functions in asexual reproduction (plural, gemmae).

GOLGI APPARATUS   A cellular organelle consisting of stacks of sacs or cisternae that are secretory in function.

GROUND MERISTEM   The primary meristematic tissue other than protoderm and procambium.

GROWTH   An irreversible increase in volume, with or without differentiation.

GUARD CELLS   Specialized epidermal cells that contain chloroplasts and surround a stoma.

GYMNOSPERM   A seed plant with seeds not enclosed by a megasporophyll or pistil.

HAPLOID   Having a single chromosome complement (set).

HAUSTORIUM   An absorptive hypha that penetrates a host cell (plural, haustoria).

HERBACEOUS   Soft rather than woody.

HETEROCYST   A transparent, thick-walled blue-green algal cell.

HETEROGAMOUS   Having the type of sexual reproduction in which the male and female gametes are morphologically distinct but both flagellate.

HETEROSPORY   The production of miscrospores that grow into male gametophytes, and of megaspores that develop into female gametophytes; the two kinds of spores may or may not differ in size.

HETEROTHALLISM   Being sexually self-incompatible, thus requiring two compatible strains or organisms for sexual reproduction.

HETEROTROPHIC   Requiring organic compounds for nutrition; see also *autotrophic*.

HOLDFAST   An attaching cell or organ in algae.

HOLOZOIC   Phagotrophic, that is, obtaining food by ingesting solid, complex organic particles.

HORMOGONIUM   In blue-green algae, a trichome segment (usually motile) that can grow into a new trichome.

HOST   An organism on which a parasite is growing.

HYPHA   One branch of mycelium in a fungus.

HYPOCOTYL   The portion of the plant axis between the cotyledonary node and the primary root.

INDUSIUM   See *false indusium* and *true indusium*.

INFLORESCENCE   An axis bearing flowers, or a flower cluster.

INTEGUMENT   The tissues covering the megasporangium in ovules.

INTERNODE   The region of the stem between two nodes.

ISOGAMOUS   Having the type of sexual reproduction in which the gametes are morphologically indistinguishable.

KARYOGAMY   Nuclear union.

KELP   A large seaweed (some of which are more than 100 ft long) of the brown algae.

LIP CELLS   Thin-walled cells that interrupt the annulus in certain fern sporangia.

LEAF GAP   A parenchymatous interruption in a stele, associated with departure of a leaf trace.

LEAF PRIMORDIUM   A miniature leaf in the bud.

LEAF SCAR   A scar at the node of a woody plant that remains after leaf abscission.

LENTICEL   A region in the bark of woody stems where gaseous interchange occurs.

MACROPHYLLOUS   Having leaves with branching veins, the traces of which are associated with gaps in the stem stele.

MEGASPORANGIUM   The sporangium in which megaspores are produced.

MEGASPORE   A spore arising by meiosis in which all four products potentially can grow into female gametophytes; often, but not always, larger than microspores.

MEGASPOROCYTE   The megaspore mother cell, which forms megaspores after meiosis.

MEGASPOROPHYLL   A leaf bearing one or more megasporangia or ovules.

MEGASTROBILUS   The strobilus in which megaspores are produced.

MEIOSIS   A process involving two successive nuclear divisions, in which the chromosome number is halved and genetic segregation occurs.

MEIOSPORANGIUM   A sporangium in which meiosis occurs.

MESOPHYLL   The photosynthetic tissue, interspersed with veins, that is located between the lower and upper epidermis of a leaf.

METABOLISM   The normal, functional chemical processes occurring in living organisms.

MICROPHYLL   A leaf with an unbranched vein, the trace of which leaves no gap in the stem stele.

MICROPYLE   A passageway between the apexes of the integument or integuments of an ovule.

MICROSPORANGIUM   A sporangium that produces microspores.

MICROSPOROPHYLL   A leaf bearing one or more microsporangia.

MICROSPORE   A product of a microsporocyte, often, but not always, smaller than the megaspore of the particular species, that produces a male gametophyte.

MICROSTROBILUS   A strobilus that produces microspores.

MITOCHONDRION   A double-membrane-bounded cytoplasmic organelle, the site of energy release in cellular respiration.

MITOSIS   Nuclear division involving chromosomes that are replicated and distributed equally between the daughter nuclei.

MITOSPORANGIUM   A sporangium in which the spores arise by mitotic, rather than meiotic, nuclear divisions.

MONOECIOUS   Producing both microspores and megaspores on one individual.

MULTIPLE FRUIT   A fruit developing from the maturing ovaries of more than one flower.

MUTATION   A sudden change in an organism that is transmitted to offspring.

MYCELIUM   The collective term for the hyphae of a fungus; the somatic or vegetative thallus of a fungus.

MYCORRHIZA   An either superficial or internal association of a root or rhizome with a fungus.

NITROGEN FIXATION   The use of gaseous nitrogen as the source of the nitrogen required in metabolism.

NODE   Point of attachment of a leaf to a stem; also point of branch emergence.

OBLIGATE PARASITE   An organism that cannot exist apart from a host.

ONTOGENY   The development of an individual.

OOGAMOUS   Having the type of sexual reproduction that involves a large, nonmotile egg and a small, motile sperm.

OOGONIUM   A unicellular gametangium that contains an egg.

OPEN BUD   A bud without bud scales that is continually unfolding.

OPERCULUM   The coverlike apex of a moss capsule, freed by rupture at the annulus.

OVARY   The ovule-bearing region of a pistil.

OVULE   A megasporangium covered by an integument.

PALYNOLOGY   The study of spores and pollen grains.

PARAMYLON   A β-1,3-linked glucan.

PARAPHYSIS   A sterile structure among reproductive cells or organs (plural, paraphyses).

PARASITE   An organism living in, upon, or at the expense of another.

PARENCHYMA   Thin-walled living cells with large vacuoles, that are active in either photosynthesis or storage.

PARTHENOGENESIS   The development of an embryo without gametic union.

PATHOGENIC   Disease-causing.

PENICILLIN   An antibiotic produced by *Penicillium chrysogenum*.

PERENNIAL   A plant that grows and reproduces during more than one growing season.

PERIANTH   (1) In flowering plants, the collective term for sepals and petals. (2) In liverworts, the leaves or other tissue surrounding a group of archegonia.

PERICYCLE   A thin zone of living cells just within the endodermis.

PERIDERM   A corky layer and its generator, the cork cambium, at the surface of organs that are undergoing secondary growth.

PERIPLAST   A complex and often ornamented plasma membrane.

PERISTOME   Cellular or acellular structures at the mouth of the capsule in many mosses, involved in spore dissemination.

PETAL   A colored, usually sterile appendage of the angiospermous flower; see also *corolla.*

PETIOLE   The stalk that attaches the leaf blade of a plant to the stem.

PISTIL   A megasporophyll, carpel, or group of united megasporophylls in angiosperms.

PHAGOTROPHIC   Obtaining food by ingesting solid organic particles.

PHLOEM   Living, thin-walled cells, typified by sieve areas in the walls of some of the cells, that function in food-conducting.

PHOTOAUTOTROPHIC   Able to use light energy in synthesizing protoplasm from inorganic compounds.

PHOTOTAXIS   Movement stimulated positively or negatively by light.

PHYLLOTAXY   The pattern of arrangement of appendages (leaves, flower parts, and so forth) upon an axis.

PITH   The parenchyma cells at the center of certain stems and roots, inside the zone of primary xylem.

PLACENTATION   The pattern of ovular attachment.

PLANKTONIC   Suspended, free-floating, aquatic microorganisms.

PLASMODIUM   An unwalled, ameboid, multinucleate mass of protoplasm.

PLASMOGAMY   Union of sex cells or gametes.

PLASTID   Any of a group of photosynthetic lamellae bounded by two membranes.

PLUMULE   The terminal bud of an embryo; epicotyl.

PLURILOCULAR   Having a multicellular structure, each cubical cell producing a single reproductive cell.

POLAR NUCLEI   The nuclei of the angiosperm female gametophyte that migrate to the center from the poles of the gametophyte.

POLLEN GRAIN   A microspore containing a mature or immature male gametophyte.

POLLEN CHAMBER   A depression at the apex of the megasporangium, formed by cellular breakdown, in which pollen grains are deposited.

POLLINATION   The transfer of pollen from the microsporangium to the micropyle of the ovule (in gymnosperms) or to the stigma of the pistil (in angiosperms).

POLLINATION DROPLET   A droplet of fluid at the micropyle involved in pollination.

POLYPLOID   Having two or more times the basic chromosomal complement.

PRIMARY ENDOSPERM NUCLEUS   The nucleus formed by the union of two polar nuclei (or a secondary nucleus) with a sperm, in angiosperms.

PRIMARY MERISTEM   The three meristematic derivatives (protoderm, procambium, and ground meristem) of the apical meristem.

PRIMARY MYCELIUM   The haploid mycelium produced by the germination of a basidiospore, as in a mushroom.

PRIMARY ROOT   The embryonic root after seed germination.

PRIMARY TISSUE   A tissue that has differentiated from a primary meristem.

PROCAMBIUM   The part of the primary meristem which differentiates into vascular tissue and cambium (if present).

PROKARYOTIC   Lacking membrane-bounded nuclei, plastids, Golgi apparatus, and mitochondria.

PROTHALLIUM OR PROTHALLUS   The gametophyte of vascular cryptogams, especially that of ferns.

PROTODERM   The part of the primary meristem which differentiates into epidermis.

PROTONEMA   The product of spore germination in mosses and certain liverworts, the precursor of the leafy gametophores.

PROTOSTELE   A solid core composed of xylem surrounded by phloem in the plant axis.

PROVASCULAR TISSUE   The procambium.

PSEUDOPLASMODIUM   An aggregate of amebae in cellular slime molds.

RADICLE   The primary or embryonic root.

RECEPTACLE   A fertile area on which reproductive organs are borne.

RED EYESPOT   The stigma in the motile cells of certain algae.

RHIZOID   A unicellular or multicellular absorbing organ lacking vascular tissue.

RHIZOME   A fleshy, elongate, nonerect stem that is often, but not always, subterranean.

RHIZOPHORE   A root-bearing organ or region.

ROOT CAP   A covering of parenchymatous cells over the apical meristem of the root.

ROOT HAIR   An absorptive unicellular protuberance of the epidermal cells of the root.

SAPROPHYTIC   Obtaining food by absorbing soluble nonliving organic matter.

SECONDARY MYCELIUM   The product of fusion of the hyphae of two compatible primary mycelia, as in mushrooms.

SECONDARY ROOT   A branch from the primary root.

SECONDARY TISSUE   Tissue that originates from a secondary meristem (either the cambium or the cork cambium).

SEED   An embryonic sporophyte embedded in the female gametophyte (in gymnosperms) or in the endosperm, or gorged with digested products of the endosperm (in angiosperms), enclosed within the remains of the megasporangium and covered with one or more integuments.

SEPAL   Any of the lowermost sterile appendages, usually green, on a floral receptacle.

SETA   The stalklike region between the foot and the capsule, in liverwort and moss sporophytes.

SEXUAL REPRODUCTION   Reproduction involving nuclear union and meiosis, and often, plasmogamy.

SIEVE CELL   A single cell with sieve plates or areas.

SIEVE TUBE   A series of sieve cells.

SIMPLE FRUIT   A fruit derived from a single pistil (simple or compound) of a single flower.

SIMPLE LEAF   A leaf with an undivided blade.

SIRENIN   A secreted substance that attracts male gametes in sexual reproduction of *Allomyces*.

SIPHONOSTELE   A hollow cylinder composed of xylem and phloem.

SOMATIC   Vegetative; not reproductive or germinal.

SORUS   A group or cluster of plant reproductive bodies.

SPERM   The motile male gamete or male nucleus.

SPERMATIUM   A minute, nonflagellate male gamete.

SPIRILLUM   A spirally twisted bacterium.

SPORANGIOPHORE   (1) In certain molds, a hypha bearing a sporangium at its apex. (2) In seedless vascular plants, a branch bearing sporangia.

SPORE MOTHER CELL   See *sporocyte*.

SPOROCARP   A hard, nutlike structure containing sori of heterosporous sporangia in ferns.

SPOROCYTE   A cell that gives rise meiotically to a tetrad of spores.

SPOROPHYLL   A leaf bearing one or more sporangia.

SPOROPHYTE   The diploid, spore-producing alternant of the alternating generations.

SPUR SHOOT   A lateral, dwarf shoot in certain woody plants.

STAMEN   The microsporophyll of angiosperms.

STELE   The vascular tissue of axes.

STIGMA   (1) The red eyespot of algae. (2) In angiosperms, the receptive region of the pistil.

STOLON   An elongate, horizontal stem rooting at the nodes as it passes over the soil surface.

STOMA   A minute, intercellular fissure in the epidermis, surrounded by guard cells.

STROBILUS   A stem with short internodes and spore-bearing appendages.

STYLE   The portion of a pistil between the stigma and the ovary.

SUBERIN   Cork.

SYNERGIDS.   Sterile cells associated with the angiosperm egg.

TAPROOT   An elongate, deeply growing primary root.

TETRAD   A group of four (often used in the term "spore tetrad").

TETRASPORANGIUM   In red algae, a sporangium that gives rise to four spores after meiosis.

TETRASPORE   The product of meiosis in a tetrasporangium.

TETRASPOROPHYTE   In the red algae, the diploid plant that produces tetraspores.

THALLUS   The plant body of algae and fungi, and the gametophytic stages of liverworts and sometimes other seedless plants (plural, thalli).

TRACE   A vascular connection from the stele of an axis to an appendage.

TRACHEID   A single-celled, lignified, nonliving, water-conducting element of xylem.

TRANSDUCTION   Genetic modification (in bacteria) effected by the DNA of viruses (bacteriophages).

TRICHOME   (1) A chain of cells, in blue-green algae. (2) An epidermal hair, in vascular plants.

TRUE INDUSIUM   A thin layer of epidermal outgrowth covering receptacle and sporangia in certain ferns; see also *false indusium.*

TUBER   The enlarged tip of a rhizome, filled with stored food (usually starch).

TUBE NUCLEUS   The nucleus of the pollen tube, other than the sperm nuclei.

UNILOCULAR   Having a single cavity.

VACUOLE   A cavity filled with fluid (the cell sap) within a cell.

VALVE   (1) Half of a diatom frustule. (2) A segment of the capsule wall of liverworts and hornworts at dehiscence.

VASCULAR BUNDLE SCAR   The scars of vascular bundles, visible within leaf scars.

VASCULAR TISSUE   Xylem and phloem.

VEGETATIVE   Somatic, not usually reproductive.

VEIN   The strand of xylem and phloem in a leaf.

VENATION   The pattern of vein arrangement in leaves.

VERNATION   The pattern of arrangement of embryonic leaves within the bud.

VESSEL   A series of perforated, lignified, conducting cells of xylem.

WATERBLOOM   A dense population of planktonic algae.

WOOD   Secondary xylem.

XYLEM   Lignified, water-conducting tissue.

ZOOSPORANGIUM   A sporangium that produces zoospores.

ZOOSPORE   A motile, asexual reproductive cell formed by a nonmotile organism.

ZYGOTE   The cell produced by the union of two gametes.

ZYMASE   An intracellular enzyme complex that degrades sugar to ethyl alcohol and carbon dioxide.

ALEXOPOULOS, C. J. *Introductory Mycology*. New York: John Wiley & Sons, Inc., 1962. A well-illustrated general account of the fungi.

ALEXOPOULOS, C. J., AND H. C. BOLD *Algae and Fungi*. New York: The Macmillan Company, 1967. A brief discussion of algae and fungi for the general reader.

ANDREWS, H. N. *Studies in Paleobotany*. New York: John Wiley & Sons, Inc., 1961. A survey of fossil plants and their relationships to extant forms; includes an introduction to palynology.

BENSON, L. *Plant Classification*. Boston: D. C. Heath & Company, 1957. A comprehensive treatment of the classification of vascular plants and the criteria on which the classification is based. Also included are instructions for identifying plants and preserving specimens. The book closes with a consideration of some aspects of plant ecology and a discussion of the floras of North America.

BOLD, H. C. *Morphology of Plants*. New York: Harper & Row, Publishers, 1967. A summary of plant structure and reproduction with reference to algae, fungi, liverworts, mosses, and vascular plants, both seed-bearing and seedless. Includes discussions of systems of classification and of plants of the past.

DELEVORYAS, T. *Morphology and Evolution of Fossil Plants*. New York:

Holt, Rinehart & Winston Inc., 1962. A brief treatment of the nature of fossil floras.

DELEVORYAS, T.   *Plant Diversification.* New York: Holt, Rinehart & Winston Inc., 1962. Selected topics in the evolution of plants.

EAMES, A. J.   *Morphology of the Angiosperms.* New York: McGraw-Hill Book Company, 1961. A comprehensive treatment at an advanced level of the anatomy and reproductive process in the flowering plants.

ESAU, K.   *Plant Anatomy.* New York: John Wiley & Sons, Inc., 1965. A detailed and comprehensive account of the gross and minute structure of vascular plants, with copious illustrations.

FOSTER, A. F., AND E. M. GIFFORD, JR.   *Comparative Morphology of Vascular Plants.* San Francisco: W. H. Freeman and Co., Publishers, 1959. A summary, at a somewhat advanced level, of the structure and reproduction of vascular plants, and a discussion of general topics in plant morphology.

MEEUSE, B. J. D.   *The Story of Pollination.* New York: The Ronald Press Company, 1961.

PARIHAR, N. S.   *An Introduction to Embryophyta.* Allahabad, India: Central Book Depot, 1967, Vol. I (*Bryophyta*) and Vol. II (*Pteridophytes*).

SCAGEL, R. F., R. J. BANDONI, G. E. ROUSE, W. B. SCHOFIELD, J. R. STEIN, AND T. C. TAYLOR   *An Evolutionary Survey of the Plant Kingdom.* Belmont, Calif.: Wadsworth Publishing Co., Inc., 1965. A comprehensive account of the plant kingdom emphasizing phylogeny and groups of organisms.

SMITH, G. M.   *Cryptogamic Botany,* Vols. I and II. New York: McGraw-Hill Book Company, 1955. A two-volume, advanced-level treatment of representative algae, fungi, liverworts, mosses, ferns, and other seedless vascular plants.

SPORNE, K. R.   *The Morphology of Gymnosperms: The Structure of Ferns and Allied Plants,* 2nd ed. London: Hutchinson & Co. (Publishers) Ltd., 1966.

SPORNE, K. R.   *The Morphology of Pteridophytes: The Structure and Evolution of Primitive Seed-plants.* New York: Hillary House Publishers, Ltd., 1966.

STANIER, R. Y., M. DOUDOROFF, AND E. A. ADELBERG   *The Microbial World,* 3rd ed. Englewood Cliffs, N.J.: Prentice-Hall, Inc., 1970. A comprehensive introduction to microbiology.

Abscission layer, 91
Acetabularia, 27
Achlya, 49, 50, 51, 64, 163, 164
Acrasiomycota (cellular slime
    molds), 5, 45–46
Actinomycetes, 43
Actinostele, 85
Adaptation, 8
Adder's tongue fern, 120
Adiantum, 112, 114, 117, 119
Aecia, 54
Aeciospores, 54
Aesculus, 80
Agar, 12
Agaricus, 55
Age of ferns, 121, 167
Akinete, 23
Algae, 2, 5, 11–37, 78, 98
    cellular organization, 16

Algae (**cont.**):
    classification, 14, 15
    defined, 11, 12
    divisions of, 22
    evolution of, 36–37
    form and organization, 14
    major groups, 15
    reproduction, 18–22
Algin, 12
Allium, 80
Allomyces, 48, 49
Alternation of generations, 76, 93,
    94, 110, 164
Amebae, 46
Anabaena, 23, 24
Ananas, 156
Angiosperms, 7, 98, 124, 126, 141–
    159 (*see also* Anthophyta;
    Flowering plants)

Angiospermy, 125, 158, 159
Annual plants, 70, 78
Annual ring, 83, 84
Annulus, 114, 115
Anther, 147, 148, 149
Antheridiophore, 66
Antheridium, 12, 34, 50, 62, 63, 64,
    68, 70, 71, 95, 103, 109,
    115, 116, 117
Anthoceros, 67–68, 71
Anthophyta (angiosperms; flower-
    ing plants), 1, 2, 7, 98, 124,
    126, 141–159
Antibiotics, 43
Antipodal cell, 151
Apical cell, 107
Apical meristem, 78, 81, 86, 114,
    143
Apical notch, 114

Apogamy, 117
Araucaria, 133, 134
Archegoniophore, 65
Archegonium, 12, 62, 63, 64, 68, 70, 71, 94, 103, 109, 115, 116, 117, 132, 133, 135
Aristolochia, 82
Arthrophyta (horsetails and sphenopsids), 7, 93, 98, 106–109 110, 111
Ascomycota (sac fungi; Ascomycetes), 5, 47, 52, 53–54, 55, 57
Ascus, 52, 54
Aspergillus, 52, 53
Atactostele, 85
Autumnal coloration, 91
Axillary bud, 79, 81
Azolla, 112, 118, 120, 165

Bacillariophyceae, 34–35 (*see also* Chrysophycophyta; Diatoms)
Bacillus, 40
Bacteria, 2, 5, 10, 23, 38–43, 98 (*see also* Schizomycota)
Bacteriochlorophyll, 42 (*see also* Chlorophyll)
Bacteriology, 43
Bacteriophages, 42
Barberry, 55
Basal cell, 153
Basidiocarp, 54, 56, 57
Basidiomycota (club fungi; Basidomycetes), 5, 54–57
Basidiospore, 54, 55, 56
Basidium, 54, 55, 56
Berberis, 55
Binary fission, 23, 32, 34, 162
Bioluminescence, 56
Black mold, 51
Blastophaga, 151
Blue-green algae, 5, 15, 43 (*see also* Cyanophycophyta)

Botrychium, 120–121
Bracket fungi, 57
Bread molds, 5 (*see also* Zygomycota)
Bristlecone pine, 84, 133
Brown algae, 5, 15, 27–29 (*see also* Phaeophycophyta)
Bryophyta (mosses), 1, 2, 5, 60, 68–76, 98, 103, 163
Buckeye, 80
Bud, 70, 79, 81
    covered, 128
Budding, 52
Bud scale, 81
Bud scale scars, 80, 81
Bulb, 80

Calamites, 122
Calamophyton, 122
Calathospermum, 159
Callithamnion, 30, 32
Calyptra, 64, 68, 71
Calyx, 145
Cambium, 81, 82, 83, 84
Canal, 33
Capitulum, 146
Capsule, 65, 66, 67, 71, 72
Carinal canal, 107
Carpel, 141, 159
Carpogonium, 30
Carpospore, 31
Carposporophyte, 65
Carrageenin, 13
Caulerpa, 27
Cedrus, 133
Cell division, 18
Cell republic, 161
Cellular organization, 2, 8
Cellular slime molds, 5, 45–46 (*see also* Acrasiomycota)
Cellulose, 15, 81
Cell wall, 6, 8, 15
Central canal, 107
Chara, 34

Charophyta (stoneworts), 5, 15, 34
Chemoautotrophic organisms, 39, 41
Chitin, 46
Chlamydomonas, 12, 14, 17, 18, 19, 20, 21, 25, 36, 64, 163, 164
Chlorella, 24, 25
Chlorococcum, 24, 25
Chlorophycophyta (green algae), 5, 15, 18, 23–27, 37
Chlorophyll, 15 (*see also* Bacteriochlorophyll)
Chlorophyll *a,* 166
Chloroplast, 16
Chromosome, 19
Chroococcus, 23
Chrysolaminarin, 15
Chrysophycophyta (chrysophytes), 5, 15, 34–35 (*see also* Diatoms)
Chytridiomycota (chytrids), 5, 47–48
Cilia, 14, 135
Circinate vernation, 96, 112
Cladoxylon, 121
Class, 14
Classification, 2, 4–7, 14, 125–126, 165–166
    artificial, 2
    natural, 2
    phylogenetic, 2
Clonal culture, 18
Club fungi, 5 (*see also* Basidomycota)
Club mosses, 7, 93–105, 122 (*see also* Microphyllophyta)
Clump formation, 17
Clumping, 18
Coal-age forest, 104
Coccus, 40
Codium, 27
Coenocytic hyphae, 46
Coleus, 81
Colonies, 14
Columella, 68

Companion cell, 82, 83
Compound pistil, 141, 145
Conceptacle, 29, 30
Coniferophyta (conifers), 7, 128–134, 147
Contractile vacuole, 17
Corm, 80
Corn (*Zea mays*), 145
Corolla, 145
Cortex, 81, 107
Coscinodiscus, 35
Cotyledon, 133, 153, 157
Covered bud (*see* Bud, covered)
Cucurbita, 83
Cuticle, 82
Cutin, 82
Cuttings, 86
Cyanophycean starch, 15
Cyanophycophyta (blue-green algae), 5, 15, 16, 17, 18, 22–23, 43
Cyathea, 113
Cycadeoidea, 139
Cycadophyta (cycads), 7, 125, 128, 134–136, 137, 147
Cycas, 134, 135
Cyperus, 89
Cyrtomium, 78
Cystocarp, 31, 32

Darwin, Charles, 2, 159
Dawsonia, 69
Deuteromycota (imperfect fungi), 5, 47, 53, 57
Diachea, 44
α,ε-Diaminopimelic acid, 23
Diatomaceous earth, 12, 34
Diatoms (Bacillariophyceae), 12, 34–35 (*see also* Chrysophycophyta)
Dichotomous development, 63
Dictyostele, 85
Dictyostelium, 45, 46
Differentiation, 78

Dinoflagellates, 5, 15 (*see also* Pyrrhophycophyta)
Dioecious plants, 135, 145
Dioon, 134, 135
Diploid stage, 21, 164
Disc flower, 146
Division, 14
DNA (deoxyribonucleic acid), 7, 17, 23, 40
Double fertilization, 148, 150, 152, 158
Drimys, 159
Dryopteris, 112, 114, 115, 116, 117, 119
Duckweed, 1

Ectocarpus, 12, 27, 28, 36, 37
Egg, 17, 26, 151, 152, 164
Eichornia, 8
Elater, 65, 109
Elodea, 142
Embryo, 106, 116, 132, 133, 137, 148, 153, 154, 158
Embryogeny, 147, 152–154
Emplectopteris, 139
Endodermis, 87, 107
Endoplasmic reticulum, 6, 8, 17, 23, 41
Endosperm, 152, 153, 154, 155, 157, 158
Endosporic gametophyte, 104
Endospory, 126, 127
Enzymes, 10
Ephedra, 128, 137, 138, 140
Epicotyl, 153
Epidermis, 81, 90, 107
Epiphyte, 142
Equisetum, 93, 103, 107–109, 110, 113, 114, 122, 123, 126, 163
Eremosphaera, 24, 25
Escherichia, 41
Essential elements, 39
Eucalyptus, 78

Euglena, 10, 33
Euglenoids, 5, 15 (*see also* Euglenophycophyta)
Euglenophycophyta (euglenoids), 5, 15, 18, 33, 34
Eukaryotic organisms, 36
Euonymus, 88
Eupenicillium, 53
Eurotium, 53
Eustele, 85, 107
Evolution, 9, 161, 165–169

Fagopyrum, 157
Family, 14
Fermentation, 53
Ferns, 1, 2, 7, 111–123 (*see also* Pterophyta)
Fertilization, 71, 128, 135, 136, 137, 147, 151
Fibers, 82, 84
Fig, 151
Filament, 14, 16, 147
Flagellum, 14, 15, 17, 18, 19, 33, 41
Floridean starch, 15
Flour, 155
Flower, 142, 143, 156
Flowering plants, 1, 2, 7, 141–159 (*see also* Angiosperms; Anthophyta)
Food chain, 1
Foot, 65, 67, 71, 116
Fossils, 11, 61, 78, 92, 104, 122, 166–169
  algae, 11, 12
  angiosperms, 159
  bacteria, 43
  ferns, 121
  fungi, 58, 59
  gymnosperms, 139, 140
  liverworts, 61
  mosses, 61
Fragaria, 80, 156
Fragmentation, 18, 23, 162

Fruit, 124, 125, 141, 142, 156, 157, 158
  aggregate, 156
  multiple, 156
  simple, 156, 157
Frustule, 34
Fucus, 16, 27, 29, 30, 164
Funaria, 68, 69, 72
Functional megaspore, 127, 131, 132, 148, 149, 150, 151
Fungi, 1, 2, 5, 10, 46–59, 98
  importance of, 58, 59
  sensu lato, 5
  sensu stricto, 5

Gametangia, 49
Gamete, 12, 17, 18, 19, 20, 28, 31, 44, 163, 164
Gametogenesis, 147, 150–151
Gametophyte, 21, 28, 64, 67, 73, 76, 77, 95, 99, 100, 103, 108, 109, 110, 114, 115, 116, 117, 118, 119, 120, 123, 158, 163, 164
  female, 102, 103, 104, 105, 106, 126, 127, 132, 133, 135, 148, 151
  male, 102, 103, 106, 126, 127, 130, 131, 132, 148, 149, 150, 151
Gemma, 65, 162
Gene, 19, 20
Generative cell, 149, 150
Genus, 14
Geologic time, 98
Germ (of seed), 153
Germination, seed (*see* Seed, germination)
Gill, 55
Ginkgo, 89, 125, 128, 136–137, 140, 147
Ginkgophyta, 7, 136–137
Gladiolus, 80
Gnetophyta, 7

Gnetum, 137, 138, 140
Golden algae, 15
Golgi apparatus, 6, 8, 17, 23, 41
Gonyaulax, 12
Grape fern, 120
Green algae, 5, 15, 23–27 (*see also* Chlorophycophyta)
Ground meristem, 81, 86
Growth, 78
Guard cell, 82, 89, 90, 108, 112
Gymnosperms, 7, 98, 124–140
Gymnospermy, 125, 158

Haircap moss, 69
Hairs, epidermal, 83
Haploid stage, 20, 21, 164
Haplostele, 85
Haustorium, 47
Hepaticites, 61
Hepatophyta (liverworts and hornworts), 1, 2, 5, 60–68, 76, 98, 103, 163
Herbaceous plants, 81
Hermaphroditic organisms, 163
Heterocyst, 23
Heterogamous organisms, 20
Heterogamy, 17, 49
Heterospory, 103, 104, 105, 114, 120, 126, 165
Heterothallism, 51
Heterotrophic organisms, 38
Holozoic organisms, 39
Homospory, 103, 165
Hormogonia, 23
Hormone, 51, 143, 152
Hornworts, 5, 60, 76, 103 (*see also* Hepatophyta)
Horsetails, 7, 107 (*see also* Arthrophyta)
Hydrodictyon, 25
Hypha, 46, 54
Hypnites, 61
Hypocotyl, 153

Imperfect fungi, 5, 57 (*see also* Deuteromycota)
Indusium, 114
Inflorescence, 145, 146
Integument, 127, 149, 153
International code of botanical nomenclature, 5, 14
Internode, 34, 79, 106
Iris, 80, 142, 156
Isoetes, 96, 105, 106, 165
Isogametes, 44
Isogamous organisms, 20
Isogamy, 164

Juniperus, 133

Karyogamy, 18
Kelp, 14, 16, 27, 28, 162

Laminaria, 28, 29, 36
Laminarin, 15
Lamproderma, 44
Land plants, 77
Larix, 133
Leaf, 87–91, 116, 122, 123
  compound, 89
  simple, 91
Leaf gap, 85, 88, 112
Leaf primordium, 79, 87
Leaf scar, 80, 81
Leaf trace, 88, 112
Lederberg, Joshua, 41
Legume, 42
Lemna, 1, 78, 142
Lenticel, 81
Lepidodendron, 104, 105, 122
Lichens, 1, 57, 58
Life cycle, 20, 26, 33, 45, 48, 53, 56, 64, 69, 117, 123, 166
Life, origins of, 9

Lignification, 82
Lignin, 81
Ligule, 105
Ligustrum, 90
Lilium, 149
Linear tetrad, 148, 149, 150
Lip cells, 114
Liverworts, 1, 2, 5, 60–68, 76, 98, 103, 163 (*see also* Hepatophyta)
"Lower" plant, 161
Luciferase, 56
Lycoperdon, 57
Lycopodium, 96–100, 103, 104, 110, 122, 163, 167
Lycopods, 98

Macrophyll, 88, 110, 112, 162
Maidenhair tree, 7, 136–137
Mannitol, 15
Marchantia, 61, 65–66, 67
Marsilea, 113, 118–119, 120, 165
Medullosa, 139
Megasporangium, 103, 105, 119, 127, 131, 132, 149, 153, 165
Megaspore, 102, 103, 106, 119, 126, 127, 148, 149, 165
Megasporocyte, 103, 130, 131, 148, 149, 150
Megasporogenesis, 147
Megasporophyll, 101, 102, 105, 141, 142, 143, 145, 150
Megastrobilus, 129, 130, 131, 132, 135
Meiosis, 7, 19, 20, 28, 29, 30, 34, 36, 45, 52, 55, 56, 64, 93, 99, 103, 108, 114, 126, 130, 150, 164, 165, 166
Meiosporangium, 48
Metabolism, 6
Metasequoia, 133
Merismopedia, 23, 162
Mesophyll, 89, 112
  palisade, 89, 90

Mesophyll (**cont.**):
  spongy, 89, 90
Micrometer, 40, 135
Microphyll, 99, 110, 162
Microphyllophyta (club mosses), 7, 93–107, 109–111, 122, 162
Micropyle, 135, 149, 152
Microsphaera, 54
Microsporangium, 103, 105, 119, 130, 131, 143, 149
Microspore, 102, 103, 119, 126, 127, 130, 131, 145, 148, 149, 165
Microsporocyte, 130, 147, 148, 149
Microsporogenesis, 147
Microsporophyll, 101, 102, 105, 130, 131, 143, 145
Microstrobilus, 130, 137
Mitochondrion, 6, 8, 17, 23, 41
Mitosis, 20
Mitosporangium, 48
Mnium, 70
Monoecious plants, 130, 145
Moonwort, 120
Morchella, 53
Morel, 53
Morphologist, 2
Mosses, 1, 2, 5, 60, 68–76, 98, 103, 163 (*see also* Bryophyta)
Mucilage canal, 135, 137
Muramic acid, 23
Mushroom, 55–56
Mutation, 165
Mycelium, 46, 55, 56
Mycorrhiza, 93, 94
Myxomycota (slime molds), 5, 43–45

Naval stores, 128
Navicula, 35
Needle, pine, 128, 129
Neurospora, 53, 59
Nitrobacter, 41, 42

Nitrogen fixation, 12, 23, 42, 43
Nitrosomonas, 41, 42
Node, 34, 79, 106
Nonvascular plants, 61–76, 124
Nostoc, 23, 24, 67
Nucleolus, 17
Nucleus, 16
Nutrition, types of, 38, 39

Oedogonium, 12, 25, 26, 36, 37, 64
Oenothera, 149
Oil, 15
Ontogeny, 14, 162
Oogamy, 17, 20
Oogonium, 26, 34, 50
Oomycota (water molds), 5, 47–51
Operculum, 72, 75
Ophioglossum, 120–121
Order, 14
Oscillatoria, 16, 23, 24, 162
Ovary, 143, 150, 155, 156, 157
Ovule, 127, 128, 130, 131, 132, 136, 141, 144, 147, 148, 149, 150, 152, 158

Palaeolyngbya, 12
Paleobotany, 167
Palynology, 147
Pandorina, 163
Paramylon, 15
Paraphysis, 54
Parasite, 38, 55
Parasitism, 47
Parenchyma, 82
Parthenogenesis, 21
Pathogenic bacteria, 42
Peat, 75, 76
Peat moss, 73
Pectin, 15
Pelargonium, 83
Penicillium, 52, 53
Penicillin, 53

Peptidoglycans, 15
Perennial plants, 70, 78
Perianth, 145
Pericycle, 87
Periplast, 33, 34
Peristome, 61, 72, 74
Petal, 144, 145
Petrifaction, 166
Peziza, 53
Phacus, 34
Phaeophycophyta (brown algae), 5, 15, 27–29
Phagotrophic organisms, 39
Phaseolus, 154
Phloem, 76, 77, 81, 82, 85, 107, 112, 161
   primary, 83, 84
   secondary, 83, 84
Photoautotrophic organisms, 38, 41
Photoperiod, 143
Phycomycetes, 47
Phylloglossum, 96, 97
Phylogeny, 92
Phylum, 5
Physarum, 44
Pigments, 15
Pilularia, 118, 119
Pinnularia, 35
Pinus, 84, 128–133, 135
"Pipes," 107
Pistil, 141, 142, 144, 145, 150, 156, 158, 159
Pistillate flower, 145, 146
Pisum, 154
Pith, 81
Placentation, 144, 150
Planktonic algae, 12
Plasmodium, 44, 45
Plasmogamy, 18, 49
Plastid, 6, 8, 16
Plectonema, 22
Plectostele, 85, 99
Plumule, 153
Plurilocular gametangia, 28
Podocarpus, 133, 134
Polar nuclei, 151

Pollen chamber, 131, 132
Pollen grain, 127, 130, 131, 135, 136, 149
Pollen sac, 151
Pollen tube, 128, 131, 132, 148, 150
Pollination, 127, 129, 135, 137, 147, 151, 152, 158
Pollination droplet, 132, 135
Polyploid race, 73
Polyporus, 57
Polysiphonia, 30, 31
Polytrichum, 68, 69, 71, 163, 165
Pond scum, 11
Porella, 61, 66, 67
Postelsia, 29
Powdery mildew, 54
Primary endosperm nucleus, 152
Primary mycelium, 55, 56
Primary tissues, 81
Procambium, 81, 86
Prokaryota, 39, 43
Prokaryotic organisms, 18, 23, 26
Pronuba, 151
Prothallus, 115, 116
Protista, 14
Protoderm, 81, 86
Protonema, 69, 70, 72
Protoplasmic continuity, 16
Protostele, 85, 87, 99, 101
Provascular tissue, 81
Prunus, 157
Psaronius, 122
Pseudoplasmodium, 46
Pseudopodium, 75
Psilocybe, 56
Psilocybin, 56
Psilophyta (psilophytes), 7, 93–96, 98, 109, 110, 111, 122, 162
Psilophyton, 122
Psilotum, 93–96, 103, 107, 120, 122, 163
Pteridium, 113
Pteridophyta, 122
Pterophyta (ferns), 1, 2, 7, 98, 111–123
Puccinia, 54, 55

Puffballs, 57
Pyrenoid, 33
Pyronema, 53
Pyrrhophycophyta (dinoflagellates), 5, 15
Pyrus, 157

Quercus, 84

Radicle, 153
Ranunculus, flower of, 144
Raphanus, 86
Rattlesnake fern, 121
Ray flower, 146
Receptacle, 114, 144, 145
Red algae, 5, 15, 29–33 (*see also* Rhodophycophyta)
Red eyespot, 17
Red tide, 12
Reduction, 87, 161
Redwood, 133
Regeneration, 73
Regnellidium, 118, 119
Reproduction:
   asexual, 18, 57
   sexual, 6, 7, 12, 17, 23, 26, 30, 36, 44, 45, 49, 50, 51, 57, 63, 70, 74, 95, 99, 103, 105, 109, 116, 119, 132, 137, 148
Reservoir, 33
Resurrection plant, 99, 100
Rhizoid, 47, 51, 69, 74, 93, 103, 109, 114
Rhizome, 69, 80, 87, 93, 112
Rhizophore, 100
Rhizophydium, 47
Rhizopus, 16, 51, 163, 164
Rhodophycophyta (red algae), 5, 15, 29–33
Rhodospirillum, 42
Rhoeo, 90
Rhynia, 93, 94, 122

Riccia, 61–64, 65
Ricciocarpus, 61–64, 65, 162
Ricinus, 155
Rockweed, 27, 30
Root, 69, 78, 82, 85–87, 116
Root cap, 86
Root hairs, 86, 87
Rusts, 54–55

Saccharomyces, 52
Sac fungi, 5 (see also Ascomycota)
Salvinia, 112, 118, 120, 165
Saprolegnia, 49
Saprophytic organisms, 38, 99
Sargassum, 29, 31
Scenedesmus, 25
Scheffeleria, 88
Schizaea, 96
Schizomycota (bacteria), 2, 5, 10, 23, 38–43, 98
Scouring rushes, 107
Sea lettuce, 26
Seaweed, 11
Secondary growth, 83–84
Secondary mycelium, 55, 56
Seed, 125, 126, 128, 132, 136, 137, 141, 148, 151, 153, 154
dormancy, 158
germination, 133, 154, 155, 158
Seed coat, 153, 154
Seed ferns, 121, 126, 159
Seedless vascular plants, 92–123 (see also Vascular plants)
Seedling, pine, 133
Seed plants, 92, 124–159 (see also Vascular plants)
Selaginella, 96, 99–104, 105, 110, 113, 119, 126, 127, 130, 162, 163, 165, 167
Self-incompatability, 51
Sepal, 145
Sequoiadendron, 78, 83, 84, 133
Seta, 65, 67, 71
Sex organs, 12

Shelf fungi, 57
Shield fern, 112
Sieve cell, 82
Sieve plate, 83
Sieve tube, 82, 83
Sigillaria, 104, 105, 122
Simple pistil, 141, 145
Siphonostele, 85
Sirenin, 49
Slime molds, 5, 43–45 (see also Myxomycota)
Solanum, 80
Solenostele, 85
Somatic phase, 45
Sophora, 88, 89
Sorus, 114, 119
"Spanish moss," 142
Spawn, 55
Species, 14
Sperm, 17, 26, 135, 136, 137, 150, 152, 164
Spermagonium, 54
Spermatium, 30, 32
Sphagnum, 73–76
Sphenophyllum, 122
· Sphenopsids, 7 (see also Arthrophyta)
Spike mosses, 93
Spirillum, 40
Spirogyra, 16, 26, 51
Sporangiophore, 51, 107, 108
Sporangium, 114, 115, 120
Spore, 64, 68, 72, 99, 108, 114, 163
Spore formation, bacterial, 40, 41
Spore mother cell, 64
Sporocarps, 118, 119
Sporocyte, 64, 68, 95, 99, 108, 114
Sporogenesis, 147
Sporophyll, 97, 99, 145
Sporophyte, 21, 28, 61, 64, 66, 67, 68, 70, 71, 73, 76, 77, 95, 99, 100, 103, 106, 109, 110, 116, 117, 126, 153, 164
Spur shoot, 129, 130, 136
Stalk, 65
Stamen, 144, 145

Staminate flower, 145, 146
Stamnostoma, 159
Starch, 15
Stele, 84, 85, 87
Stem, 78, 79–85, 116
Stigma, 17, 33, 145, 151
Stolon, 80, 118
Stoma, 82, 83, 89, 90, 108, 112
Stoneworts, 15 (see also Charophyta)
Strobilus, 99, 101, 102, 104, 108, 125, 126, 143
Stromatopteris, 96
Style, 145
Stylites, 96
Suberin, 87
Suspensor, 133, 153
Synergid, 151
Syringa, 79

Taproot, 137
Tatum, Edward L., 41
Taxodium, 133
Teliospore, 54
Tetrasporangium, 31, 32
Tetraspore, 31
Tetrasporophyte, 31, 32
Tilia, 83
Tmesipteris, 96, 122
Toadstool, 55
Trace, 81
Tracheid, 82, 83, 113, 129, 184
Trachelomonas, 33
Tracheophyta, 92
Tree ferns, 111, 112, 113
Triceratium, 35
Trichogyne, 30, 32
Tube nucleus, 150
Tuber, 80
Tubular green algae, 16, 27

Ulothrix, 25, 36

Ulva, 16, 26, 36, 162, 164
Unilocular zoosporangium, 28
Urediniospore, 54
Usnea, 58

Vacuole, 6, 8, 18, 23
Vallecular canal, 107
Valve, 34
Vascular bundle, 82, 83, 85
Vascular bundle scar, 81
Vascular plants, 77–165
    adaptations of, 91
Vascular ray, 83, 84
Vascular tissue, 60, 69, 83, 88, 95
Vegetative phase, 45
Vein, 88, 90
Venation, 89
Vessel, 82, 84, 113

Viruses, 42
Volvox, 14, 25, 163, 164

Waterbloom, 12
Water ferns, 117, 118
Water molds, 5, 49–51 (*see also* Oomycota)
Welwitschia, 137, 138, 140
Whisk fern, 93–96
Williamsonia, 139
Wood, 84, 129

Xylem, 60, 69, 77, 81, 82, 84, 85, 107, 112, 161
    primary, 83, 84, 87
    secondary, 83, 84, 87, 106, 125, 129

Yeasts, 52
Yew, 134
Yucca, 151

Zamia, 134–136
Zea mays, 55, 83, 86, 153
Zoosporangium, 24
Zoospore, 18, 24, 25, 28, 47, 49, 50, 163
Zygomycota (bread molds), 5, 47, 51–52
Zygote, 18, 19, 20, 26, 28, 29, 30, 36, 44, 69, 71, 78, 99, 103, 109, 116, 119, 132, 152, 153, 161, 164
Zymase, 53